The Dimensions of
Legal Reasoning

The Dimensions of
Legal Reasoning

Developing Analytical Acuity from Law School to Law Practice

Timothy P. Terrell

Professor of Law
Emory University School of Law

CAROLINA ACADEMIC PRESS

Durham, North Carolina

ISBN: 978-1-63282-094-5
eBook ISBN: 978-1-63282-095-2

Library of Congress Cataloging-in-Publication Data

Names: Terrell, Timothy P., 1949- author.
Title: Dimensions of legal reasoning : developing analytical acuity from law
    school to law practice / Timothy Terrell.
Description: Durham, North Carolina : Carolina Academic Press, [2016] |
    Includes bibliographical references and index.
Identifiers: LCCN 2016038548 | ISBN 9781632820945 (alk. paper)
Subjects: LCSH: Law--Methodology. | Semantics (Law) | Law--Philosophy.
Classification: LCC K212 .T43 2016 | DDC 340/.19--dc23
LC record available at https://lccn.loc.gov/2016038548

Carolina Academic Press, LLC
700 Kent Street
Durham, North Carolina 27701
Telephone (919) 489-7486
Fax (919) 493-5668
www.cap-press.com

Printed in the United States of America

This book, like everything else I do, is dedicated to my wife, Mary.

Contents

Part III
Adding Depth to Each Dimension

Preface

Integrating the Strands that Produce the Rule of Law

This book is about a complex form of reasoning, usually labeled "thinking like a lawyer," to which I heard general allusions in my first days of law school. Although I remember being impressed by the idea, I didn't understand it then, nor could I pin it down by the time I graduated. It remained a mystery even when I began teaching law myself. Now, much later than I care to admit, I think I have a better perspective on this phenomenon, and on why it is such a perplexing challenge to grasp. This book is my effort to unpack this mental process so that others might appreciate it, and indeed exploit it, earlier than I did.

But who are these "others" to whom this book is addressed?

A very wide range, as it turns out. Although the analysis of legal reasoning to be developed here is indeed ambitious, the topic is approached in stages of intellectual and professional growth. These are the "Parts" identified in the Table of Contents. Initially, the story is about early experiences in law school, but we progress step-by-step to encompass the full range of complex legal issues confronting practicing lawyers and judges.

The ultimate purpose of the book follows from this surprising breadth. The text seeks to improve the analytical perspectives at both ends of this professional spectrum. Law students ought to be given a better chance to appreciate earlier than they usually do the mental agility, rather than memorization prowess, that law practice will actually expect of them. Concomitantly, experienced lawyers ought to have a more explicit understanding of the professional acumen they bring to bear when they analyze issues and construct arguments, so that they can deploy that skill more effectively and explain it more clearly as they train their younger colleagues.

But one group of legally experienced readers deserves special attention: my academic colleagues, who are the bridge between law students and law practitioners. They present a special challenge for this book because any of them who have labored in and around the topic of legal reasoning will have a rational concern about the breadth of the project here.

The range of topics to be developed in these pages is indeed quite wide. We will engage, describe, and sometimes critique several areas of "legal theory" that their own separate bodies of respected literature. These include abstract inquiries into "What is law?" as a social and philosophical matter; more practical examinations of legal reasoning as a professional activity; theories of language and interpretation of constitutional and statutory texts; some specific legal doctrinal areas, such as landlord-tenant law, privacy law, and so on. As a consequence, one could argue that there is not one book here, but several—each of which is insufficiently developed. For my purposes, however, this breadth is both justified and important.

My animating thesis is that a proper appreciation of legal reasoning requires that all these lines of scholarly inquiry be integrated rather than separated. Each must take account of all the others. Thus, the challenge for this book is to address each of these underlying intellectual strands *enough* to bring to light their inherent and necessary overlap. I do not consider myself alone or unique in this regard: A quintessential example of this kind of analytic ambition is the body of work produced by Prof. Ronald Dworkin,[1] in which he made claims to comprehensive descriptive and normative accuracy across a swath of legal issues as he developed his theory of adjudication. I hope to use and extend aspects of his academic agenda.

Given this simultaneously broad and deep pedagogical ambition, two caveats must be quickly acknowledged to limit, and make more reasonable, the book's scope.

First, the purpose of this book is *not* to improve anyone's "knowledge" of the law in the sense of making legal rules or doctrines more certain, less complicated, less contentious, or anything of that sort. I seek instead to explain better *why* the legal world is unavoidably uncertain, complicated, and contentious. Concerning the law's substance, then, this book does not intend or hope to explain why, for example, there is an exception to the several exceptions to some general rule. I more modestly intend to explain why such complexities arise.

Second, this book has no intention of being a work of psychology, trying to capture all the thoughts and motivations of all (or any subset) of lawyers and judges. The legal system is populated, after all, with humans rather than robots, so personal idiosyncrasies like bias, animus, and ignorance can certainly be important elements in "explaining" any specific legal argument or opinion.[2] However, these "imperfections," if you will, will not be directly addressed in the analysis here. My interest is instead in unpacking the elements of what might be characterized as a kind of idealized psychology: the most comprehensive examples of legal analysis in controversial situations.

This level of thoughtfulness can nevertheless involve very different understandings of facts and social values, leading to conflicting conclusions. But this inconsistency is not a failing. The underlying justification for legal reasoning is *not* based in any of its *results*, compatible or otherwise, welcome or otherwise. It is instead grounded in the *process itself* that precedes the results. What we mean by the guiding principle of the "rule of law" is, then, actually neither rules nor law, but the sophisticated thinking that leads to them.

Although this may seem perplexing, the key to understanding legal reasoning, I will contend, is to appreciate legal complexity—in fact, to revel in it—rather than to try to eradicate or soften it. This book will not help someone find "Rule X" in a legal source that then easily and clearly resolves a legal question. (For example, how many witnesses does local law require for a valid will?) Most anyone could do that. Instead, the book is intended to help a lawyer confront the situation where no "Rule X" seems to exist to fix things, and thus must be invented; or, more troubling, where you have found that decisive "Rule X" but you don't like it, and thus must do what you can to avoid or overcome it. (Back to the example: The will you want to challenge has two witnesses, but one of them was age 16, and local law has never considered this situation.) That's hard, particularly when you nevertheless claim to be paying homage to the rule of law.

As a consequence, despite the abstract nature of much of the book's analysis of legal reasoning, the ultimate success of this enterprise will be assessed quite practically: Does the analytic model developed here make you, the reader, better able to understand and then employ legal material more effectively in complex circumstances, whatever result you are trying to achieve?

We'll see. You have the right to remain skeptical.

Notes

1. We will review much of Prof. Dworkin's work in Chapters Three, Six, and Seven. *See infra* ch. 3, 6, 7.

2. This observation is prompted by the discussion of such factors in many sources analyzing legal and judicial reasoning, and in particular that found in Judge Richard Posner's important book, How Judges Think, and the numerous responses that text has provoked. *See* Richard Posner, How Judges Think (2008). This point is developed further in Chapters Three and Six. *See infra* ch. 3, 6.

Acknowledgement

I would like to acknowledge the remarkable support I received in the careful review and completion of this book by two outstanding research assistants, Carla Elias-Nava and Brian Wilson. Their attention to the details within my thinking and prose was appropriately annoying.

The Dimensions of
Legal Reasoning

Part I

Initial Analytic Steps

The Introduction and first two Chapters of the book set the foundation for all that follows. The Introduction, not surprisingly, describes and summarizes the approach of the text as a whole, while the first two Chapters develop pictures of the initial stages of law students' assumptions about and struggles with "the law" as they begin their professional legal journeys. The key lesson to be drawn from these early efforts will be how much more there is to the craft of lawyering than just stuffing one's head with data.

Introduction

Art and Angst Amid Ambiguity: Appreciating Disagreement

To say that someone "thinks like a lawyer" is to many people an insult.[1] It suggests a kind of pedantic fussiness, a version of an unfortunate personality that parents sometimes attribute to a quarrelsome child ("That kid's gonna grow up to be a lawyer."). But the phrase actually denotes a remarkable, but not well-understood, mental acuity exercised in very challenging circumstances. Indeed, it is a special ability, I will argue, that is *unique* to the legal profession[2]—for three reasons, each of which will be reflected in the discussions throughout this book.

Legal Reasoning as Unique

First, although the reasoning process in which lawyers—at least good lawyers—regularly engage is certainly multilayered, that is also true of any number of other challenging mental exercises. What is special about legal reasoning is the additional difficulty that each of its layers—layers that I will be labeling "text," "context," "hypertext," and "subtext," or, in plainer English, words, circumstances, values, and political structure—is *unstable*. Each is not only subject to its own internal conflicts, but also constantly affected by the other layers and, through them, by the world beyond the realm of "legal" data. The analytic result is therefore always intriguingly controversial and precarious.

Some might consider that message rather disquieting—that to be a lawyer is to revel in human disharmony rather than to bring people together in satisfied repose. I do not, however, mean at all to preach despair. I am not suggesting that lawyers exist to *produce* disagreement. To the contrary, the controversies and difficulties lawyers encounter preceded them—discord and friction were already and always there. Thus, we will instead emphasize *opportunity*: Appreciating the structure and nuances of legal reasoning provides a unique insight into the nature of human disagreement, revealing multiple avenues for its possible successful resolution. This book is therefore not directly about developing good legal answers; it is more about first being able to see all the questions that the complex nature of legal reasoning generates.

These questions, however, lead directly to the second distinct challenge associated with legal thinking: Part of the reason for so much unavoidable legal contentiousness is the fact that the information that lawyers must confront and conquer is not simply data in a conventional sense. It is instead material organized by and around multiple *abstract concepts* (what is "consideration," after all, or "ownership," or "jurisdiction"?). And those concepts are layered: They have constituent parts that are themselves abstract concepts that may actually conflict and compete with each other. As a result, dealing with legal concepts demands a special analytic facility.

Third, although lawyers, again like all professionals, claim to have a "thorough" understanding of the circumstances regarding which people have sought their advice and counsel, that quality is particularly difficult to demonstrate when those circumstances are both controversial and very abstract. To be thorough here, then, does not mean to be perfect or complete or anything else absolute. It connotes instead a special, practical analytic sophistication. An impressive mastery over *legal* circumstances demands that lawyers perceive, and make others perceive, that our often contentious circumstances nevertheless have a *structure* of some meaningful kind (rather than being chaotic), and that in turn that structure rests on some identifiable, and respected, *foundation* (rather than being idiosyncratic or arbitrary).

The model of legal reasoning to be developed here, therefore, has the ambition of establishing each of these professional qualities—coping with the instability of basic information, developing practical abstractions, and being carefully methodical all the while. But we shall do so in the opposite order: We will first identify a structured foundation to this analytical enterprise that will then allow us to appreciate and use abstract concepts that then can be practically effective despite lingering social disagreements.

Beyond Text and Context

After some important preliminaries in the first three Chapters, where key images are developed that become anchoring themes throughout the text, Chapter Four presents the substance of my alternative approach. The analysis will separate legal reasoning into the four component parts noted earlier; beginning, as any discussion of law must, with the two traditional fundamentals, and unavoidable facts, of "text" and "context." Regarding the former, law is expressed in words brought together into groups that must be examined not only as clusters but individually as well. Regarding context, those words must be applied to real people, also in clusters and individually, in actual situations that can get quite messy. But there is much more to reasoning about the law than these initial two (rather obvious) categories suggest.

Once texts and contexts are properly appreciated, two additional elements will need to be added to the mix. One (labeled here "hypertext") will involve the normative values that are embedded within words and situations, and that therefore establish *why* any of the analysis of law actually matters. The other ("subtext") recognizes the political circumstances (judges, legislatures, and so on) within which legal issues are identified, created, and resolved. And as if things weren't bad enough at that point, we will discover that each of these four dimensions—words, circumstances, values, and political structure—is plagued by its own particular internal struggle or debate. The analytic result is strikingly complex.

Legal reasoning also does not take place in a vacuum, of course. It is applied to real people trying to establish real social relationships. Understood appropriately, then, "thinking like a lawyer" certainly involves as well "thinking like an advocate." In the vast majority of practical professional circumstances, legal reasoning is not an arid, abstract, impersonal exercise, but a very practical assessment of how best to present a client's point of view—perhaps to an adversary and, as necessary, to a dispute-resolver, but just as often to a friendly audience simply hoping to understand the relevance of law to their situation. Thoughtful and careful advocacy is thus certainly at the core of the lawyer's professional skill.

Legal Reasoning as Art

A skill, moreover, that I will claim is akin to "art."[3] I do not use this reference lightly, however, as if legal reasoning were "colorful" or "entertaining," or perhaps "obscure" or "personal" (as in, for example, "you know it when you see it" or "in the eye of the beholder"). To the contrary, I intend an analogy that is much more serious. Art is not simply things or objects, but a special kind of experience—one that many encounter, but few can (or even attempt to) understand, much less articulate. Similarly, legal reasoning is not the mere connecting of informational dots (an image to which we will turn in Chapter Two), but a unique synthesis of that information, which again few seriously attempt to understand. We will make that effort, however, and thereby demonstrate the practical importance of these very abstract concepts.

As an initial step, let us define "art" as the phenomenon of things "transcending themselves."[4] For example, dance, as an art form, is bodily movement that somehow becomes more than its physical actions—the movements and gestures and postures communicate far more than a body ordinarily seems capable of (indeed, athletic talent will sometimes reach this level, as when a particularly spectacular or impressive effort is made, as in "turning that double play was a thing of beauty"). Painting, similarly, is colored substances on a surface that become something much more to us than simply various pigments. Poetry, by the same token, is a set of words that ascend beyond their humble roots in mere letters and phrases, communicating something far more profound—moving, inspiring, insightful, upsetting. The words, like bodies and tinted oils, become more than their ordinary, objective component parts.

Legal reasoning, at its most comprehensive, has that quality. It is not merely an exercise of fitting "facts" together with "law" as if the two were children's blocks that, properly stacked, might look like a house. Instead, both of these categories of data and regulation, although eventually and inevitably expressed in words, can transcend their ordinary foundations to become an elaborate dance, impressive portrait, or insightful poem: The facts establish a story; the law resolves the story appropriately; and that resolution guides the assessment of later stories—with each exercise being a challenge in its own way. It is a form of thinking that somehow transcends its ordinary-looking constituent elements. It therefore becomes an "art," but—and this is the key here—rather than being "obscure" or "impenetrable" like so many of its cousins, it can be unraveled and studied, and hence made readily accessible. And exploitable.

Legal Reasoning as Angst

But not *too* readily. It is one thing to concoct legal arguments—to make facts and law dance together effectively. It is quite another to *assess* that dance—to determine whether the choreography and execution are aesthetically pleasing. This is where art turns to angst: How does one justify rating one artistic effort as better than another? Does *Paradise Lost* beat "Roses are red, violets are blue"? Does Poe trump Byron? How so? Judging, as opposed to lawyering, is its own special conundrum, deserving particular attention. Although judicial reasoning has indeed received more focus over the past few decades, the circumstances of the judge still need to be connected more directly to the difficult task laid before him or her: reaching decisions within unstable and controversial situations.

This, then, is the purpose of this book. It is intended to link rather tightly the efforts to understand, argue, and assess—to identify the elements common to both the development of a strong, comprehensive legal argument, and the criteria by which those contentions should be considered adequate or unimpressive. None of these tasks is easy. But careful study of them yields significant dividends.

Developing and Applying a Model

The two Chapters in Part I describe the basic initial steps into the world of legal reasoning. In Chapter One we begin that effort with what might seem trivial misdirection—a reference to baseball, which is actually a popular analogy for legal analysis. Although this move into sports may appear to have been made to be cute or entertaining, it is instead quite serious and useful. On the one hand, the alternative universe of baseball obviously has the standard, rudimentary elements of what is loosely referred to as a legal system: It has the text of its rules, as well as a special context of contentious competition in which those rules must be applied; difficult, close decisions (you're safe! you're out!) that must be made by a judge-like figure; and so on. But the game involves other, much deeper characteristics as well, which involve a subtle approach to its rules and complex decision-making processes, making it a more apt point of departure for the analysis of legal and judicial reasoning than has heretofore been recognized.

We will then use this example of baseball as a bridge into two initial analytic elements that set the stage for everything else. In Chapter Two, the most rudimentary qualities of legal reasoning—the "connect-the-dots" approach mentioned above—are established using the concept of "dimensional thinking." Despite its very limited utility, this level of analysis is about as far as ordinary discussions of legal reasoning extend.

The two Chapters in Part II then take us beneath and beyond these seemingly foundational, but incomplete, efforts. Chapter Three is the portion of the book that I readily acknowledge is most directly addressed to my academic colleagues—faculty and students alike—who are interested in the scholarly background of the topic of legal reasoning. It will review some, but by no means all, of the better known literature on legal reasoning—sources that have similarly argued in various ways that these initial steps need to be improved. But the suggestions by these scholars, as respected and impressive as they are, I find dissatisfying. They are not as accessible and practically useful as I think this topic requires.

Chapter Four, then, is where we start the analysis of legal reasoning afresh. There, as noted above, four separate but interconnected categories of thinking will be identified: unpacking legal "texts"; understanding relevant situational "contexts"; appreciating underlying value-based "hypertexts"; and identifying preexisting systemic "subtexts."

But as challenging as it is to have four elements to unpack, when we do so in succeeding Chapters in Part III of the book, we discover that each of them should be understood as a multi-layered form of schizophrenia (as that mental problem is popularly, rather than medically, perceived): The legal mind must confront a host of competing dichotomies that split the thought process into contending, but each legitimate, perspectives. Disagreements about the law are therefore endemic and unavoidable. Chapter Four, while it will not cure this problem, will at least establish an analytic framework that will allow us to diagnose and treat it: It will outline and organize this daunting mental process, and thus describe in detail the special difficulty facing judges and umpires alike. Because that framework has four segments—that is, the four different forms of legal schizophrenia noted above of text, context, hypertext, and subtext—Chapters Five through Eight develop the details of each in turn.

Part IV will then turn to application of the full model. Although all the Chapters in Part III demonstrate the unavoidable overlaps and interactions among these four elements, Chapters Nine and Ten will draw them together around two particularly intriguing legal topics. The former will apply this book's analytic technique to the fundamental, and fundamentally confounding, right to privacy, revealing the range of attitudinal nuance beneath it. The last Chapter will likewise unpack the continuing disagreement over the judiciary's role in interpreting the statutes and regulations produced by other branches of government. You might reasonably think such an exercise would be relatively objective and boring, yet it is anything but.

The lesson of these concluding Chapters, as in much of the book, is that readers can discover very useful lawyering insights *not* by trying to resolve these legal puzzles with confident finality, because the complex structure of legal reasoning guarantees that they won't be. Instead, the goal will be to understand the structure of disagreements to be able to participate more effectively in the debates.

Notes

1. My loving spouse, for example, after too many years of listening to my blather, tells me that the more appropriate title for this book is "The Dementia of Legal Reasoning."

2. I recognize that some of the scholars noted in Chapter Three do not believe that legal reasoning is particularly distinct from standard forms of careful thinking—except perhaps for being more forgiving of inconclusive messiness. But I disagree. I will concede throughout this book that lawyers do indeed seem to thrive in complex, controversial circumstances, yet I will argue that they approach their challenges with more structure than they themselves ordinarily recognize.

3. This idea is explored in Timothy P. Terrell, *Flatlaw: An Essay on the Dimensions of Legal Reasoning and the Development of Fundamental Normative Principles*, 72 CALIF. L. REV. 288, 310–316 (1984).

Judge Richard Posner also notes briefly in his book How JUDGES THINK a mild connection between law and art, but his approach is quite different from what I am suggesting. *See* POSNER, *supra* Preface note 2, at 63–4. His comparison of the two is based on the murkiness of the evaluations inherent in both fields ("the products of these activities cannot be evaluated objectively"). *Id.* In contrast, my linking of law and art is about better appreciating the analytic structure lying beneath the murkiness of both. In other words, while neither law nor art can be assessed "objectively," both *can* be assessed *systematically*.

4. *See* Terrell, *supra* note 3.

Chapter One

The Challenge of Calling "Balls and Strikes": The Curious Case of *Gould v. Roberts*

A few years ago, *The New York Times* reported sad news, as it regularly does, on its front page.[1] It was of a death, and an obituary followed. But this newsworthy event did not involve a politician or world leader or movie star. It was instead the story of the passing of a zoology professor: Stephen Jay Gould, Harvard's prolific author of both popular and scholarly books and essays on biology, paleontology, and evolutionary theory, who had died at the age of 60 after a long battle with cancer. Prof. Gould was such an unusually well-known scientist, teacher, and commentator that his death merited serious acknowledgement. But the obituary failed to mention, and in fact few people even know of, what may be one of his finest publications. It had little or nothing to do with science, however. It was about much more: truth, justice, language, law, and particularly the angst of judging.

In a very short, but remarkably profound, essay he published (ironically enough) in the *Times*,[2] and indeed as a eulogy for someone else, Prof. Gould presented in five paragraphs all the ingredients necessary to summarize most of any law school course in jurisprudence, even though his topic had nothing directly to do with the law. His focus was instead his other great passion outside of science and scientific theory: baseball. I have for many years used this essay as the opening foray for law students into the mysteries of clear rules that aren't, of sources of authority that implicitly claim to be complete but aren't, of decision-makers—like judges—who must cope with being "final" but also with being human and imperfect, and much more. I have also occasionally raised Gould's essay with judicial audiences to provoke conversation about the reasonableness or legitimacy of the example of quick decision-making that Gould praises and memorializes. I have happily speculated along with students and judges about what Prof. Gould may have meant by various provocative

13

passages, for he himself provided us with very little additional commentary on this essay. We are left to wonder, then, what his responses might be to the weighty issues his essay so effortlessly raises.

These issues have become timely again because of recent hearings for nominees to the Supreme Court. Chief Justice John Roberts noted during his confirmation that his modest ambition was just "to call the balls and strikes" as best he could.[3] This seemingly innocuous comment has since been criticized as being a disingenuous understatement of the nature and role of a Supreme Court justice, if not of the judicial role more generally.[4] Gould's essay is, I believe, directly relevant to this point, and reveals a profound irony underlying Justice Roberts' sports analogy: Despite the fact that both of them use the same regulatory concept (a "strike") to make their argument, Prof. Gould views baseball as subjective, and thus like the law, while Justice Roberts views the law as objective, and thus like baseball. Their perspectives could hardly be more divergent.[5]

But the situation might be even worse: One lesson that could be drawn from the distinction between Prof. Gould and Justice Roberts is that the latter may have a remarkably simplistic understanding of not only baseball, but of objectivity itself. Justice Roberts' comment is reminiscent of the famously unprofound observation by an earlier Justice Roberts—Owen—who also saw nothing particularly complicated in the judicial function: The Court was "to lay the article of the Constitution which is invoked beside the statute which is challenged and to decide whether the latter squares with the former."[6] I shall argue, through the convenient medium of Prof. Gould's essay, that this effort to minimize judicial reasoning to rote exercises of robotic comparison is demeaning to every judge in this country, including Justice Roberts himself.

Nevertheless, Prof. Gould's analysis does, oddly enough, provide a potential justification for Justice Roberts' comment, even though that would no doubt come as a surprise to both of them. It is based in appreciating the specific role of the umpire or judge within the "game" being played—a point we will explore in detail in Chapter Seven.

To demonstrate the richness and importance of Gould's article, I need do no more than allow you to read it for yourself. Without further ado, the entire essay is presented below. Thereafter I will discuss the points I believe make it relevant to legal theory in general—that is, to an understanding of law as a functioning social institution—and to theories of judicial reasoning and decision-making in particular. My comments, however, will do no more than demonstrate how much more could and should be said about his essay. With luck, then, perhaps this presentation might expand into a true discussion, giving a larger audience a chance to do justice to Prof. Gould's suggestions about justice, and to be better able to judge more acutely his assessment of judging. In particular, I think you will find that one of his most pointed observations about the judicial role—one that he probably made inadvertently—is captured in the essay's last two words.

Gould's Essay

Below is the complete text of Gould's essay, which first appeared with a different title in *The New York Times* on November 10, 1984. It was reprinted in his book *The Flamingo's Smile*,[7] along with a short following commentary by him indicating that I am not alone in admiring his article. But his commentary also indicated, as we will see later, how limited his appreciation was of the implications of his analysis.

One additional caveat, however: Gould's essay unapologetically assumes that the reader knows and appreciates the rudiments of the sport of baseball. My discussion of it will as well. If you do not have that important piece of cultural background,[8] I apologize. But not much. I provide in an endnote a depiction of the "strike zone" that the pitcher in this game missed,[9] but other than that, you are on your own.

STRIKE THREE FOR BABE

Tiny and perfunctory reminders often provoke floods of memory. I have just read a little notice, tucked away on the sports pages: "Babe Pinelli, long time major league umpire, died Monday at age 89 at a convalescent home near San Francisco."

What could be more elusive than perfection? And what would you rather be—the agent or the judge? Babe Pinelli was the umpire in baseball's unique episode of perfection when it mattered most. October 8, 1956. A perfect game in the World Series—and, coincidentally, Pinelli's last official game as arbiter. What a consummate swan song. Twenty-seven Brooks up; twenty-seven Bums down. And, since *single* acts of greatness are intrinsic spurs to democracy, the agent was a competent, but otherwise undistinguished Yankee pitcher, Don Larsen.

The dramatic end was all Pinelli's, and controversial ever since. Dale Mitchell, pinch hitting for Sal Maglio, was the twenty-seventh batter. With a count of 1 and 2, Larsen delivered one high and outside—close, but surely not, by its technical definition, a strike. Mitchell let the pitch go by, but Pinelli didn't hesitate. Up went the right arm for called strike three. Out went Yogi Berra from behind the plate, nearly tackling Larsen in a frontal jump of joy. "Outside by a foot," groused Mitchell later. He exaggerated—for it was outside by only a few inches—but he was right. Babe Pinelli, however, was more right. A batter may not take a close pitch with so much on the line. Context matters. Truth is a circumstance, not a spot.

I was a junior at Jamaica High School. On that day, every teacher let us listen, even Mrs. B., our crusty old solid geometer (and, I guess in retrospect, a secret baseball fan). We reached Mrs. G., our even crustier French teacher, in the bottom of the seventh, and I was appointed to plead. "Ya gotta let us listen," I said, "it's never happened before." "Young man," she replied, "this class is a French class." Luckily, I sat in the back just in front of Bob Hacker (remember alphabetical seating?), a rabid Dodger fan with earphone and portable. Halfway through the period, following Pinelli's last strike, I felt a sepulchral tap and looked around. Hacker's face was ashen. "He did it—that bastard did it." I cheered loudly and threw my jacket high in the air. "Young man," said Mrs. G. from the side board, "I'm sure the verb *écrire* can't be that exciting." It cost me 10 points on my final grade, maybe admission to Harvard as well. I never experienced a moment of regret.

Truth is inflexible. Truth is inviolable. By long and recognized custom, by any concept of justice, Dale Mitchell had to swing at anything close. It was a strike—a strike high and outside. Babe Pinelli, umpiring his last game, ended with his finest, his most perceptive, and his most truthful moment. Babe Pinelli, arbiter of history, walked into the locker room and cried.

The purpose of parsing this extraordinary essay[10] is not simply to acknowledge the many directions in which a conversation about it could go, but to focus more directly on how remarkably well it implicates and illustrates—and hence serves as a particularly useful introduction to—two topics fundamental to legal education: the key elements of legal reasoning and the personal challenge confronting any judge who must make a difficult, and close, decision. Reduced to their essence, both subjects are about the search for two elusive qualities: a "structure" to the analysis that will avoid the appearance of mindless whimsy, and a "foundation" that will make the structure universally applicable rather than idiosyncratic. What all lawyers and judges seek is the ability to claim that their thinking and conclusions are not chaotic and arbitrary, but patterned, coherent, and constrained, and hence respectable. One rudimentary form that this effort takes is the commonplace observation that legal reasoning is basically about consistency—"treating like cases alike, and different cases differently"[11]—but that rubric merely describes the challenge rather than resolves it. The important question is how the legal mind attempts to identify *relevant, meaningful* resemblances and distinctions, and hence how it believes it *justifies* its arguments and conclusions beyond simple assertion itself.

A Classroom Illustration of the Analytic Challenge

I believe that at this point, this summary of the implications of the Gould essay for legal (or any sort of) reasoning has become sufficiently abstruse that the discussion needs something to bring it back to earth. I will use my own experience of presenting these five paragraphs to a class of first-semester, first-year law students who I confront with a very basic legal task: Given the evident fact that "the law" is composed of words, and that "strike" is a word, I ask them simply to tell me what a "strike" is in "the law" of baseball.[12] In particular, I want them to tell me how Gould, who admits that Larsen's pitch was "high and outside" is nevertheless within the definition of that word.

Within the conversation that ensues, the entire range of elements fundamental to legal reasoning to be developed in this book—the limitations of texts, the vagaries of contexts, the unavoidable relevance of moral and political values, and the impact of political structure—all emerge.

To "define" a strike (in baseball, you will notice, not labor law[13]), the students will immediately refer to the physical space between armpits and knees and over the width of home plate, as anyone familiar with the sport would know. I then ask how they know this to be an accurate definition. They will make some vague reference to some baseball rule book that must be lying somewhere in the background, even though none of them has actually seen a copy. This, they realize, is what Gould meant by the "technical definition" of the concept. But if we assume for the moment that this rule book is indeed "official," and thus otherwise a legitimate and "authoritative" source to be consulted, how can Larsen's pitch be given the label that this book limits to certain physical circumstances? Obviously, something other than the rule book seems to matter here in giving the concept of a "strike" its *full* meaning.[14] The questions now are several: How is this possible, that the dictionary of baseball is incomplete? What is the extra-textual source for this proposition? And how does this mysterious source claim competing—and indeed in this case, superseding—legitimacy and authority? This is deep stuff, and we are only talking baseball.

The answer, of course, is that the "meaning" of a term, just as Gould asserted, also depends on context—but not just the factual circumstances in which the term is being used. This substantive sense of context is the set of circumstances *relevant* to the use of the term, the facts that somehow *matter*. These are identified only by reference to the "values" that lie behind the use of the term. I make this point to the students by asking them for the "justification" for the word "strike." I ask them for its "theory." They look at me quizzically. So I ask them why the word strike *matters* to anyone—why it is being used here. They will usually respond that it matters simply to know whether a batter is "out" or not, or something of that sort. But the next question is obvious: So what? Why does knowing "out" matter? Ah, but that is important to the *game*, they respond, satisfied that the line of questions has come to its natural and necessary end. But, I ask, what is the "game" to which they refer? Is it baseball? Or is it a critical game in the World Series? The latter is *Gould's* context. Perhaps, then, we must always connect the "fact" of the rule book definition to the "values" at stake at the moment the term is invoked to know what a strike "truly" is *in that special context*. If so, Gould is right again: "Truth is a circumstance, not a spot."

Now the fight in class truly starts. Some students are quite critical of the idea that the meaning of "strike" can float from game to game, context to context. For them, it is ordinarily a matter of notice: How would you know, as a player, that the rules are shifting? How would you know whether the umpire had the same perspective on the game that you did? How can the game be played, reasonably and fairly, in such circumstances? At this point I simply play back for them their own words, and note that instead of challenging the idea that values matter in the use of a word, they have endorsed it: They have simply invoked the competing values associated with "fairness" and fair play. The trick in this exercise, then, is not to reject the analytic move that Gould makes in appealing to the ethereal values of the World Series, but to beat him at his own game, appealing to different—and, you hope, somehow better—values. It is *your* sense of context that should really matter, not his.

Note, for example, how Gould does not refer to "fairness" to justify his praise of Pinelli, but to "justice." Is there anything important in that choice of term? Or, as students ordinarily assume, are the two words basically synonymous, communicating the same fundamental notion of "good" or "being correct"?

But we are (again) getting ahead of ourselves. For now, we should just focus on what is turning out to be an "inadequate" text—a rule book definition of a vital concept that seems to leave important questions unanswered. To simply say that now the argument shifts to "my values are better than your values" leaves students deeply dissatisfied. How, they ask, can we arbitrate between these competing claims? Gould has his values, I have mine; we are at stalemate. How can we decide whether to praise or condemn Pinelli for his call? Indeed, how could anyone *ever* argue with an umpire if the response we get is that the "values" of the game justify the call that was made? Suddenly a group of students in the room realize that they are "strict constructionists" and never knew it. They don't like the idea of the umpire altering the nature of the game on the basis of some set of values that might be quite personal to that official, and the surest way of being able to rein in this decision maker is to return to a value-neutral, "technical" approach to the concept of a strike. The rule book rules, they say, and properly so, if only to avoid intractable debates about "bad" calls.

So, they conclude, Pinelli was wrong, and so is Gould. No wonder the umpire cried: He knew he blew it, and in a big game with everyone watching.

But, I ask them, is that the way the game is *in fact* played? Is their approach consistent with the traditions of the sport and the expectations of the players? That doesn't matter, they say: It is the way the game *should* be played. "Should?" I ask. Where did that come from, in this argument ostensibly focused on the "technical," objective, rule-based definition of a strike? They look at me with consternation. The *rule* is the thing that matters here—otherwise we would have chaos: The game itself would begin to unravel. So, I observe, "values" *are* relevant here, after all, but they are now just the values intrinsic to baseball itself, and its continuation. Right, they concede, grudgingly. But do these baseball values exist independent of the participants in this sport, and the history of the playing of this game? Do the players and umpires and, perhaps, the spectators—their actions, reactions, and varying circumstances and expectations—not matter at all to the values, and hence to the rules, of their game? Does the fact, for example, that this was a World Series game not matter at all? Now in a corner, the response is emphatic: No. The "values" of baseball, to the extent they exist at all, are reflected and captured in the technical rules of the game, in any and all circumstances. That's what rules are for: to prevent dumb arguments like the one they are enduring in this class.

With any luck, at this point, some brave and unintimidated soul speaks up—quite often someone who has some personal experience with the game—and objects to this line of reasoning. That is *not* the way the game is played. The "rules" hardly capture the way the game actually unfolds and is enjoyed. Does a shortstop actually have to touch second base, while holding the ball, in the midst of turning a fast and furious double play, particularly in the context of professional games where the players are so fast? Does the "infield fly" rule actually have to be written down to be a part of the game?[15] Don't the special circumstances of the World Series, and indeed a perfect game, mold or shape the nature of the rules, or at least their application? Could we replace the umpire with a computer that is programmed with only the "technical rules" of the game? Would that still be baseball?

I applaud the student's resolve and passion, but then ask whether these contentions are an "is" or an "ought" argument: Is their opposition to the other students' analysis based on observations about the way the game is *in fact* played, or is it based on an implicit claim that the way the players actually play and understand the game is also the *right* way to play and understand the game? It seems to be both, but this is troubling, because you are not supposed to be able to derive an "ought" directly and simply from an "is": The way the players play could perhaps be labeled as *wrong* from some different, perhaps deeper, perspective. Could that perspective be, for example, "fairness"? Doesn't this batter "deserve," in some way, the application to him of consistent expectations concerning his performance? Yes, the student will concede, but *other* values might be relevant here as well—values like the "good" of the game as a whole, or the recognition of the special demands of a World Series game, or of a perfect game, or some other consideration that puts this particular batter in his appropriate "place" in this analysis: The world—and particularly the World Series—does not revolve around *him*.

But why not? Why isn't this player entitled to the same consideration regardless of circumstance? Why do his "rights" change just because the stakes have gone up?[16] Shouldn't we be even *more* diligent to "protect" him from arbitrariness when "larger" forces are said to be at work?

The discussion now usually descends into chaos, if anyone is willing to talk at all. The "strict constructionists" seem more adamant than ever to focus on the rule, and its sanctity, but for different reasons: Some emphasize the importance of the individual batter, and are concerned with his potential victimization. Some emphasize the pitcher, and argue that he should be honored with the mantel of "perfect game" only in the narrowest of circumstances. Some don't worry about the players so much as the game and its rules—these players are but momentary occupants of this space and time within the universe called baseball, and the forces that preceded them and will sustain the activity into the future should be the focus here, meaning that the "technical" rules that have both history and the dependence of the future behind them should control.

The other camp is just as adamant, and as diverse. Some see the situation quite broadly—the game and its heritage and its viability are indeed the key—but that doesn't mean that the technical rules are paramount. Quite the contrary, the larger values reflected in the game must be honored, and that means seeing a strike for what it "truly" is: merely one step in a more complex dance that has an elegance that must be recognized above all else. Others, however, are a bit leery of turning the analysis over to an abstract appreciation of some "dance" (recall the reference in the Introduction to the possible relevance of "art" to our analysis of legal reasoning), where a range of unanchored images might compete and clash. They want the steps in this dance (the rules) to be given more respect, but not to be viewed in isolation. The rules exist for *reasons* intrinsic to the game itself, and it is that set of more limited values that must be given emphasis. But values of some sort are nevertheless primary in the analysis, rather than secondary, and the umpire's job is ultimately, then, to be sensitive to those normative concerns.

Now everyone is dissatisfied, except me. I hope the class has at least recognized that the differences of opinion they have developed all spring initially from the rather simple observation that the "meaning" of a strike has varied initially on the basis of the separation of "is" from "ought"—the difference between describing the facts of the situation, on the one hand, and, on the other, justifying the values implicated by the situation. But the disagreement goes much deeper, because the facts themselves seem to be understood quite differently: Is the key circumstance the duel between pitcher and batter, or more generally the game of baseball? Or is it the *World Series* baseball game, or the *perfect* World Series baseball game? And which values ought to matter here? Fairness? Or Gould's seemingly larger sense of justice? And how do we go about choosing the values that will be infused into the analysis? In the final analysis, aren't the facts a function of the values we espouse, and the values we espouse a function of the facts upon which we focus?

On the basis of what has been said so far, there seems to be no way to assess the call made by Umpire Pinelli. Some students think it is correct, others that it is incorrect, and the "insight"—which the students hardly think it is—of the distinction between "is" and "ought" doesn't help to resolve that impasse. Instead, differences between description and justification seem equally elusive, if not simply perverse. We're back, they claim, to "I'm OK, you're OK."

Not so, I reassure the class: They are simply becoming lawyers. They are beginning to appreciate the characteristics of annoying, but quite practical, argument. Practical? they almost sneer. Okay, then, they ask me in great frustration, which is it? Was Pinelli correct or incorrect?

I can't answer that question, I tell them, until they answer another: Who's paying me?

Lights go off. The business majors smile and the theology majors groan. The worst fears of many in the class are now realized, as the crass cynicism and instrumentalism at the heart of law practice is revealed. Postmodernist emptiness wins after all.

Not so fast, I suggest. Developing an argument that will protect a client's interests is not necessarily evil or arbitrary: Would it make any difference, I ask the class, if Don Larsen or Dale Mitchell were your brother? Disagreeing with someone who is arguing for the *wrong* result isn't a bad thing at all. So, rather than assuming that the entire mental exercise is capricious, perhaps a better way out of this soup is to go in *deeper*. What might be useful would be a more sophisticated understanding of these basic camps of description (is) and justification (ought), which might reveal that they have form and symmetry as well.

That happy prospect of some kind of structure, rather than self-serving chaos, leads to the next step in a student's analytic journey. We now go beneath this classroom discussion using a quite different, but perhaps equally surprising, mental construct. As if baseball were not enough of a possible misdirection, we will next develop a pedagogical device that is entirely imaginary. But it too will prove to be a very useful starting point because of its strong connection to basic, and then more advanced, legal reasoning.

Hereafter, as more and more detail is added in succeeding Chapters to the levels of thinking that comprise legal reasoning, we will develop a comprehensive map of legal argumentation—whether for attack, defense, or dispute resolution. And we will be able to note that, remarkably, every element within it is reflected in Prof. Gould's essay. Indeed, Chapter Eight will be of particular importance, for it will focus on the singular anxiety and pressure imposed on those who must make close calls, legal or otherwise, and will revisit in some detail the differences between the visions of decision-making of Prof. Gould and Justice Roberts.[17]

Notes

1. Carol K. Yoon, *Stephen Jay Gould, 60, Is Dead; Enlivened Evolutionary Theory*, N.Y. TIMES, May 21, 2002, at A1. I should note, as a matter of full disclosure, that this Chapter, as well as portions of several others, are drawn from a previous publication: Timothy P. Terrell, *The Art of Legal Reasoning and the Angst of Judging: Of Balls, Strikes, and Moments of Truth*, 8 Nw. J.L. & Soc. Pol. 1 (2012).

2. Stephen Jay Gould, Opinion, *The Strike That Was Low and Outside*, N.Y. TIMES, Nov. 10, 1984.

3. *Confirmation Hearing on the Nomination of John G. Roberts, Jr. To Be Chief Justice of the United States*, 109th Cong. 56 (2005) (statement of John G. Roberts Jr., nominee to be Chief Justice of the United States).

4. *See id.* (Senator Joe Biden pointed out that "[Rehnquist] used the phrase 'tacit postulates.' He said that these tacit postulates are as much ingrained in the fabric of the [Constitution] as its express provisions ... Chief Justice Rehnquist made this vital point and it was about state's rights and language that didn't speak directly to them in the constitution. And he concluded that the answer was a rule he was able to infer from the overall constitutional plan. So, Judge, you're going to be an inferrer, not an umpire. Umpires don't infer. They don't get to infer. Every justice has to infer").

5. One objection to this entire enterprise of comparing baseball and the law should be confronted and put to rest. An obvious reason for the divergence of the approaches of Prof. Gould and Justice Roberts to objectivity and subjectivity is the physical differences between baseball and courtrooms: While the rules of baseball are, by and large, "objective" in the sense of being quite specific about the physical circumstances in which they are to be applied, "subjectivity" nevertheless enters the picture because an umpire must make snap decisions where human senses may not have perceived all the available data perfectly. Legal situations, on the other hand, are "subjective" in the sense that the ability of the law to predict all future circumstances to which it might be applied is impossible, and the law itself is expressed in human language that is notoriously malleable. Nevertheless, judges have the luxury of time, allowing development of facts and opportunities for reflection, to create the impression that their decisions are, all things considered, "objective" and required, rather than capricious.

Thus, umpiring and judging are connected by the fact that both seek a justification for asserting certainty in the face of uncertainty: baseball, because its circumstances put umpires under significant pressure; the law, because its constituent materials put judges under similar pressure. And that "pressure" needs to be appreciated: Umpires and judges both exist *not* for the purpose of making easy calls, but to make tough ones. Justice Roberts' use of the baseball analogy is therefore worth exploring.

I also recognize that some would argue that I am referencing the wrong sport here altogether—that the closer analogy would be the responsibility of basketball referees to make quick calls where the clarity of something like a physical strike zone is absent. *See* Eric Segall, *Justices, Referees, and Umpires: The Role of Discretion in Sports and Supreme Court Decisions*, Dorf on L. (Jan. 5, 2015), http://perma.cc/MDY8-32UN. I will let others debate that point.

6. United States v. Butler, 297 U.S. 1, 62 (1936). We will note a similar comment from Montesquieu later. *See infra* ch. 8 note 6.

7. Stephen Jay Gould, The Flamingo's Smile: Reflections in Natural History, 227–229 (1985). Prof. Gould also notes here the story behind the changes over time to the essay's title, but very little else. *Id.*

8. The possible incomprehensibility of the concept of a strike in baseball became evident to me in the law school class in which I used this essay to initiate an analysis of law and legal material. One student, from the Bahamas, for example, complained that while she understood cricket, baseball was a mystery. Another student, just arrived from France, misunderstood aspects of Gould's analysis because she thought that the key to the essay was the fact that the batter was inappropriately standing on one of the lines on the field ("with so much on the line").

9. To respond briefly to the specialized knowledge required, I will note that a strike—in the specific circumstances of Gould's essay—is a pitch by the pitcher that the batter should have tried to hit, but failed to swing the bat to make that attempt. This kind of pitch places the ball within an area where it is reasonable for the batter to make that attempt—a space over the width of "home plate" which is in front of the batter, and no higher than the batter's armpits and no lower than the bottom of the batter's knees. This area can be depicted as follows:

Figure 1.1

Official Baseball Rules, 2015 Edition, copyright © 2015 by the Office of the Commissioner of Baseball, reprinted with permission.

The point of Gould's essay, then, is that Larsen's pitch was, according to this spatial definition, not a strike (it should have been labeled a "ball") because it was too "high" and also "outside" the width of home plate. But Umpire Pinelli nevertheless called the pitch a strike anyway (and quite correctly, according to Gould). *See* Gould, *supra* note 2.

10. What a remarkable piece of work. Gould later acknowledged that he wrote it "in a quarter hour's flood of inspiration during an interminable round of speechmaking at my son's annual Little League banquet." Gould, *supra* note 7, at 227. It depresses me to realize that even after a lifetime of work, and given unlimited time, I will never be able to write like this.

This is not, by the way, the only story about the umpiring of Babe Pinelli. He himself wrote an article for a book on baseball lore in which he described an encounter with another Babe—Ruth, of course—when Pinelli was a rookie umpire and Ruth was at the close of his career. Pinelli writes that he was told that one did not call close pitches as strikes when The Babe was at bat, but he did so anyway. After being fussed at by Ruth, who claimed that "forty thousand people in this park … know that was a ball, tomato-head," Pinelli calmly responded, "Perhaps—but mine is the only opinion that counts." Babe Pinelli, *Kill the Umpire? Don't Make Me Laugh!, in* THE SECOND FIRESIDE BOOK OF BASEBALL 278 (Charles Einstein ed., 1958).

11. The idea of connecting the rules of baseball to the rule of law is hardly new, of course. *See, e.g.*, BASEBALL AND THE AMERICAN LEGAL MIND (Spencer W. Waller, Neil B. Cohen & Paul Finkelman eds., 1995); *The Common Law Origins of the Infield Fly Rule*, 123 U. PA. L. REV. 1474 (1975); Charles Yablon, *On the Contribution of Baseball to American Legal Theory*, 104 YALE L.J. 227 (1994); Gerald F. Uelman, *The Jurisprudence of Yogi Berra*, 46 EMORY L.J. 697 (1997); Paul Finkelman, *Baseball and the Rule of Law Revisited*, 25 T. JEFFERSON L. REV. 17 (2002); Neil B. Cohen & Spencer W. Waller, *Taking Pop-Ups Seriously: The Jurisprudence of the Infield Fly Rule*, 82 WASH. U. L. Q. 453 (2004).

12. This phrase is ubiquitous in legal contexts, but one of its most thoughtful discussions appears in H.L.A. Hart's classic work. *See* H.L.A. HART, THE CONCEPT OF LAW (Peter Cane, Tony Honore & Jane Stapleton eds., Oxford Univ. Press 2d ed. 1994) (hereinafter referenced in this book as "COL").

13. My Emory colleague Dean Robert Schapiro has noted to me that perhaps this entire analysis is incomplete because Gould's essay actually also depends on a theory of a "walk." The problem, he argues, is that a walk is not at the moral core of baseball, even though it is part of the duel between pitcher and batter. It is an exception to the "excellence" of play we expect of competent players. "Real men," he contends—as well as official scorers for the sport—do not "count" walks. Hence, there is a kind of hollowness and defensiveness to the expression "a walk is as good as a hit." Not really. The biggest, most memorable games turn on hitting, not walking. Consequently, in games like the World Series, perhaps a thumb is already on the scale in favor of strikes.

14. Although the same word can have different meanings in various contexts, often, as Ludwig Wittgenstein famously noted, these uses can be related by "family relationships" that connect their independent uses to shared characteristics across a range of uses in the language. LUDWIG WITTGENSTEIN, PHILOSOPHICAL INVESTIGATIONS 2–41 (G. Anscombe trans., 1953). One example he used was the word "game" that had various connotations, but nevertheless formed a "family" of applications. *Id.* I do not think the two uses of the term "strike" noted in the text have any sort of connection like this at all. They are simply distinct uses of the same six letters.

15. *See supra* note 11.

16. This is Ronald Dworkin's basic conception of "rights": You have a "right" when you are permitted to do something even though, all things considered, the community would be better off if you didn't act. This is based on his distinction between "principles," which establish individual rights, and "policies," which establish collective goals. RONALD DWORKIN, TAKING RIGHTS SERIOUSLY 90–94 (1978) (hereinafter referenced as "TRS"). We will explore these ideas in much more detail in Chapter Four. *See infra* ch. 4.

17. What one will *not* find in this book, however, is a detailed review of Justice Roberts' opinions over the many years he has served as a judge. Chapter Eight will indeed review some of his opinions, but that discussion will be limited to a few written while he was on

the Court of Appeals, not the Supreme Court. *See infra* ch. 8. A wider review of his work is not really relevant here for three reasons.

First, Prof. Gould's essay and Justice Roberts' comment at the hearing limit the direct comparison of their approaches to decision-making to a particular kind of case: one in which a single concept, like a "strike," is the central point on which a decision will turn. To broaden the analysis to all aspects of Justice Roberts' opinions would therefore be unfair to him and off-point here.

Second, we will focus on Court of Appeals decisions because they are more analogous to that of an umpire's call than would be Supreme Court opinions, which would be more akin to decisions by the Commissioner of Baseball. The best comparison, of course, would be between an umpire and a district or trial court, but Justice Roberts never served at that judicial level.

Third, using Justice Roberts' Court of Appeals decisions for the D.C. Circuit allows us to contrast his approach more directly with the reasoning of another judge who served on that same Court—Judge J. Skelly Wright—which we will do in Chapter Seven. *See infra* ch. 7.

Chapter Two

To Flatlaw and Beyond: Appreciating Multiple Analytic Dimensions

My summary of the law student discussion of the Gould essay actually moved down the path of analyzing legal reasoning a bit too far too fast, for certain very basic characteristics of the nature of law and legal systems were being assumed by these students rather than acknowledged. Therefore, a momentary step back should be taken to allow us to identify the bedrock elements already within that early discussion that will prove to be the basis for later analytic sophistication. This will involve the imaginary journey, referenced at the end of the last Chapter, to a mental location, if you will, where all law students begin to get a feel for the challenge of legal education, and, sadly, where some remain even as they graduate and embark on professional careers. I call it Flatlaw.[1]

If Flatlaw were indeed a place, it would be where the vast majority of lawyers, and most law professors, have lived and worked for their entire professional lives. It would be the community law students are trained to join, most of them believing that to dwell there is an attorney's highest professional aspiration. It would probably be where you are now as you read this. This is not to say you should be ashamed, for Flatlaw is not an easy place to reach. But it is an even harder place to leave behind. This Chapter, while initially about Flatlaw itself—what it is, where it is, how to get there, and why it is important—also contemplates the meaning and legal significance of moving beyond it. As a consequence, this Chapter will be about much more than just law, as ordinarily understood.

Of course, Flatlaw is not a physical place at all, but a region of the mind, a sector within the larger mental territory of legal reasoning that this book develops. For some readers, the origin of the label I have chosen for this location, and the foundation for the discussion to follow, are now clear: This Chapter is a celebration of a little book by Edwin Abbott entitled *Flatland*.[2] Although virtually unknown outside some circles of mathematicians and engineers, it explains in a charming Victorian manner the process of dimensional thinking to those who, like Abbott himself, were not scientists by trade or education. Flatland is an imaginary place of only two dimensions, where one of the inhabitants—the narrator of the story—struggled to understand the concepts of one and three dimensions. As I hope to demonstrate, Abbott's allegory serves well as a vehicle for describing and assessing the related mental exercise of learning to think like a lawyer.

This imaginary journey will be useful for several reasons. Once completed, it can serve as a kind of developmental roadmap by which any student of the law can locate his or her own current position in analytic technique. This is not to say that everyone would characterize the mental journey beyond Flatlaw as "progress," but at least the challenge presented by those who have ventured onward will encourage those who have not to examine and justify their decision to remain behind. The journey will also explain some of the tensions that plague the academic legal community as its members discuss the nature of the task they believe to be before them. It will lead to a more comprehensive understanding of the tensions inherent in the techniques used by courts and legislatures to find and make the law. And it will clarify the many substantive legal disputes about the nature, and limits, of legal reasoning itself.

A word of caution is in order, however. Because this book's move into and beyond Flatlaw is allegorical—that is, an abstraction, an indirect representation, a metaphor[3]—its relationship to the *precise* method by which we reach legal conclusions will be approximate. This unavoidable limitation is both a benefit and a detriment. It is helpful in that it permits our analysis to develop at a quicker pace than a more descriptively methodical technique would allow, thus giving us the opportunity to reach useful comparative conclusions about the forest without being lost in the trees. Its drawback is that, to an expert in any given legal area, the approximation of the forest may seem to distort the color and nature of its constituent, more tangible, vegetation. But rest assured that the steps in following Chapters will fill in the details that the Flatlaw image leaves open.

A. Abbott's Flatland

No summary can do justice to the wit and originality of Abbott's discussion in *Flatland*[4] of the concept of dimensional thinking. But I think the following brief description will be all that is necessary to establish an anchor for the legal analogy to come.

In Abbott's allegory, Flatland is indeed a place, inhabited by two-dimensional creatures. Fully half his book is devoted to a detailed description of these creatures and their customs, which served as commentary on contemporary English society, much in the manner of Jonathan Swift's *Gulliver's Travels* and Lewis Carroll's *Alice in Wonderland*. For example, the relative social status of any individual in Flatland was established by the number of sides in the individual's figure. Thus, soldiers and the lowest classes of workmen were isosceles triangles, and among their group relative status was determined by the acuteness of the smallest angle in the triangle. But women, according to Abbott (and the not-so-charming Victorian view), were simply straight lines, and hence had the sharpest, and most dangerous, "point" of all. Professionals were four- and five-sided figures; the narrator of the tale was himself a square. Hexagons, heptagons, and so on, represented increasingly important individuals, with the pinnacle of the society being the figure in which the multi-sidedness of the individual gave way to one curved perimeter: a circle. Priests were circles. Not surprisingly, one common ambition of the members of this society was that their children have more sides than they had themselves.

Two incidents occur in the book that give the narrating Square a unique perspective on his homeland and make the book more than a simple social commentary. The first is a dream in which the Square imagines an encounter with the inhabitants of Lineland, a region of only one dimension. As he passes through their territory, these inhabitants perceive the Square as a mere series of lines. The Square endeavors to explain his difference to the King of Lineland, but fails. The King, like his subjects, has no ability to understand the concept of "width" because his own kingdom is constituted entirely of "length."

The second incident is the Square's encounter with a three-dimensional creature. It begins when the Square witnesses the sudden appearance of a single dot, which then inexplicably grows into a tiny circle, then into a larger circle, then reduces again to a small circle, then a dot, and finally disappears. As if this were not upsetting enough, the strange creature that caused this phenomenon speaks to the Square from a vantage point outside the Square's own two dimensions, and the Square can only perceive the sound as originating within his own mind. Not surprisingly, he seriously doubts his sanity. Of course, this new creature is a three-dimensional sphere (from Spaceland, naturally) that has passed through the plane of Flatland, and the Sphere's numerous attempts to explain the concepts of "up" and "down" to the Square are as unsuccessful as the Square's own conversations with the King of Lineland. In a fit of frustration, the Sphere kicks the Square out of his two-dimensional plane. To the Square's amazement he floats above his world, looking down on its inhabitants. He is able for the first time to see the angles formed by their sides, and he can look into their closed houses. After all, these structures have walls that block the view only from within Flatland's two-dimensional plane.

Upon his return to Flatland, the Square communicates his startling encounter to others only to be met with disbelieving hostility. His attempts to explain the dimension of "up" into which he has traveled are taken as evidence of insanity. His descriptions of his fellow inhabitants of Flatland as two-dimensional figures, and his assertion of the ability to see into closed houses, confirm their suspicions. Unable to convince even his intelligent young hexagonal grandson of the accuracy of his perception of another dimension, the poor Square is ultimately confined to a mental institution where he languishes away the remainder of his life.

What has this allegorical description of dimensional thinking to do with the special phenomenon of legal reasoning? The remainder of this Chapter explores the possible connections, and attempts, in essence, to put perspective in perspective.

B. Reasoning From Dotlaw to Linelaw

Although the parallels are not precise, Abbott's *Flatland* suggests the following general description of some basic stages in the development of the ability to "think like a lawyer."

In the beginning—before law school, that is—the "law" appears to be simply discrete official pronouncements by various government functionaries: statutes (you need two witness for a valid will), regulations (you cannot smoke in here), court decisions (you can sue for damages in situation X but not in Y), and the like. Even the Constitution can seem to be little more than an elaborate list of particular powers and limitations (regulate interstate commerce, respect free speech, each state gets two Senators, and so on). From this perspective, one can easily imagine the law to be like a dimensionless array of propositions—just "dots" of information—making the popular term "a point of law"[5] appropriate indeed. Non-lawyers consequently perceive law schools as places for the study of Dotlaw, if you will, where students discover (in an archaeological sense)[6] the various bits of special information in the array; the bar examination is imagined in turn to be a test of how many bits or dots the candidate has memorized; and the practice of law is basically identifying and using those dots most beneficial to the lawyer's clients.

Law school changes these perceptions rather quickly (at least for most students). Tentatively at first, and then with more and more acumen, students realize that the more dots they discover, the more patterned the dots seem to become, until at some point the first mental breakthrough is achieved: Rather than chaos, the dots suggest linear connections. Court decisions seem to have important similarities; statutes and decisions seem sometimes to work together, sometimes to clash; officials are constantly noting and assessing the work of other officials. At this point, dimensional thinking has begun, and the student approaches each new legal topic as an exercise in discovering and developing lines of connectivity.[7] The task now becomes not simply finding and listing bits of legal data, but establishing the *links* between various cases or statutes, or both, which ultimately provide a picture of the "path of the law"[8] in a given area.

At the beginning of the student's discovery of what I will call Linelaw, the exercise of forging the connective links is rudimentary and simplistic, based on some feature shared by two or more legal "points," such as a set of cases all involving injured children, or broken promises, and so on. But as modest as this first step is, it is fundamental to the entire analytic enterprise upon which the student will embark. It introduces the two most foundational and well-recognized features of legal reasoning: the use of analogies and deducing conclusions.

Analogical reasoning is simply about consistency: As lawyers put it, "Treat like cases alike, and different cases differently." Deduction is about rationality: Given a true major premise, A, and a true minor premise, B, then true conclusion X must follow. But both these summaries just shift the struggle to the next, and obvious, step: What is "likeness" (the lines) and what are the "premises" (the dots)?

Note how this works within Dotlaw, where the thinking could not be simpler: The rule (major premise) says "do Z"; but (minor premise) you did not do Z; you are therefore (conclusion) in trouble. That sequence is now one of the dots in your legal array of the law of Z (which you must, as a student, presumably memorize). But as the initial legal premise and the relevant facts become more complicated, the appropriate conclusion becomes correspondingly less certain and more troubling. Dots, by themselves, are very limited bits of information in what is obviously a complicated universe.

To feel better about this perplexing murkiness, students can compare this sequential logic to other preexisting examples, where they hope to find consistent results. If they do—if they find that their struggles with connecting more complex propositions is similar to the efforts of others—they quite happily know at least that their reasoning has strength in numbers. They are reassured when their thinking does not stand alone and is not therefore vulnerable to being exposed as idiosyncratic. In searching for connections, Linelaw has emerged. The dots seem not only to string together, but in doing so, to validate each other.

The situation for the student, however, becomes more and more disconcerting when the dots of legal data begin to appear to be like complex molecules of many factors, suggesting multiple potential connections. A particular case decision, for example, might seem to share a similarity with others by involving an injured child, but it might also concern (like yet other cases) dangerous machinery or precarious bridges, or slipping and drowning in a puddle of rainwater.[9] Initially, many students seem to ignore (or want to ignore) this mass of possibilities and focus instead on only the most obvious common feature that is uniquely legal in character: the actual pronouncement or "rule" about human behavior made by a particular decision or statute, which constitutes its "point of law." The common feature may be nothing more than, for example, features of products that are particularly dangerous to children. In that comfortably simple situation, the line the student develops may appear quite "straight," linking injury-based cases of this kind. Later, the student may rethink the connection to reflect further data: The common feature may become a more general duty of due care to avoid harm to others of any age, and as a result, the initially imagined connective line between cases may seem inadequate—it at least begins to "curve" or change direction as a result of causation problems. This growing dissatisfaction with Linelaw's strict unidimensional character—where, as in Abbott's Lineland, only "back and forth" movement is possible—means that new analytic perspectives are being perceived.

As another illustration of the nature of these "lines" of legal data, consider an array of judicial decisions or statutes answering questions about ownership claims to wild animals: for instance, whether physical possession of the animal is necessary or sufficient,[10] whether marking the animal makes a difference,[11] whether the unusualness of the place where the animal is found is relevant.[12] These rules, or "dots," become a "line" when some connective tissue is discovered. At first the student may see nothing more than the fact that all these legal pronouncements have to do with animals, but the first true bit of legal cartilage will appear when he or she makes the slightly more sophisticated observation that all these rules address the problem of owning something that does not remain stationary or respect boundaries. Indeed, the student may discover that link only by comparing one subject, like wild animals, to an apparently unrelated subject, like the ownership of oil, natural gas, and water,[13] and thereby realizing that the patterns of the dots in the two areas are remarkably similar.

No matter how this initial observation is made, the student's limited objectives within Linelaw are first, to establish that in various areas of the law there are relationships among discrete rules of law, and second, to identify the "correct" relationships—correct not in the sense of being unique, but in the simple descriptive sense of being satisfactorily consistent and coherent.[14] A couple of potential dividends might come from this initial, superficial exercise. A linear pattern established by points of legal data could allow the student to predict where the next point in the sequence will or ought to be,[15] and also to identify aberrations within the pattern. For example, a progression like that shown in Figure 2.1 may indicate to the student that a particular decision or statute may have been a "mistake":

Figure 2.1

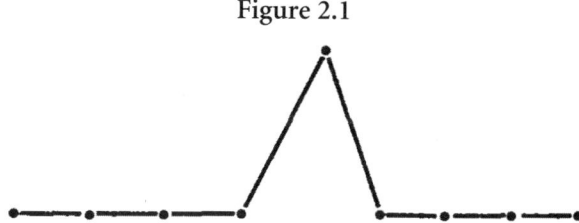

But it does not take most students long to perceive more and more factors associated with any area of law, and the complex linkages that might be possible. This new awareness has two effects: first, it makes possible configurations far more complicated than simple continuous lines; second, it suggests that while points of law may be very "close" to one another in the array, they may be parts of quite distinct lines, as demonstrated in Figure 2.2:

Figure 2.2

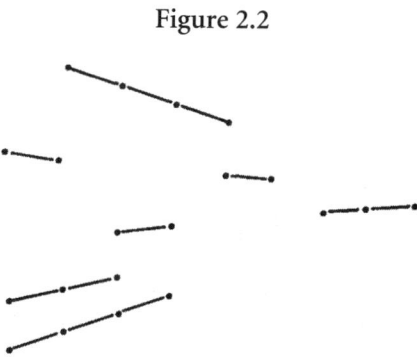

A chaos nearly as troubling as the original formless array of unconnected points now plagues the student. It is the law school's primary and unique function to give the student the ability to produce order and coherence from the mass of data that, as the student guessed or as others told her, contains connections and patterns of some kind. The question, of course, is *what* kind, and the teacher of law, depending upon her style, perhaps answers it, or gives the student the opportunity to discover answers, or devises some combination of the two educational techniques.

C. Reasoning Toward Flatlaw: From Lines to Shapes

In doing so, the teacher now gives the student a glimpse of Flatlaw by showing him or her both the need for and the possibility of another dimension of legal reasoning. This analytic element might be introduced in two steps. The student, through diligent study, may have discovered a number of points of law that seem to represent only a series of lines, as in the diagram above. The law professor, on the other hand, will reveal these dots and lines to be portions of a larger mental structure, as shown in Figure 2.3:

Figure 2.3

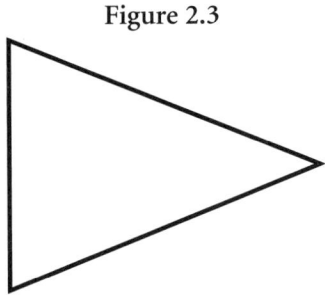

Thus, the single-dimensional nature of the student's reasoning is exposed. Thinking of the law only in terms of lines, the student was able to perceive the two-dimensional triangle only as a series of such lines. Further diligent study may have revealed more points, and hence more lines, but even the convergence of a number of lines at a single point would have been taken as only a curious and interesting pattern rather than as part of a complete figure. To move from dots and lines to figures is to move from one kind of reasoning to another—from Dotlaw and Linelaw to Flatlaw.

The example of wild animals used earlier is as good as any. The student may have perceived that the separate lines or rules associated with ownership claims to wild animals and oil and natural gas are not only similar but parallel or converging in some sense, and may have found this interesting and somewhat informative. But the professor sees this pattern as fundamental to the broader concept or doctrine (the "triangle") of ownership itself or "property" law. The particular challenge within this doctrine that the student is studying turns out to be the more general one of owning things that, unlike land, do not necessarily stay still.

Inducing students to make the mental leap from Linelaw to Flatlaw is only possible if the teacher convinces them of two things: first, that each discrete point of law captures a complex of relevant considerations that make "broader," two-dimensional, rather than simply "linear," interconnections possible; and second, that specific interconnections do in fact exist—that is, that the "law" in any given area is more than just a tangle of lines of rules. This is not an easy task, for a number of reasons.

The sophisticated teacher may be convinced, for example, that the geometric figure that depicts an area of law breaks down into chaotic lines at certain places: One illustration could be the caselaw that constitutes the doctrines of real covenants and equitable servitudes, which is often said by scholars to be a hopeless jumble, counseling thorough reconsideration and reordering.[16] This upsetting assessment can then have equally troubling implications. It can induce a certain skepticism about the validity of the "legal figure" (doctrinal area) itself, suggesting that the links filling in the "gaps" between various lines may be nothing more than a figment of the instructor's overactive legal imagination. There is also the problem of handling "mistakes"[17] identified by the teacher as being outside the figure and hence unworthy of serious consideration. How else, for example, can we view a decision like *Plessy v. Ferguson*[18] that endorsed institutionalized racism? Again, debates about these "mistakes," which call into question attempts to gather lines into comprehensive shapes, may in turn call into question the validity of the entire analytic enterprise of attempting to make sense of the daunting data called "law."

Related to these problems are the difficulties posed by the inevitable debates among academics about what kind of geometric figure is correct—some arguing that it must be a square, others that it must be a circle, and so on—and by scholarly disagreements about the size or inclusiveness of the figures involved. For example, where one scholar sees two shapes, another might see one (as shown in Figure 2.4):

Figure 2.4

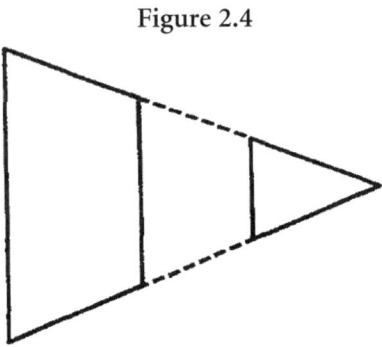

Yet another may believe the vision of these scholars is altogether too limited, or that the "direction" in which they have the law "pointing" is incorrect (as seen in Figure 2.5):

Figure 2.5

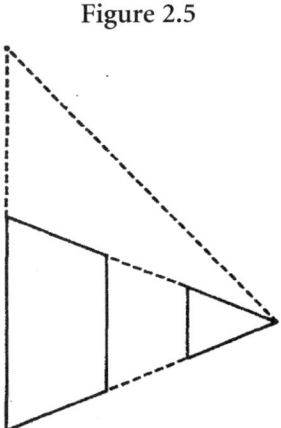

Examples of disconcerting struggles like these will be examined in the last two Chapters of this book, which will discuss quite different understandings of the shape, if you will, of two doctrinal areas—the right to privacy (Chapter Nine) and methods of statutory interpretation (Chapter Ten). At times, the sum total of these debates may for some call into question this entire dimensional analogy.

But simply because flatlawyering may not produce "perfect" doctrinal shapes to which everyone can agree does not at all mean that this analytic exercise is misguided or worthless. Quite the contrary, as I noted earlier, much of the practice of law is the rather straightforward identification of existing legal dots, developing them into coherent patterns of guidance, and reporting those results to, or imposing them on, others. Often it is not, and need not, be any fancier. Indeed, the vast bulk of law journal comments written by law students reflect this approach. The student identifies lines of cases that develop in some way inconsistently and seeks to resolve any resulting anomalies by revealing a missing or inadequate piece of logic in a court's thinking. Or, the student may conclude that two competing lines of cases are both apparently legitimately logical and reasonable, and thus requiring a difficult policy judgment that must be made by someone. All of this can be useful and necessary fundamental legal work. Indeed, much of the next Chapter will observe important contributions to legal theory that have labored to understand these seemingly mundane analytic tasks in impressively sophisticated ways.

Yet beneath that literature, I would argue, is a struggle that the Flatlaw analogy helps elucidate—if we recognize the limits that are inherent in its two-dimensional approach to legal reasoning.

D. The Need for a Next Step

We must start by noting that all the analytic problems encountered within Linelaw that led us to Flatlaw resurface anew. For example, how does a Flatlawyer explain "change" in the law? Any observer will notice that, as a matter of historical fact, particular rules, or whole sets of rules, disappear entirely, appear suddenly, or change their configuration in startling ways.[19] If your entire analytic universe is "shapes," how do these configurations alter themselves? And more fundamentally, if one remains in the two dimensions of Flatlaw, how do you have enough perspective to "know" what the shapes actually look like as a whole—much like the residents of Flatland who were unable to "see" the actual shapes of others?

Most telling of all, perhaps, is the Flatlawyer's challenge of confronting and resolving inconsistencies within the mass of legal data itself. In this situation, which goes all the way back to the dots being examined, to be able to make a shape out of the data that isn't simply an ugly hodgepodge of some sort, but something more pleasingly elegant, some dots will have to be considered unworthy of respect, and hence excluded. For example, imagine this not-uncommon legal possibility: Let's say a state supreme court is confronted with an appeal that raises the question of whether a confession by a criminal defendant was voluntary or inappropriately forced by the police. In searching for "like cases," the court discovers two decisions in neighboring states in which those supreme courts were presented—also in cases there of "first impression"—with the same factual circumstances (different defendant and police officers, of course, but the same characteristics and behavior by both). But these two courts reached completely opposite results—one declaring the confession voluntary and admissible, the other the contrary. Which of these decisions should this court decide to follow? In the absence of other immediately relevant "legal data" considered by the two other courts, how would *this* court determine which of the two is "better reasoned" and therefore should be included in its shape of this area of law?

Regarding this and all the other conundra noted above, one possible conclusion could be that there are simply *no* meaningful resolutions to these difficulties. You could, for example, adopt one form or another of nihilism—legal material is in fact arbitrary and its rationales unknowable. It is all based on "what the judge had for breakfast"[20] or something similar, so that the only thing worth studying is the psychology of judges (judicial behavioralism[21]).

In the alternative, to avoid this kind of despair, note that you probably have the sense that to resolve the conflict between the competing State judicial decisions discussed above, you would want somehow to go "beneath" or "above" these "points of law" to assess them. But what does that mean, and how is it analytically possible in the narrow confines of Flatlaw? The answers are based on a need to recognize that Flatlaw is only an intermediate stop in the journey through legal reasoning. As impressive as this mental effort is—integrating dots (bits of legal data) into shapes (more comprehensive legal doctrines)—it is still too limited to handle adequately the problems of conflicts, uncertainty, and skepticism that plague conscientious attempts to produce truly comprehensive analytic results.

E. Transcending Flatlaw: From Shapes to Objects

The analytical challenge here will require a fundamental rethinking of legal dots and lines themselves. We become, in effect, the Square who encounters, with the help of the Sphere, an entirely new dimension, although we risk, when we talk about this, being labeled by our professional community as insane. This step is daunting enough, I believe, to justify, again, an indirect, rather than head-on, approach, using a different analogy. I raise it here partly because it is famous, and thus perhaps familiar to many readers, but also because, while dramatic and intriguing, it is also, for legal reasoning, inapt. But there are important lessons to learn from its defects nevertheless.

One could argue that the traveler to the lands beyond Flatlaw would find his or her experience similar to that described by Plato's "Allegory of the Cave."[22] In this dialogue, Socrates proposes that most of the world can be compared to a cave in which the inhabitants are chained, unable to escape, unable to see direct sunlight, and unable to turn their heads to see one another. Their world is made up of the shadows of themselves and other objects in the cave created by the indirect light that manages to reach them. Reality, then, is entirely two-dimensional, for all objects appear as only flat, shadowy forms. Socrates then speculates on what would happen if some of the prisoners were released and forced to face the true reality hitherto hidden from them. Rather than an experience of great joy, it is initially one of pain and hesitation:

> Consider, then, what would … happen … When one was freed from his fetters and compelled to stand up suddenly and turn his head around and walk and to lift up his eyes to the light, and in doing all this felt pain and, because of the dazzle and glitter of the light, was unable to discern the objects whose shadows he formerly saw, what do you suppose would be his answer if someone told him that what he had seen before was all a cheat and an illusion, but that now, being nearer to reality and turned toward more real things, he saw more truly? And if also one should point out to him each of the passing objects and constrain him by questions to say what it is, do you not think that he would be at a loss and that he would regard what he formerly saw as more real than the things now pointed out to him?
>
> Far more real, he said.
>
> And if he were compelled to look at the light itself, would not that pain his eyes, and would he not turn away and flee to those things which he is able to discern and regard them as in every deed more clear and exact than the objects pointed out?
>
> It is so, he said.[23]

And the pain gets worse. When the prisoner reenters the darkness of the cave, to which his eyes are now unaccustomed, those who have never been out think he has lost his sense of reality. Therefore, ventures outside the cave are considered unhealthy and not worth the effort.[24] Yet, as depressing as this image is, Plato concludes the allegory by arguing that those to whom the nature of sunlight has been revealed have a special responsibility to their fellow prisoners. They must return to the darkness and take on the burden of leadership of their unenlightened fellows as best they can, for they alone will know the true reality of the images perceived in the cave.[25]

Using this allegory, the traveler who has departed Flatlaw could argue to the remaining residents that they see only the shadows of true legal reality. To this traveler, something beyond the law, having another dimension creating the depth of solid objects, generates the flat geometric configurations perceived in Flatlaw. Thus, the residents of that realm, she contends to anyone who will listen, are experiencing the law in a distorted, reduced form, as the two-dimensional shadow of a three-dimensional object (as shown in Figure 2.6):

Figure 2.6

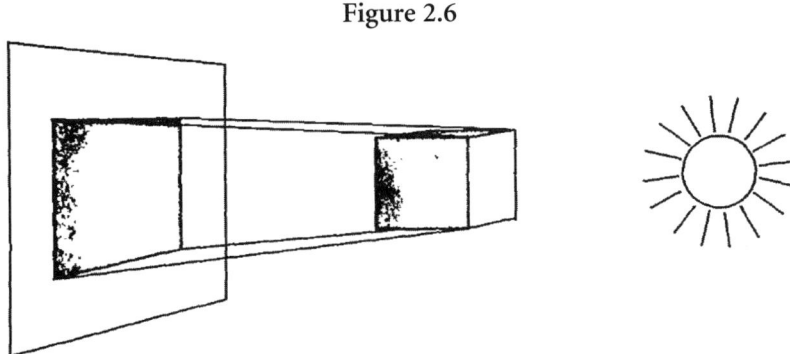

Thus, she argues, distortion, misconstruction, and limited understanding are inevitable.

But this is a very poor image of the nature of Flatlaw. Note initially what it says about "the law" itself: that legal data isn't "real," but instead the insubstantial shadow of some other "actual" reality (the cube above). The law is not part of that reality, but instead a distant and separate "product" of it. The law does not participate in this other reality but is driven entirely by it. Thus, lawyers, in discussing the law, are merely "shadow-boxing" rather than doing anything profound. They are puppets, to mix metaphors once again, with someone else pulling the strings. And it gets worse. The shadow, which reduces a three-dimensional object to just two dimensions, must necessarily also distort the reality of the object. I suppose we do at least now have an explanation for legal "change:" As the object or the light source moves, the shadow will change shape. But this doesn't help much. Why and how is the object or light moving? And assuming we can come to grips with the substance of this dominant reality (the cube), what is the light source, whose radiance is blocked by the cube, supposed to represent?

Perhaps most damning of all, note what kind of pitiable people Plato must invent to make the allegory work. They are trapped and constrained, *forced* to see nothing but shadows. They have no ability to engage with each other to improve their sense of their circumstances. They, like the shadows, are purely passive.

Such people are not those I envision as engaged in legal reasoning. Flatlawyers may have their analytic limitations, as I will argue, but they are far from being so pathetic. We therefore need to establish an image that is not so unnecessarily insulting to the ordinary practice of law.

A better understanding of the significance of moving beyond Flatlaw would be to take Plato's idea of a limited two-dimensional perspective and treat it instead as a *slice* of a larger, but not separate, three-dimensional reality (see Figure 2.7):

Figure 2.7

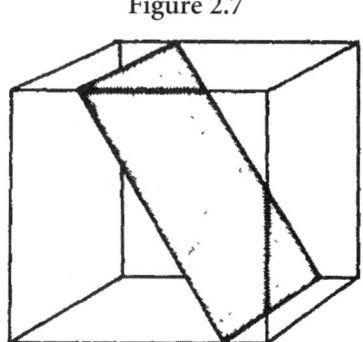

Although the slice is only a piece of this object, it is at least part and parcel of it. That slice (the law) can now interact with all the other elements that constitute the cube. Indeed, it will become interesting to discern how "thick" the slice of the law is—how much stuff other than traditional legal "dots" and "lines" the law can aggregate unto itself. And we can still have plenty of disagreements about the "shape" of any aspect of law as the slice is viewed as residing in different places or resting at different angles within the object, or the shape of the three-dimensional object changes.

This version of the traveler beyond Flatlaw is nevertheless still quite a profound challenge to those remaining in that realm. The claim now is not simply that the number, or *quantity*, of inter-connective lines among the legal dots they identify is insufficient, but that the *quality* of their information, in effect, is defective. To do their analytic job fully, the dots must reach out in new directions—to a new dimension—altogether.

And just as in Abbott's story and Plato's allegory, the traveler would expect Flatlaw residents to be less than enthusiastic about his revelation because it calls their most fundamental assumptions into question. Flatlawyers' first reactions might be rejection and hostility, for as it turns out, the Flatlaw approach to the law has a long and strong tradition on which it is proudly based. In fact, that background is well illustrated by some of the attitudes expressed in that first-year discussion of the call by Umpire Pinelli in the Gould article.

Recall the relentless emphasis by some students on baseball's rule book. The legal dots in that objective source are all "connected" simply by being in the book. That is your doctrinal "shape." End of story. So to be a successful law student (or good lawyer or umpire or judge), just memorize the book.

Discussions of the law among Flatlawyers thus become conversations within closed self-referential systems, like mathematics. Axioms in that discipline work together simply because the discipline says so. Nothing extraneous to mathematics needs to be referenced to demonstrate that $2 + 2 = 4$. The analytic picture is already complete. From this kind of perspective, the law, just as simply, tells you what the law is. The lines of connection among the legal dots all remain singularly within the dimension of the law itself.

The form that this reasoning takes among legal scholars and commentators will be developed in more detail in Chapter Three, but for present purposes, we should realize that Flatlaw is about a particular subset of connections among the data of the law—connections that are rooted in the existing institution of the law itself. These ties are what Ronald Dworkin called "institutional support"[26] or "fit" that a given rule enjoys within the legal system, or what Neil MacCormick described as the law's necessary consistency and internal coherence.[27] It is not as if Flatlawyers are therefore simplistic robots, for they might indeed also consider the social or moral consequences of a rule in the real world. But they would only do so to the extent that such consequences have been declared by some law-creating authority to be relevant to the application of the rule.

Linelaw and Flatlaw are therefore both closely related and different: the former because each depends on this concept of institutional support to identify points and then connect them to form lines and figures; the latter because of increasing analytic sophistication. To take another example: Where the student sees lines of cases dealing with offer, acceptance, consideration, and so forth, the professor sees, and tries to communicate to the student, a geometric figure called "the law of contract," which contains these lines but connects them through broader concepts (nevertheless quite "legal" in character), such as "agreement," "reliance," and "expectation."[28] But note: To do all this, no one need look beyond legal texts themselves. It is why Flatlaw is the special province of most law students and many practicing lawyers, for to have what appears to be a full professional conversation, the range of topics is constrained and comfortably traditional.

Hence, discussions with those challenging this world-view can be tense. Flatlawyers might argue that the view of the traveler beyond this realm is the one that is distorted and unreal because it questions whether the positive, objective legal sources are true embodiments, or *the* embodiment, of the law. To make matters worse, travelers beyond Flatlaw have the unfortunate tendency to look down, literally as well as figuratively, on their colleagues who have remained behind. Scholars who believe themselves to be operating beyond Flatlaw can be viewed as calling into question the worthiness of much of the enterprise that brought us to Flatlaw in the first place. They sometimes seem to suggest that only *they* possess truly profound and significant legal knowledge, and are therefore entitled to special respect.[29]

Putting those dynamics aside, it is nevertheless the case that only an effort to transcend Flatlaw can respond adequately to the open questions about legal reasoning noted earlier. Consider again the phenomenon of change. Because the law is not a static physical form but a dynamic social institution, change implies not only differences from time to time but also development or progress in a certain direction. This in turn implies that no two-dimensional depiction of the law can ever be "final," no matter how accurate. But how would a resident of Flatlaw explain this lack of finality? If the law only refers to itself, where is this pressure for change coming from, and what shape will it take?

Closely related is the simple fact that traditional objective (text-based) sources and statements of the law seem to "run out"[30] at certain points—not every circumstance has been, or can be, anticipated in advance. If law is only what legal institutions say it is, how would the Flatlawyer argue that the law can extend itself to capture new situations that appear beyond its present boundaries? How could she presume to offer more than the simplistic conclusion that a court confronted with a new situation "does the best it can in the circumstances"?

And to return to the geometric analogy, how could two residents of Flatlaw argue about which geometrical figure properly represents an area of law? For example, does the right to privacy limit the government's authority to produce security, or does the need for security inherently limit any right to privacy? If both Flatlawyers are devoted to being as descriptively accurate as possible, and assuming that neither is depending upon faulty data, how could they disagree concerning the final product? How could each label the other as using a shape (doctrine) that is legally mistaken?

On this last point, note more fundamentally that Flatlawyers cannot "see" the figures they are discussing, just as the residents of Flatland could not perceive each other as actual figures, but merely as sets of lines receding from the observer at various angles. It was only when the Square was kicked into a third dimension that he could actually understand various figures *as* figures. So too, the characterization of legal debate as involving different two-dimensional figures suggests that there must be yet another dimension from which these figures may be perceived more fully and clearly.

The point of this image of law as a slice, then, is this: A thorough knowledge of and facility with data inside this singular sliver still only means you are good at the current version and content of the sliver. It is thus largely a static exercise. You would not have much of a sense of the law as a dynamic enterprise—understanding where the elements in this plane may have come from or how or why that sliver might be reconfigured or redirected in the future.

F. The Nature and Content of the Next Step

What, then, is this new perspective that permits the traveler to depart Flatlaw and enter another dimension of legal reasoning? Stated most generally, it is the recognition that legal rules and institutions are only evidence of or data indicating larger social phenomena associated with the concepts of other disciplines. These phenomena include: community standards of morality and justice, economic efficiency, group behavior, social and political forces, primal or sociobiological urges or necessities, and so on—in essence, any other discipline that might find a home on a campus where a law school sits. From these new perspectives, "institutional" law—the doctrines regularly and traditionally employed by courts and legislatures—may well appear as only an imperfect shadow or slice representation within the larger "object" perceived by these others. To return once again to earlier examples, the rules associated with ownership of property could be viewed as data within a larger economic picture,[31] or the rules of contract could be seen as part of a deeper philosophical structure defining the normative implications of promises.[32]

So why does this additional dimension matter? What is its impact on our appreciation of the slice of this larger object that is "the law"? The answer lies in the sense of dynamism noted above, and can be multiple and complex. This wider perspective could help explain the background and current content of the legal slice; or, as different competing non-legal forces within the object are identified, help elucidate and clarify tensions and disagreements within legal discussions; or, as normative disciplines focused on values rather than data are referenced, help morally justify or condemn current legal doctrine; and on and on. The third dimension guarantees that "the law" will, and must, be perceived as more than what is in the current rule books.

One important characteristic of the third dimension in legal reasoning is subject to misunderstanding, however: I would argue that this new element does *not* include references simply to historical "changes over time." While attention to chronological development of rules and principles is certainly not irrelevant to legal analysis, it does not *in itself* permit the leap in perspective that the third dimension demands. Instead, historical analysis is a creature of Flatlaw; while it may seem to produce a three-dimensional picture of an area of law by adding the reference to "time," this picture is in fact made up of a series of planes or slices that remain two-dimensional. The more detailed the historical inquiry, the more slices that may be revealed, and consequently the more "depth" the picture may appear to have. But the mental process involved does not look beyond the positive, institutional sources of law. While from this perspective law becomes more than a single or incidental shadow or slice of a larger social phenomenon, it nevertheless remains simply a series of such two-dimensional figures.

Of course, this criticism applies only to historical analysis at its worst when it is divorced from analysis of other social forces that *generate* the "sweep of history." Such forces could be, for example, the struggle of various groups for economic advantage, or the growing concern for efficient use of resources, or the tensions generated within various forms of social structure, or the changing philosophical views of humanness and human dignity.[33] Each of these analytic points of view, and certainly any combination of them, places law and legal institutions in a more comprehensive context. (In fact they attempt to place *all* historical detail within this context.) In this expanded form, an historical analysis of any area of the law is in fact a search for data and evidence to support a larger theory, and thus qualifies as an exercise in third-dimensional reasoning.

G. Difficulties with the Third Dimension

To some readers, lumping together the wisdom and insight of various social sciences and liberal arts may seem a bit cavalier, but I hasten to remind these readers that the object of the current exercise is not to produce a finely tuned model of all individual mental processes, but rather to give some sense of the levels of complexity and sophistication that may exist in legal reasoning in particular. Nevertheless, some may find especially disturbing the fact that my third dimension of legal reasoning lumps together in the "nonlegal disciplines" category academic pursuits that are not only widely diverse in analytic method but entirely different in focus and purpose. In particular, careful scholars take great pains to differentiate between objective, descriptive, positive analyses of observable events, on the one hand, and subjective, theoretical, normative assessments of those events, on the other.[34] As we noted in the preceding Chapter, these two distinct approaches are ordinarily labeled, respectively, as "facts" and "values." The former attempts to depict what "is," while the latter seeks to justify a vision of what "ought" to be. To some, the former might be said to be about "law," the latter about "justice." The former seems the province of the social sciences, while the latter is the subject of philosophy and ethics.[35] Yet in this move beyond Flatlaw, these very distinct exercises are placed in the same category, with the obvious implication that in some way they have more in common than they have in conflict.

That will only be true temporarily—just for the purposes of this Chapter's task of introducing the multiple layers constituting legal reasoning. Later these quite different analytical agendas will indeed be appropriately separated. But for the moment, amalgamating these disciplines is justified if the vantage points they provide for viewing legal data are both sufficiently similar to make them a cohesive group, and also sufficiently distinct from our earlier perspectives to constitute a new perspective "at right angles" to that of the paradigmatic Flatlawyer.

I believe they are. From the point of view of the early student of law, these other disciplines naturally tend to lump together as a group because they all treat legal material as bits of evidence in the search for a more fundamental reality. These academic inquiries are then identified conveniently in law school curricula as "Law and _____" courses. Not surprisingly, devotees of particular disciplines within this vast realm of our third dimension would find this sort of forced association with other academic traditions uncomfortable (if not downright unsanitary). But rest assured, we will fix that.

One possible, but unfortunate, implication of consolidating all nonlegal disciplines into this additional dimension is that, because they afford perspectives that reduce law to mere evidence of a larger theory, these disciplines are somehow of a "higher" order of analysis. Therefore, the impression could be that traditional institutional, doctrinal legal analysis is inherently inferior and must worship at the shrines of these nonlegal perspectives. In effect we are back to Plato and his cave-dwellers.[36] We can expose the fallacy of this argument, however, by returning to our starting point.

We began with "points" of law and defined the first and second dimensions as the forms of reasoning that give some larger life to these bits of legal data. It follows that when we have exhausted purely "legal" analysis, we can give a larger life to legal concepts by reasoning about them from extralegal approaches. By the same token, we should understand any other discipline through the same progressively expansive forms of reasoning. For example, the first dimension of economic analysis would be the rudimentary connection of bits of economic data in various simple lines of cause and effect; the second dimension would reveal more sophisticated geometric figures reflecting an understanding of more complex economic factors. To arrive at a third dimension the economist would have to view the economic data as part of some larger social whole—which would include information not only about legal doctrine, but other disciplines as well. For example, to make an argument that understanding the economic forces in any given situation is a "good" idea—not just an analytically possible idea—then the economist would necessarily have to move beyond economics *itself* to, for example, philosophy to justify his or her myopic dedication to economic data and economic analysis.

Therefore, it would be a mistake to believe that we could short-cut our way to a full and accurate sense of legal reality by simply *starting* with the narrative provided by the conclusions of some other discipline. For an economist to analyze a complex legal concept without reference to the dot-like rules and "lines" of rules that form that concept would be in effect to treat this material simplistically as a tiny blip of economic data, or a dimensionless "point" to be connected with other economic "points." The economist would have fallen back into limited one-dimensional reasoning. Thus, it is a mistake for the practitioner of *any* discipline to suggest sophisticated or expansive conclusions without having first done the difficult groundwork that makes such leaps possible. Beginning an analysis at either end of the dimensional scale is necessarily a first, and quite rudimentary, step.

While our allegorical model may place these many disciplines together in the third dimension, it does not predict that the views of the law the disciplines generate will be the same or even similar. To the contrary, as we will see in later Chapters, debates about law in the third dimension will be even more intense than they are in Flatlaw. From the point of view of this analytic allegory, the conflict will now turn on two very different, but related, issues. First, what three-dimensional object most completely represents the reality within which positive legal sources exist? Second, what two-dimensional figure ("slice" not "shadow") is the best reduction of the object for revealing ("is") or proposing ("ought") the correct connections among these Flatlaw data?

The shapes could be anything: pyramids, cubes, cylinders, multisided monstrosities, or spheres. Perhaps one could visualize the model of law proposed by each separate discipline as a particular and distinctive shape. Indeed, one might even attempt to rank the disciplines hierarchically, as Abbott ranked the inhabitants of his Flatland, according to the number of sides or separate surfaces each discipline's model possesses. More sides would suggest more complexity, and hence a more accurate representation of three-dimensional reality. Or quite the opposite, all disciplines might aspire instead to explain as much data as possible with as few basic propositions, or sides, as possible, making the competition one of elegant simplicity rather than daunting complexity.[37]

As noted earlier, given the number of three-dimensional constructs proposed by various disciplines, a multitude of two-dimensional reductions—that is, translations into the standard doctrinal concepts of Flatlaw—will be possible. Different solid objects and different angles within objects will of course produce very different slices. And this debate about the object's form can take place even within a single non-legal discipline (not all economists view their analytic approach the same way). While such reduction from object to slice inevitably involves a certain amount of distortion, the translation from three to two dimensions is nevertheless necessary whenever the traveler beyond Flatlaw attempts to communicate with the Flatlawyers who remained behind. If the traveler wants them to understand her "larger" view of the law, she must demonstrate the accuracy of her view by connecting it to the legal data manifest in Flatlaw and evident to its inhabitants. Otherwise, the travelers just end up talking to themselves rather uselessly.

Although our present dimensional approach to legal reasoning might initially have seemed rather cursory, it in fact both depicts and predicts the great complexity of legal debate. It suggests as well why the participants in these debates sometimes cannot understand why they arrive at different results: They simply fail to perceive that they see legal problems from fundamentally different perspectives.

H. Going Further: Rethinking the Dots, Lines, Shapes, and Objects Themselves

But as important as this multi-dimensional insight is, it is still only one piece of an even larger analytical exercise. All that has been depicted thus far are, in effect, "stick figures" rather than portraits of real people. All the diagrams have been straight lines connecting simple dots, and then more lines connecting to other dots and lines to form easily perceived (even if complicated) shapes and objects—first in two dimensions, then in three. But what remains unexplained and unexplored is the nature of these "dots" of legal information and the connective lines *themselves*. It is as if we have discovered that physical matter is composed of atoms, but we now realize that far more important insights about our circumstances will be afforded by unpacking these particles to see what makes *them* work. Or, depending on what sort of metaphor you prefer, we need to put some flesh on what to this point seems a rather robotic image, bringing the dots, lines, shapes, and objects to life.

Although I hope to achieve that objective in Chapter Four, we need one more preliminary foundational step to demonstrate that the preceding extended discussions of both Prof. Gould's comments on baseball and our development of a dimensional model are not purely idiosyncratic whimsy on my part. Chapter Three will demonstrate, to the contrary, that these fundamental struggles with legal reasoning are indeed reflected in, and vital to, the traditional, much respected literature of legal theory.

Notes

1. I developed this image in Terrell, *supra* Introduction note 3.

2. EDWIN A. ABBOTT, FLATLAND (5th ed. 1963). Of course, it is by no means rare for an author to explain a difficult philosophical concept by means of an analogy. *See, e.g.*, Joel Feinberg, *The Nature and Value of Rights*, 4 J. VALUE INQUIRY 243 (1970), in which to demonstrate the nature and importance of "rights," Professor Feinberg imagines a place called " 'Nowheresville' " in which the concept of a right does not exist. *Id. See also* Laurence H. Tribe, *Ways Not to Think About Plastic Trees: New Foundations for Environmental Law*, 83 YALE L.J. 1315 (1974).

3. *See also* GEORGE LAKOFF & MARK JOHNSON, METAPHORS WE LIVE BY (1980). The authors argue that metaphor is a critical means by which members of different cultures can negotiate and establish common meanings to achieve communication. *Id.* Persons engaged in different types of legal reasoning may also need to negotiate common meanings, and I hope that the metaphor of Flatlaw will be included in that negotiation.

4. The references in the text in this area are drawn from ABBOTT, *supra* note 2, at 8–12, 45–48, 57–68, 70–86, 102–108.

5. In fact, there is a game on the market called "A Point of Law" that, much in the nature of the Multistate Bar Examination, describes a fact situation giving rise to a legal conflict and asks the player to choose one of four possible legal resolutions. The simplicity of the answers, however, generally insures that only a layperson could guess the correct response.

6. Professor Edward Dauer offers the following anecdotal evidence on this point:

> I opted for the Law some fifteen years ago. About eleven years ago I headed west for my first academic appointment—Assistant Professor of Law at a fair-sized university in Ohio. I was consumed with self-congratulation, poised to produce the greatest legal scholarship the world had ever seen. My brother-in-law, whom

I saw just before I left, asked me a question: "What does an academic lawyer do besides teach classes a few hours a week?" I laid it all out for him, with a proud underscore beneath the phrase "We do legal research." "What in the world is legal research," he asked, "other than reading cases and statutes that someone else wrote. You look for undiscovered laws hiding under rocks?"

Edward Dauer, *Law and the Life of the Mind*, 27 YALE L. REP., Winter 1980–1981, at 13.

7. To give some idea of what sorts of patterns might be discerned, note that the following configurations of four "points of law" could be linked in several different ways as shown in Figure 2.8:

Figure 2.8

Precisely what these different patterns represent (for example, different notions of logical priority or necessity) is not critical to the idea that the student begins early in his or her training to establish simple links among rules of law.

8. While I play on Holmes' famous phrase, I do not mean to limit his description of the law to the rudimentary description of Flatlaw I give in the text. *See* Oliver W. Holmes, Jr., *The Path of the Law*, 10 HARV. L. REV. 457 (1897), *reprinted in* COLLECTED LEGAL PAPERS 173 (1920).

9. *See* EVA H. HANKS, MICHAEL HERZ & STEPHEN S. NEMERSON, ELEMENTS OF LAW 103–161 (2d ed. 2010) for a nice collection of cases involving these factual elements in the context of the doctrine of attractive nuisance.

10. *See, e.g.*, Pierson v. Post, 3 Cai. R. 175 (N.Y. Sup. Ct. 1805).

11. *See, e.g.*, E.A. Stephens & Co. v. Albers, 81 Colo. 488, 256 P. 15 (1927).

12. *See, e.g.*, Mullett v. Bradley, 24 Misc. 695, 53 N.Y.S. 781 (N.Y. App. Term 1898).

13. An introduction to doctrines in these areas can be found in virtually every property law casebook. *See, e.g.*, JESSE DUKEMINIER ET AL., PROPERTY 37–40 (8th ed. 2014).

14. At this stage one would also try to formulate a pattern that conforms as closely as possible to any officially stated logic or rationale.

15. The pattern into which the points fall contains the rudiments of a deeper theory of the law. That is, any pattern must show a certain coherence or consistency to be a pattern and not a formless jumble, but this coherence or consistency cannot itself *justify* the pattern. We are forced to ask another "Why?" Why must we have coherence or consistency here? The answer to that question will necessarily be found outside the realm of Linelaw, and indeed outside the realm of Flatlaw as well.

16. THE RESTATEMENT (THIRD) OF PROPERTY § 4.8 (2000) is famous for its effort to eliminate various details of the law of covenants and servitudes. *See generally id.* at §§ 3, 5, 6.

17. *See, e.g.*, TRS, *supra* ch. 1 note 16, at 118–23.

18. Plessy v. Ferguson, 163 U.S. 537 (1896).

19. There are countless scholarly explanations of historical development in the law. One of the more controversial is MORTON HORWITZ, THE TRANSFORMATION OF AMERICAN LAW, 1780–1860 (1977). Another is GRANT GILMORE, THE AGES OF AMERICAN LAW (1977). The Flatlaw analogy, however, is *not* designed to depict developments in the law over time. Although one could describe the growth of sophistication in a given area of the law as progress from one dimension to another, what I am attempting to describe is the development of legal reasoning in any particular *individual*.

20. Flatlaw is, then, the realm of the legal realists as well as the legal positivists. *See* Yosal Rogat, *Legal Realism, in* 4 ENCYCLOPEDIA OF PHILOSOPHY 420–21 (Paul Edwards ed., 1967). I will have much more to say about this in Chapter Three. *See infra* ch. 3.

21. For an extensive compilation of articles on the subject of judicial behavioralism, see 4 INT'L ASS'N FOR PHIL. L. & SOC. PHIL., PLURALISM AND LAW: PROCEEDINGS OF THE 20TH IVR WORLD CONGRESS, LEGAL REASONING (Arend Soeteman ed., 2004).

22. Plato, *Republic, Book VII, in* PLATO: THE COLLECTED DIALOGUES 747 (P. Shorey trans., E. Hamilton & H. Cairns eds., 1973).

23. *Id.* at 748.

24. *Id.* at 749.

25. *See id.* at 751–52.

26. We shall examine this idea further in Chapter Six. *See infra* ch. 6.

27. *See* NEIL MACCORMICK, LEGAL REASONING AND LEGAL THEORY 105–06, 166, 196, 206 (1978).

28. *See generally* ARTHUR L. CORBIN & JOSEPH M. PERILLO, CORBIN ON CONTRACTS §§ 1–274 (1952).

29. Judge Richard Posner has noted this phenomenon. *See* Richard A. Posner, *The Present Situation in Legal Scholarship*, 90 YALE L.J. 1113, 1117–19 (1981).

30. This, in a sense, is what Dworkin seems to mean by a "hard case": "Legal positivism provides a theory of hard cases. When a particular lawsuit cannot be brought under a clear rule of law, laid down by some institution in advance, then, the judge has, according to that theory, a 'discretion' to decide the case either way." TRS, *supra* ch. 1 note 16, at 81. Dworkin, of course, argues that this theory of adjudication is inadequate, that this sense of " 'strong discretion' " does not accurately characterize our system of law. *Id.* We will explore this further in Chapters Three and Six. *See infra* ch. 3, 6.

31. Of the one million or so sources on this topic, you might see, e.g., WERNER HIRSCH, LAW AND ECONOMICS: AN INTRODUCTORY ANALYSIS 23–62 (2d ed. 2015); LAW AND ECONOMICS 77–187 (Robert Cooter & Thomas Ulen eds., 4th ed. 2006).

32. *See, e.g.,* CHARLES FRIED, CONTRACT AS PROMISE (1981) (discussing moral principles underlying contract law).

33. *See, e.g.,* within the vast literature on such topics, LAW, SOCIETY, AND HISTORY (Robert W. Gordon & Morton J. Horwitz eds., 2011).

34. *See, e.g.,* Peter Westen, *The Empty Idea of Equality,* HARV. L. REV. 537 (1982).

35. There have been attempts to "bridge" the "is-ought" gap, however. *See* ALAN GEWIRTH, REASON AND MORALITY 1–7 (1978); Alan Gewirth, *The "Is-Ought" Problem Resolved,* 47

PROC. & ADDRESSES AM. PHIL. ASS'N 34 (1974), *reprinted in* ALAN GEWIRTH, HUMAN RIGHTS 100 (1982).

36. *See* Posner, *supra* note 29.

37. To the extent the goal of the dimensional analogy is the generation of a useful scientific, explanatory theory, it can be argued that simplicity is preferable. *See, e.g.*, Milton Friedman, *The Methodology of Positive Economics, in* PHILOSOPHY AND ECONOMIC THEORY 26 (F. Hahn & M. Hollis eds., 1979):

> In so far as a theory can be said to have "assumptions" at all, and in so far as their "realism" can be judged independently of the validity of predictions, the relation between the significance of a theory and the "realism" of its "assumptions" is almost the opposite of that suggested by the view under criticism. Truly important and significant hypotheses will be found to have "assumptions" that are widely inaccurate descriptive representations of reality, and, in general, the more significant the theory, the more unrealistic the assumptions (in this sense). The reason is simple. A hypothesis is important if it "explains" much by little, that is, if it abstracts the common and crucial elements from the mass of complex and detailed circumstances surrounding the phenomena to be explained and permits valid predictions on the basis of them alone. To be important, therefore, a hypothesis must be descriptively false in its assumptions; it takes account of, and accounts for, none of the many other attendant circumstances, since its very success shows them to be irrelevant for the phenomena to be explained.

Id.

Part II

Adding Wider Perspectives

All law students perceive at some point that their initial assumptions about the nature and quality of the "law" they are trying to master are rather naïve and unsatisfying. But they then confront a choice that is rarely recognized by them, or identified for them by more experienced lawyers.

On the one hand, while every law student acknowledges subliminally that legal material is indeed dauntingly unclear and disconcertingly manipulable, many (too many) assume that studying "legal theory" further to examine these phenomena will add little or nothing of practical value to their efforts to cope. They believe they will survive sufficiently, both now and later, not worrying about the murkiness at the base of their profession.

If their ambition is to "get by," then I must confess they are largely correct.

On the other hand, some (but too few) have a sense that extra profit may lay in mining this material more deeply. The next two Chapters are addressed to that group. Each depicts and summarizes insights that are possible with more abstract appreciation of the "law" and legal systems. Chapter Three discusses some of the existing traditions in this line of inquiry, and develops in some detail the approaches that are particularly useful—and in turn most related to this book's alternative analytic approach. But one of its primary lessons will be that these scholarly efforts, while impressive, may not be entirely satisfactory. Chapter Four then presents the themes that constitute this book's alternative, and gives preliminary examples of the additional perspectives into law and law practice that can result.

Chapter Three

The Traditions of Legal Reasoning: Developing Analytical Legitimacy Despite Substantive Disagreement

At this point, any student of the law and legal systems who is still reading this book—that is, who has been convinced that there is indeed something to be gained by looking "beneath" legal data—needs to hit the "pause" button. It is important to take a breath and appreciate the fact that others have preceded you in this enterprise, and that their prior work might be useful. And this is true for this book as well. We should take a moment to place the present analysis within a background of its own, identifying previous scholarship in legal theory that will give us some perspective on the alternative framework suggested here. That is more of a challenge, however, than might otherwise be assumed, simply because the topic of legal reasoning, as a general proposition, has been examined countless times by numerous scholars in many ways. The task here will be to identify common elements within this vast literature that are most useful for a practical understanding of the modern demands of this professional responsibility.

We will do so in two steps. Part A below discusses quite generally the most widely respected commentaries on legal reasoning that have become paradigmatic—points of departure for the rest of us, as it were. We can establish there the analytic themes at the foundation of this interrelated, mutual scholarly enterprise. Part B will then develop in much more detail a perspective on legal reasoning that is particularly important to the remaining portions of this book: the debate between two eminent scholars—H.L.A. Hart and Ronald Dworkin. We find in their disagreements evidence of Chapter Two's Flatlaw phenomenon and efforts to transcend it and, as a consequence, support for the multidimensional approach to legal reasoning developed in later Chapters.

A. Legal Theory's Common Traditions

1. Three Questions and Four Shared Themes

Every serious analysis that deserves the label "legal theory" (as I hope this book does) engages one or more of three very basic topics—each of which can most easily be appreciated if we simply analogize this scholarship to the study of architecture. To "analyze" a building, you would:

- identify the particular specific materials that constitute this edifice— wood, steel, glass, plastic, etc. (like the dots of pre-Flatlaw);

- examine and appreciate the ways in which these materials are arranged and connected so as to produce the standing structure, as opposed to remaining simply a pile of bricks and debris (thus, the lines and then interconnected figures of Flatlaw); and

- assess the final product for its adequacy on whatever grounds—beauty, utility, and so on (in turn, the solid objects perceived by transcending Flatlaw).

To translate all this into legal theory, the first category has traditionally involved the seemingly simple (but actually quite complex) question, "What is law?" What building materials—pronouncements, propositions, directives, and so on—deserve the label "law," as opposed to being merely idle hopes or, at the other extreme, terroristic threats? To put this in its most practical and immediate terms (which, however, overlaps with the next category): What could you cite to a court as a legitimate item of authority on which the judge could in turn rely to reach a decision? Or, in contrast, when could a judge respond to an argument by saying "That's a very interesting point, counselor, but it isn't *law*"? (To express this response in terms of the architecture metaphor above: "Counselor, you claim that you are presenting me with concrete on which I can construct an edifice, but you have offered me sand.")

Regarding the second category, the focus of study becomes the legal *system*— the structure as a whole rather than separate bricks and I-beams. Questions now revolve more around the concept of the "rule of law," as distinguished from "rule by fiat" or decree. Why, and at what point, in other words, do we have courts (or legislatures) in the first place that can use (or create) the "law" stuff (concrete rather than sand)? What makes anything they say in any way controlling? Here the constituent elements become a functioning social institution.

And for the final category, assuming you could identify law and establish your legal system, what makes either of them worthy of respect? When do we move from pronouncements that are merely controlling to ones that are, for whatever reason, compelling? And how and why does this occur?

You will note, of course, that the previous two Chapters raised all these issues implicitly: What makes a "strike" or "ball" a baseball "rule"? How do these dots coalesce into the game of baseball? Once the rules and game are established, why did Umpire Pinelli nevertheless cry after that final call? Did he denigrate the game in some way? Embarrass himself? And then, of course, how does any of this help us understand sophisticated, practical *legal* reasoning?

Theorists of the legal variety usually confine themselves to the first two categories of issues, leaving the third to moral and political philosophers. But as we have already seen, that question of law's worthiness is never far from any of these discussions, and it will play an important role in this book's effort as well. To study legal *reasoning*, then, we will need to engage and integrate all three analytic activities. Initially, however, we have to see how difficult that task is.

The traditional background academic literature in legal theory that focuses on the categories of law and legal system is quite diverse. A summary list of just the "classics" in this realm, in rough historical order, would probably begin with Karl Llewellyn and his daunting "bramble bush" perspective on law study and the development of legal arguments;[1] then note the debate between H.L.A. Hart and Lon Fuller on the "internal" morality (if any) of the law,[2] and add here a review of Fuller's wonderful hypothetical judicial struggle with the "Case of the Speluncean Explorers;"[3] next pay homage to the very careful examination of practical lawyering in the materials developed by (a different) Henry Hart and Albert Sachs;[4] add the short but insightful summary of legal reasoning developed for lawyer and non-lawyer audiences alike by Edward Levi;[5] certainly include a discussion (as noted earlier) of the debate between H.L.A. Hart and Ronald Dworkin;[6] perhaps go so far as to include the interconnection between legal "rights" and legal "remedies" developed by Guido Calabresi and Douglas Melamed in their justly famous work in law and economics;[7] and note as well the recent thoughtful commentaries by Steven Burton,[8] Jeremy Waldron,[9] Judge Richard Posner,[10] and Frederick Schauer.[11]

All these sources have become well-known and much studied because they share, among each other and in large measure with this book, certain important perspectives and assumptions basic to a study of legal reasoning. For our purposes, I identify four such commonalities that are far more important than the detailed differences among them.

Respectful disagreement. All legal theory begins with the important assumption, noted at the beginning of this book, that law and legal systems exist in a world of disagreement, even among reasonable people. Law and lawyering, in other words, did not cause this disagreement; contentiousness preceded whatever legal social institution is to be examined. So there will always be differences of opinion about the appropriate *outcome* in a dispute, *and* there will be, just as inevitably, differences of opinion about the appropriate *methods* to use to reach that outcome. With all this fussing at law's core, legal theorists engage in their debates nevertheless because they believe fundamentally that disagreements need not be disagreeable—that all their arguing and quarreling ought to be able to be carried on by reasonable people who hold reasonable, even though differing and indeed competing, beliefs about the proper way to analyze and understand a situation. The task of theories of legal reasoning, then, in this difficult context, must be to respect and ground this reasonableness, to organize and structure the range of human disagreement rather than attempt to eliminate it.

Absence of substantive legal "truth." Consistent with this background, all these well-known sources preach the message that studying the phenomenon of legal reasoning is interesting and important *not* because its purpose is to discover and establish some underlying "truth," the way scientific method and reasoning strive to do. Instead, all the scholarly classics are efforts to examine how legal reasoning operates within a realm where fundamental truth is *absent*— where all conclusions remain contingent and challengeable, and "discretion" is unavoidable.[12] Each emphasizes, disconcertingly to the uninitiated, that the study of law is something that changes as it is being studied. Prof. Levi perhaps put the proposition most directly: "Therefore it appears that the kind of reasoning involved in the legal process is one in which the classification changes as the classification is made. The rules change as the rules are being applied. More important, the rules arise out of a process which, while comparing situations, creates the rules and then applies them."[13]

Disagreement over law's normativity. Even though legal theorists do not ordinarily endorse a singular appropriate substance for all of the law, they nevertheless acknowledge that normative values, like justice, fairness, dignity, and so on, do at least matter to our understanding of what law and legal systems might be. They differ widely, however, regarding everything else associated with such values—Which values matter? Where do they come from? Why do they matter? How and to what extent? Resulting questions become, for example: Can a judge impose his or her *personal* values in deciding a case? Could any individual legitimately condemn an entire legal system because it fails to reflect and implement his or her personal values? Can a judge identify relevant values through an opinion poll? Could a legislature do so? A particularly useful example of this issue will be developed in this Chapter's next section, where the Hart-Dworkin debate is developed.

Presence of "process faith." Nevertheless—and here is an important key to legal theory in general and legal reasoning in particular—despite all this contingency about the normative substance in the legal world, respectful disagreement among commentators is possible because the law's malleability—its vast range of possible processes and moral conclusions—is *not infinite*. The assumption is that the legal world travels on identifiable patterns and internal propositions of appropriate, objective, *logical* analysis. After all, the topic here is legal *reasoning*, not legal goofiness or legal arbitrariness. Legal theory has therefore always endorsed analytic techniques fundamental to establishing coherence in fluid circumstances: the use of analogy ("treat like cases alike, and different cases differently"), deductive and inductive reasoning,[14] and theories of language,[15] all of which will be examined later.

This is most evident, perhaps, when the inquiry turns more pragmatically (largely under the influence of Prof. Dworkin) into a search for a "theory of adjudication:"[16] examining how judges can reach appropriate decisions (and in turn how lawyers can make appropriate arguments) in "hard" cases[17]—those in which clear, obvious, uncontroversial rules are *not* available to resolve a matter easily (or where a lawyer does not *want* an otherwise clear rule to resolve the matter). This disquieting context will get special attention in Part B below. As a general observation, however, literature in this context has developed at length a large number of distinctive theories of what could be called "legal coherence," in which legal data and legal analytic processes are variously combined. Examples would include realism,[18] positivism,[19] anti-positivism (or interpretivism),[20] formalism,[21] rule-skepticism,[22] and so on, only a few aspects of which will be relevant to this book's analytic agenda.

2. Developing Strategic Argumentation

The perspective I seek to add to this immense literature is perhaps best summarized this way: I want to enhance existing theories of adjudication with a theory of *strategic argumentation*. I believe a very useful initial step to take in understanding the phenomenon of legal reasoning is to avoid focusing myopically on the work of the repairmen of the complex machinery of the legal system—judges and similar dispute resolvers, who constantly strive to make that engine appear to be operating smoothly. Although being familiar with what these officials say and do is certainly important, the task of examining their output should include attention to the prior question of why this machinery seems to need constant tinkering in the first place. Everyone, not just law students, seems to understand that legal questions do not always have obvious and easy answers, and that smart people seem naturally drawn to the professional challenge of concocting these answers. But *why*, on both counts? As the saying goes, the law doesn't seem to be rocket science. Is the problem simply that there is so much of it?

What interests me is the further observation that because any legal dispute will necessarily have at least two contending sides, we need to appreciate not just what constitutes legal disagreement, but *skillful* and *conscientious* legal disagreement. In other words, because one side is going to "lose" this argument, how do these unfortunate lawyers (or dissenting judges) nevertheless retain a sense of professional integrity? One way to appreciate this point is a challenge I give my first-year law students: If you want to learn how to "be a lawyer"—and not just learn "the law"—focus as much attention on the losing arguments in the cases in your casebooks as the winning ones. Ask yourself: How did the losing sides (or dissenters) concoct their arguments with a straight face? What made these losers think they might win, or have anything professionally useful to say?

Before we plunge into how this perspective might be developed by Professors Hart and Dworkin in Part B, let me give you two examples of other academic work that help further bring out the distinction between this book and the prior literature.

a. Prof. Schauer's Version of Process Faith

Prof. Frederick Schauer is certainly the most prolific commentator on the common core element in the literature of "process faith," noted above. Not only does he believe that the basic reasoning foundations of analogy and deduction are at the core of any attempt to understand and justify a legal system, he has given these elements much more attention, and much more substance, than others. Because I, too, will be giving serious emphasis to expanding the simple idea of "treating like cases alike," but from a different angle, it is worth taking a moment to note his approach in more detail. Our approaches have much in common, but they also diverge in important ways.

We'll start with the common ground. In his many articles,[23] and now a recent book,[24] Prof. Schauer explores the sequence of analytic steps that produces the complex matrix of the common law. Although it is always dangerous to summarize a nuanced study of a topic this abstract (and one that Prof. Schauer continues to address apace), his argument basically reduces to an observation that a judicial decision links to others through a series of three mental exercises: The legal mind *characterizes* the problem at hand, then *compares* the current matter to existing legal authority within that context, and then *assimilates* the new decision into that context. In effect, the effort is to connect this new case to all three temporal perspectives: the past—the preexisting contexts that have been recognized as appropriate perspectives or categories of legal thought; the present—the relationship of the current case to those existing categories; and then the future—the way the new case is perceived to affect the way life (legal and otherwise) will be led in light of the new decision. Prof. Schauer does not contend that these steps are necessarily taken in this order, or that each is somehow rigidly separated from the others. They blend. As he puts it at one point:

> Reasoning from precedent, whether looking back to the past or ahead to the future, presupposes an ability to identify the relevant precedent. Why does a currently contemplated decision sometimes have a precedent and sometimes not? Such a distinction can exist only if there is some way of identifying a precedent—some way of determining whether a past event is sufficiently similar to the present facts to justify assimilation of the two events. And when we think about precedential effect in the future of the action we take today, we presuppose that some future events will be descriptively assimilated to today's.[25]

What we need, then, is "an organizing standard specifying which similarities are important and which we can safely ignore"[26]—what he calls "rules of relevance."[27] In turn, these rules will "be explained as a choice among alternative characterizations,"[28] and these characterizations will be viewed with reference to assimilation—the spin "the future ... will place [on] today's facts."[29] And, as you would expect, the question then becomes whether there are any "rules" of assimilation as well—that is, preexisting categories of some sort "in the larger consciousness surrounding a particular decision making individual or institution"[30] that constrain or direct that activity as well.

This is a complex and interesting picture of thinking within the context of legal issues, and it can be seen at work in Stephen Jay Gould's analysis in Chapter One of Umpire Pinelli's called third strike. The "characterization," or category, at stake might be simply that of baseball's traditional, physical understanding of a "strike," or it might instead be "a strike in a big game toward the end of a spectacular effort by a pitcher." Which category is chosen depends on how we compare the game in question to games of the past, and

that assessment may or may not support this distinction between the two categories. And the category we choose, and the comparison we make, will also
depend on how we assess the impact the "strike" call will have on the game of
baseball as it will be played in the future.

I can accept all of Prof. Schauer's analysis to this point, but it seems that
we ought to ask additional questions: Is there more that might be said about
this process? Are there more precise ways of capturing the categorizing, comparing, and assimilating that no doubt seem to be occurring within the legal
mind? Can we identify, in other words, the typical analytic strategies that
lawyers—and more generally, all very careful thinkers—use "underneath"
Prof. Schauer's steps? Can we articulate *how* the categorizing, and so on, unfolds in a particular lawyer's or judge's mind so that we can compare and contrast that thought process to the thinking of others? Prof. Schauer does not
seem to believe so, for at one point he observes that "the rules of precedent
are likely to resemble the rules of language—a series of practices not substantially reducible to specifics."[31]

Here I disagree. Although "specifics" in the sense of precise maps of analytical
process may well be impossible, "specifics" in terms of additional *structure*
within that process *is* quite possible. More important, however, it is also quite
necessary, as a matter of both legal and political theory: The question that lies
beneath Prof. Schauer's depiction of categorizing and assimilating and so on
is *why*—with so many smart people doing these identifiable mental tasks so
regularly and for so long—*why* do we nevertheless continue to disagree so
profoundly about appropriate outcomes in so many cases? We can understand
that litigants will disagree simply because they have competing interests they
wish to vindicate by any means at their disposal. But why do *judges* disagree,
when presumably they do not have a personal motive to do so? Why does social consensus develop so grudgingly, if it develops at all?

I argued back in the Introduction that "thinking like a lawyer" is a "unique"
form of reasoning for several reasons. Prof. Schauer agrees with that proposition generally, but not entirely. He does note that while other forms of reasoning may well use the different pieces that constitute the full scope of legal
thinking, few (if any) use *all* of them.[32] But in addition, lawyers and judges
are unique, he believes, because of their willingness to accept, in the context
of all the ambiguities within each of the reasoning elements, that the results of
their efforts will not necessarily produce any sort of perfect outcome—the
idea of "no legal truth" noted earlier. They will accept suboptimal results just
to keep the system moving and operating, letting the future deal with glitches.[33]
I agree with all of this, but I would like to take a step further: Is it possible to

develop a theory of legal reasoning that identifies in more detail the nature of these constantly imperfect legal results?

b. Prof. Fuller's Descriptive Challenge

Another intriguing way to express this conundrum of accepted legal messiness that more closely ties to the Hart-Dworkin debate to which we will next turn is an analytic exercise developed many years ago by Prof. Lon Fuller. He challenged his Harvard Law students to put the following three words in the correct order: rule, right, remedy.[34]

You should note immediately that there are six different possible permutations available: You could start with any of the three, then go to either of the remaining two, and then put the remaining term last. But which ordering is the "correct" one? For most law students, the immediate assumption is that rules establish rights, which in turn define appropriate remedies. But is that inevitable? Why can't an appreciation of an individual's rights *precede* and ground relevant legal rules, which then produce even more compelling remedies? Indeed, why can't we turn all this on its head, the way most any practicing lawyer would, by focusing first on what remedies a client needs so that the lawyer can justify the fee he or she will charge for their work, and then develop the rights that support that remedy, and then look (and argue) for the rules that officially achieve that result. (And it is certainly possible, of course, that judicial reasoning could be characterized in this way: A judge determines first the outcome in a matter that he or she wants, then builds the foundation in rules and rights necessary to make that result seem both appropriate and perhaps inevitable.)

Prof. Fuller's elements of rules, rights and remedies are thus the *substance* of what is being, in Prof. Schauer's approach, categorized, compared, and assimilated. But the two lists not only overlap, they seem to blur into each other disconcertingly. For example, are the processes of categorizing or comparing rights and rules the same, or somehow distinct? We clearly need some more steps.

B. Appreciating the Hart-Dworkin Debate: Of Rules, Principles, and Policies

Those will be supplied—even though they will still not be sufficient for our purposes—by examining commentaries by two eminent legal scholars who spent their careers developing alternative structural analyses of legal reasoning as a special professional skill.

The much-discussed debate between H.L.A. Hart and Ronald Dworkin goes to the core of what it means to "think like a lawyer," and why that concept remains controversial. Both of these scholars paid careful attention to all three of the basic questions of traditional legal theory listed in this Chapter's preceding section—"law," "system," and law's "normativity"—reaching very different conclusions on all three. Yet neither of these academic icons can be declared the "winner" of this contest, for they approached the underlying foundation of legal reasoning itself from such different perspectives. And those perspectives are conveniently summarized by the Flatlaw analogy: Prof. Hart is the quintessential Flatlawyer, emphasizing law's special legitimacy against those who would try to push law beyond its appropriately limited dimensions. But he nevertheless notes as well the uncomfortable implications of that narrow view. Prof. Dworkin, in contrast, made his name challenging these limits, arguing for the inevitable relevance to the law of factors outside its narrow, traditional confines. Yet that ambitious agenda produces its own range of questionable results for conscientious lawyers and judges.

1. Hart and the "Central Case" of Law

Prof. Hart's seminal book, *The Concept of Law*,[35] remains the best statement of the "positivist" approach to law and legal analysis—a label to be explained in a moment. The task he set for himself was to identify the key characteristics that would constitute the "central [set of] elements"[36] that would *define* the word "law" as it is used in standard discussions of that social phenomenon. That is, he did not seek to identify *everything* that people might call "law"—instead, only the quintessential, most widely agreed-upon examples that would anchor any conversation about the subject of law. By clarifying that starting point, he believed analysis of what could be included in the discussion of legal guidance would be improved.

Now immediately, this might seem a remarkably esoteric, if not simply boring and pointless, question to explore—unless you bear in mind the very controversial endpoints to which Hart is building throughout his book. Two key issues on people's minds at the time (the 1950s and early 1960s) would be addressed at the end of his text: First, could the pronouncements by a regime as evil as that of Nazi Germany—directives that have the trappings of "law"—enjoy that label even if monstrous in substance? If they could, how could Nazi leaders be punished after World War II for following pronouncements that are "legal"? Second, regarding another development arising from that great conflict, given the ongoing struggles among nations after the war to organize themselves, can we meaningfully talk about "*international* law"? Is it even in the same category as familiar domestic, national law, or is it just wishful thinking?

Hart's goal was to develop pragmatic, unsentimental answers to both issues, neither of which would necessarily be welcomed by anti-Nazis and in-
ternationalists.

a. Law as Derived From Psychological Fact

As a first step in appreciating the relevance of Hart's work, however, we
should make the analytic circumstances a great deal less dramatic, even perhaps mundane, which will allow his effort to be more universal and practical.
Assume the following hypothetical, which we will make about *you*:

Scientists have recently discovered that the planet Mars is indeed inhabited,
and the study of Martian civilization has begun. (If this version of the hypothetical is too goofy for you, make the discovery about something that has indeed happened: a tribe of indigenous people in the rain forest of the Amazon River
in Brazil has been encountered who have otherwise never interacted with other
human beings.) You have been asked by the organizers of this project to determine whether the Martians (or the tribe) have "law." How would you conduct
the investigation? What would you look for to determine whether our word "law"
has any relevance to how these alien creatures (or indigenous people) are acting?

If you still think this example so outlandish as to be trivial, bring it back to
the modern examples noted above: A regime claims to have "law" permitting
what would anywhere else be murder or rape or theft. Or perhaps the decrees
aren't quite as heinous: cutting off hands as a punishment for theft, inflicting
the death penalty in cases of capital murder, forbidding women to drive cars,
permitting only certain races to vote, and so on. You might certainly consider
all these to be examples of "bad" law, but could you argue that they are not
law *at all*? Remember your hypothetical task: If any of these examples were
present on Mars (or within the tribe), would your answer be any different?

Note how all three of the earlier questions associated with legal theory come
into play: What is entitled to the label "law"? How does the concept of a "system" of directives become relevant? Do the normative values associated with an
official pronouncement influence the answer to either of the other two questions?

Hart's impressive analysis employed the background analytical perspective labeled "legal positivism,"[37] which is based in turn (to some extent but
not entirely) in "logical positivism." In very summary form, this approach
divided the world between, on the one hand, facts—objective, "positive,"
identifiable, concrete data—and, on the other, values—slippery, often personal, always mere opinions about "right" and "wrong." The former are capable of rigorous, careful study; the latter are not. Hence, if a concept like
"law" was to be pinned down usefully—meaning that conversations about

it become anchored and organized appropriately—it had to have the *facts* of its definition identified with great care. This will require in turn, rigorously gathering evidence of the way people are *in fact* using that word. Any normative values that might lurk at its edges would be considered more distracting than relevant. Facts, you see, can be determined to be true or false; values cannot.

Hart's study of law, then, focused on the facts of psychology and sociology, and eschewed philosophy. If he were given the Martian hypothetical, he wouldn't be concerned with whether he liked what the Martians were doing with various directives. The focus would be simply on what they were *actually* doing, period. And that doing, through directives, would be "law"—*if* those directives had certain fundamental, observable, positive characteristics.

The first and most basic of those features for Hart, like his nineteenth-century predecessor John Austin, would be rooted in psychology. Austin had claimed that law was grounded quite simply in coercion—threats of force and punishment: You could determine if a society had "law" if you could identify a powerful order-issuer who could intimidate citizens into following directives.[38] Hart, in contrast, found this approach unnecessarily crude and superficial. Austin, he argued, had in effect put at the "center"—the focus—of the study of law efforts to make bad people behave appropriately. In contrast, to his considerable credit, Hart turned this psychological perspective upside down: The vast bulk of official directives, he observed, were (as a matter of fact) actually aimed at good people who are generally complying with such directives rather than chafing against them.[39] These people just want to know what to do to get along in society. So, to identify the true "center" of the law—its anchoring example—the focus should be on this compliant person, rather than the outlaw.

To do that, a new, improved psychology was necessary. Hart labeled it the "internal point of view."[40] To study law properly, he argued, you needed to assume that people were obeying directives, not because they feared punishment, but because this guidance was, quite simply, considered by them to be the "right thing to do." These individuals had simply "bought into" (internalized) the legitimacy of the directives. Precisely *why* they thought this guidance was appropriate was not really relevant—it could be because the directives generally gave them an advantage over others, or were morally pleasing, whatever. The key was simply the *fact* that these citizens did not need to be intimidated into following the rules, whatever they were. They were simply interested in what the society's rules were so they could follow them.

This revised psychology then leads directly to an improved sociology: In contrast to the hierarchical community imagined by Austin's approach (a monarch demanding fealty), Hart imagined society as a basically cooperative group of people who have internalized a sense of appropriate behavior within their community, and in turn a sense of the appropriateness of the social rules developed to constitute and direct that community. "Law," then, becomes primarily directive rather than coercive.

The sequential sociological picture that emerges in Hart's analysis of the origins and end-points of his central case of law can be summarized in the schematic presented in Figure 3.1:

Figure 3.1

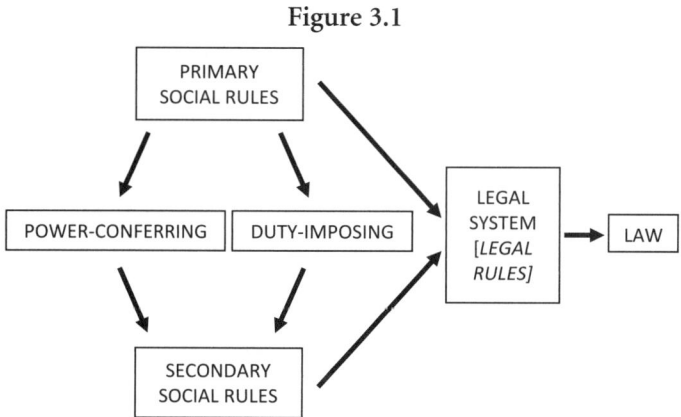

For Hart, our image of "law" that anchors our conversation about the topic (its "central case") does not simply appear one day. It emerges through a series of social developmental steps. We start with a "pre-legal" primitive society that coalesces around (that is, develops an internal point of view of legitimacy about) certain basic *social*—not yet legal—"primary rules"[41] that allow these people to live together in peace. These rules would take two forms: "duty-imposing"[42]—don't kill, don't steal, and the like—and "power-conferring"[43]—the basic elements of economic exchange, like property ownership, contract concepts, the rules of inheritance, and so on. All of this fledgling social interaction would, however, be too unclear and haphazard to sustain itself, so this community would develop (that is, again, generate an internal point of view about) three types of "secondary"[44] social rules aimed at its officials that would regulate the primary rules: a "rule of recognition"[45] that would identify the society's rules; then "rules of change"[46] that would establish a legislative method for modifying the rules from time to time; and finally "rules of adjudication"[47] that would resolve disputes about the application of the social rules.

This double-action internal point of view—one for the people and one for officials—would then come together to form this society's legal system, which in turn would be the origin and foundation for everything that would deserve to be called *legal*, as opposed to merely social, rules. Hence, your task as the investigator of Martian society is clarified: If you find these social elements—ordinary citizens accepting the legitimacy of their community, and officials following and imposing directives that they and the citizens believe to be legitimate as well—you have discovered the Martian legal system, and in turn what that community considers "law."

Note, then, how Hart addressed the basic questions at the foundation of legal theory: He actually started with the second—what is a legal system?—then moved back to the first: Legitimate "law" turns out to be whatever is produced within and by this legitimate legal system. But what about the third issue? Does it matter to the definition of law and systems what the moral content of these directives might be? If not, could Nazi Germany therefore have a "legal system" capable of producing what we must concede is "law"? Would this then insulate Nazi officials from *legal*, as distinguished from moral, criticism and condemnation? In other words, what of "justice"? Does it have no place in the positivist world?

b. Justice as a Fact Rather than a Value

Indeed, according to Hart, discussions of justice are relevant, even to a positivist, *if* that concept is understood, like everything else in his approach, factually (psychologically and sociologically), rather than in the normative sense usually attributed to it. Hart removes any moral content that "justice" might be assumed to have by making it procedural rather than substantive: The "central case" of justice in a legal system, he contends, possesses three objective definitional elements[48] that ensure that it is functioning in such a way that the critical "internal point of view" of citizens and officials about the system's legitimacy will be established and maintained:

(1) *consistency and impartiality*: A properly functioning legal system is one in which its laws treat "like cases alike, and different cases differently" through the actions of officials who are considering and applying these laws impersonally and impartially. This kind of pleasant orderly, unbiased predictability, based in a very abstract sense of *prima facie* equality, is enough for an operating sense of justice, and need not be given any further normative substance.

(2) *appropriate compensation*: In resolving disputes, justice would require this legal system to respond to "wrongs" by consistently and impartially compensating victims for their losses. These transgressions, however,

need not be defined by any particular morality—they would be based instead on whatever conventional morality actually exists in this community and time. It has no more substantive content than these citizens (Martians, Nazis, whomever) have *in fact* given it. Maiming or murdering, then, might not be considered "wrongs" in this society in certain circumstances, in which case justice would exist even if these inflictions went uncompensated.

(3) *common good*: This central case of justice *might*, however, include one piece of possible substance, but it turns out it does not. Hart added to his discussion of justice that the legal system would be conscientiously attempting to enhance the "common good." But again, Hart's reference here is to a "good" that has no content other than what this society has *in fact* given it. Its substance could be morally pleasing, or it could just as easily be racist, sexist, or anything else you don't like. "Justice," then, would be achieved when this legal system pursued whatever social "good" this community has defined for itself. It remains purely procedural. Whatever substance the concept of justice has, then, is given to it by forces *outside* the legal system, not from within it.

The result of this analysis is now clear. Hart's sense of law and legal systems *does* have a normative element of a sort, but it is limited only to the value of *order*. What matters to him in legal theory is describing how the social institution of the law begins and is sustained over time, and these phenomena are due entirely to a healthy internal point of view. That attitude is in turn founded on only those values that will cause a community to form and then not fall apart, not any *particular* norms of human behavior that might philosophically justify this social arrangement. His focus remains on whether a community sufficiently *exists*, not whether we would call it good or bad.

So, back to the basic issue Hart's legal theory must confront: Did the Nazis indeed have not only *valid* law, even though monstrous, but "justice" as well? Hart must (and does) forthrightly answer affirmatively,[49] by the Nazis' own understandings of procedural regularity and the "good." They had the requisite social order and stability through an internal point of view that established the foundation for what Hart claimed was the key to his legal theory.

c. Law, Justice, and Iniquity

But, having reached this uncomfortable conclusion, Hart quickly emphasizes that there is one more important step in considering the Nazi regime: We must distinguish between, on the one hand, the objective "validity" (the "lawness") of these reprehensible, but appropriately created and implemented, directives, and, on the other, the separate question of whether they ought to be obeyed. Some directives may simply be, as Hart put it, "too iniquitous to obey."[50]

Even so, these iniquitous directives nevertheless remain "law." Your decision to engage in civil disobedience is simply a function of your own personal morality—not a morality that is embedded within the law or the legal system. So the question of when you can justifiably disobey remains, for Hart, completely open. He has no philosophy to suggest to fill this void—*except* the "value" of systemic order *itself,* in contrast to chaos or arbitrariness.

And Hart believes he has no responsibility as a *legal,* as opposed to a moral or political, philosopher to argue in favor of any other value. For him, the study of "law" is the study of directives that, *as a matter of fact,* function as accepted guidance for citizen behavior. That task requires you to exclude any reference to the moral content of the system's pronouncements. The careful study of Martians and Nazis demands that you do so.

What counts as "legitimate" law, then, for Hart is simply a function of two levels of facts: for ordinary people in this legal system, we need *efficacy*—the fact that the rules, as a matter of the internal point of view, are being followed far more often than not—and for society's officials, we need *validity*—the fact that these administrators believe, based as well in an internal point of view, that their announcements and directives are equivalently appropriate.

But if this is the analysis we must follow regarding the study of any particular community (the Martians, Nazi Germany, etc.), we *ourselves* do not have to connect our allegiance to that society. We as observers need not accept and participate in its specific "internal point of view" psychology. As outsiders, with our potentially very different *external* point of view, we could scoff at and criticize this community's rules of behavior. We nevertheless as visitors to this place might decide to follow these silly or evil rules anyway just to avoid trouble (like wearing expected clothing or participating in religious ceremonies while in a particular country). But it is also important to note that you could be a citizen of this community and *still* have an external point of view—you could be so alienated by the morally disheartening rules of your community that you fail to develop the expected internal point of view in the first place. You could, in other words, *as a lawyer* in this place advise your clients to follow rules that you believe to be illegitimate—you could in effect be a critical legal scholar,[51] rejecting what this deluded community of yours mistakenly *thinks* is legitimate law, but study and use it anyway.

You can now predict, can you not, what Hart's struggle will be in the last chapter of his book with the concept of *international* law. At the mid-twentieth-century point at which he was writing, there is not much of a legal *system* that could be said as a descriptive, objective matter to be producing pronouncements that enjoy an *international* "internal point of view" concerning their legitimacy. No objective, cold-blooded psychology or sociology would establish that foundation—it really would be wishful thinking. But, Hart concludes more sympathetically, there is at least enough evidence of a positive direction in these regards to let us characterize international law as in the neighborhood of traditional "law" (it can at least be said to be in the set), even if it is not yet at the level of a "central case."

d. Law as Archaeology

So what, then, is "legal reasoning," more narrowly, for a positivist like Hart? How would a positivist teach you to advise clients, or argue to a court—in Nazi Germany or on Mars (or in the Amazon jungle)? Legal analysis becomes, more akin to archaeology than any other discipline. It is an effort in *discovery*. A good lawyer is one who can:

- uncover through diligent digging and sifting (research),
- from within the mountain of "positive," identifiable, data of official pronouncements of the legal system (statutes, judicial decisions, administrative rulings, academic articles, and so on),
- the key legal nuggets or artifacts most relevant for an official to use to give direction to, or assess the behavior of, a citizen—or at least the most predictive of how an official might use this information.

Whether you like the result of your efforts is of no consequence. All you are concerned with are the "sources" of law, not their moral or political substance.

And if you find this a bit circular and empty—that is, that law is the stuff that comes from a system that is itself identified by the stuff it produces—Hart's response is quite unflinching and pragmatic: "[A]ll that succeeds is success."[52] The test for law's legitimacy is law's acceptance by those (people and officials) on whom it is imposed. Law becomes a closed system, like mathematics, which is entirely self-referential and self-justifying. It needs no other "outside" foundation for its existence or legitimacy.

This summary, I dare say, is an accurate depiction of the nature and maximum extent of "legal reasoning" to which most law students and lawyers would admit they aspire. It is the realm of Chapter Two's Flatlaw. It is the foundation for Justice Roberts' comment in Chapter One of just wanting to "call the balls and strikes." It is the endorsement of the order of Prof. Fuller's elements that law students find most comfortable: "Tell me the rules, which might give me some sense of rights, which then dictate appropriate remedies." The thinking is something like this: "My job is only to discover the rules out there in the ether of the legal system, and understand them sufficiently so that the best you can expect of me is to communicate them to you (client or court) to allow you to make your own decision. A strike is a strike, and a 'point of law' is exactly what it purports to be, and that result is not my fault. What more can you demand of me?"

Much more, I would hope. Are these rules, rights, and remedies all that uninteresting?

2. *Dworkin's Revised Psychology from Normativity*

Prof. Dworkin's approach to law and legal reasoning, developed over many years,[53] is fundamental, far-reaching, and directly relevant to this book's agenda. As we will see, the circumstance of the "hard case," noted above, becomes the centerpiece of his alternative analytic vision: What should a lawyer or a judge do when guidance gets murky? To answer that question, you have to develop a more sophisticated sense of the murk.

Just as Hart based his theory on its contrast with John Austin's inadequate psychological picture of the legal system's human subject, so too Dworkin sought to expand and deepen Hart's understanding of that element within legal theory. And just as Hart did not claim that Austin was entirely wrong and thus should have his work ignored, so too Dworkin will claim that Hart's view is not so much inaccurate as incomplete. Hart has missed, according to Dworkin, the important role played in legal reasoning by abstract, non-"positive," normative components—the third issue in the previous list of basic questions within legal theory—that make law, legal systems, and legal reasoning all much more complex (and, I would argue, more interesting).

a. Rules and Judicial Discretion

As a preliminary matter, we must be careful to note that Hart's analysis was not at all so superficial as to claim that legal analysis, even in the sense of objective archaeological digging, would always yield legal certainty or clarity, like an identifiable artifact. To the contrary, because of the slippery nature of language itself (which we will examine with more care in Chapter Six) and the unpredictability of future events, legal guidance even for an arch-positivist would necessarily be at times unclear, approximate, and controversial. All legal rules, Hart acknowledged, would have "open texture"[54]—which can be depicted in the Figure 3.2:

Figure 3.2

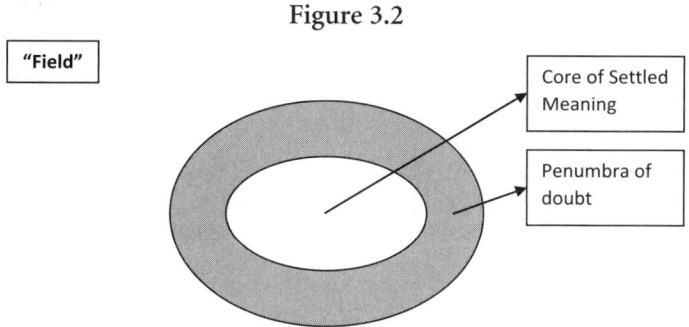

Rules would have a "core of settled meaning,"[55] or certainty, where there is widespread, perhaps even unanimous, agreement that the rule applies in particular cases. These cases are then surrounded by a "penumbra of debatable cases,"[56] instances in which reasonable people believe that applying the rule is possible but not certain. And these cases are in turn surrounded by, we could say, a "field" of situations in which there is agreement that the rule does *not* apply. All rules, then, are inevitably to some degree ambiguous.

The implication of this critical area of uncertainty is Hart's further argument that, concomitantly, judges, just as inevitably, have discretion in these penumbral circumstances to apply the rule or not, as they see fit, as best they can, as they try to treat like cases alike.[57] This inherent judicial authority is in turn nevertheless considered as legitimate by the patient population of good people out there because courts so often announce their decisions in such a way as to give the impression that the case was actually in the core area of certainty. From that air of confidence, lack of clarity is the exception, not the rule, so to speak. To his credit, Hart acknowledges that all this appearance of confident certainty is, however, merely a "pious fiction,"[58] which has been accepted by society because, as we noted earlier, "nothing succeeds like success."

Most fundamentally, the diagram above that acknowledges unavoidable rule ambiguity also applies to Hart's foundational starting point for the legal system—the "rule of recognition." Even the most fundamental rule of them all, which identifies all the other rules within this legal system, is *itself* ambiguous, and hence subject to judicial discretion. Judges, then, get to decide for themselves *both* which pronouncements direct them *and* what that direction is. The legitimacy of judicial authority is, then, obviously circular: It is based on nothing more than their internal point of view, which is itself based on a sense of judicial legitimacy. Despite the fact that Hart's "central case" of law is therefore itself inherently ambiguous, he nevertheless contended that it was objective and value-free *enough* to anchor and organize the controversies that remained (like Nazi legalism and international norms).

Prof. Dworkin responded that even at this core there was a fundamental defect: failing to recognize the importance of the psychology of normativity itself. People, and particularly judges, simply do not think, Dworkin argued, in Hart's neutralist form. And most dramatically, Dworkin claimed that the kind of discretion that Hart imagined the judiciary enjoyed—what he called "strong discretion"[59]—simply did not exist. Legal reasoning was not limited to Hart's archaeology, but instead included difficult and controversial moral sifting and assessment. If there was a fundamental psychological "internal point of view" establishing the legitimacy of law and legal systems, it was much more normative than Hart ever acknowledged (or would accept).

For Dworkin, two important analytic features about legal material were missing from Hart's approach:

- Within legal reasoning there was more guidance for behavior that had to be considered than just the specific, familiar, narrow legal "rules" on which Hart focused. These additional players were abstract "principles,"[60] as Dworkin called them, which performed several analytic functions that Hart's model did not address.

- And this previously unidentified constituent ingredient had the quality of being inherently value-*filled*, rather than value-free. These principles reflected our "rights" as citizens.[61] Hence, according to Dworkin, Hart had failed to "take rights seriously" (which becomes the appropriate title of Dworkin's single most famous book) at every level of legal theory.

b. Principles within Legal Reasoning

The idea that "law" would contain something more than narrow directives is not all that startling. From Hart's own perspective, you could imagine that positivist legal material could be depicted as a range of levels of relevance, as in Figure 3.3:

Figure 3.3

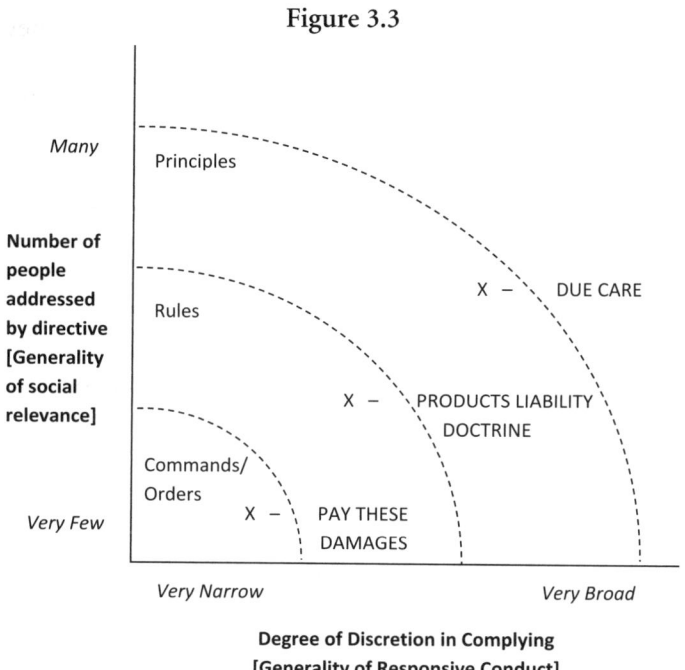

Directives could vary by the number of people to whom they apply, and by the degree of specificity of the behavior required by the directive. So at one extreme you have "commands," much like what John Austin seemed to have in mind, as in hierarchical military situations: "You, soldier, go attack that hill." No discretion or ambiguity there, with the ranges of both actor and action reduced to one. The legal system equivalent would be an order by a court: "Defendant, pay the following amount of damages." At a mid-range you would encounter the familiar rules of the legal system—definitions of negligence in torts or consideration in contract law, and so on, which are meant to guide a range of behavioral acts and be relevant to a much wider range of people—all drivers of automobiles and all business people, for example. At a yet higher level of abstraction you could imagine very broad pronouncements, like "due care" and "meeting of the minds," that seem to be universal in character and very broad in possible substance. So the Dworkinian idea that the farther reaches of this diagram need a new label is not something immediately compelling—principles could just be more abstract and general rules.

Dworkin argued, however, that these "principles" were something differ-ent. They had an independent role to play in the legal mind, and thus deserved special, separate attention. Here is a possible analogy: Dworkin imagined the "law" to be like a large brick wall. The bricks in the wall—the aspects of this edifice that you see most obviously and immediately—are Hart's "rules," while the substance that actually holds the wall together, giving it its shape and strength, is the mortar running between all the bricks. This glue binding the legal system's guidance into an actual social institution is Dworkin's conception of principles. Positivists, in contrast, Dworkin would argue, see the law as sim-ply a pile of bricks, and legal reasoning as the unimpressive enterprise of pil-ing up these dissociated, distinct pronouncements as and when necessary.

The concept of principles added quite different, and quite useful, dimensions to the process of "thinking like a lawyer." The edifice of legal guidance could now be perceived as a meaningful structure, constituted by distinct analytic elements that acted in different ways, although ordinarily in concert. If Dworkin can con-vince you that these principles are indeed something separate and special, the interaction between them and legal rules will be both complex and revealing.

c. Principles as Separate From Rules

The obvious initial question is whether principles are in fact actually some-thing other than just very abstract rules. Dworkin used a number of judicial decisions to illustrate how developments in the law that were otherwise per-haps startling and innovative could best be understood as shifting from one mode of thinking to another. In these cases, existing legal rules are re-engi-neered to reach results that the rules alone would not have supported. In *Riggs v. Palmer*,[62] inheritance rules that should dictate that a legal heir will receive a deceased ancestor's property are suddenly perforated with an exception, never before announced, where the heir kills the decedent. Similarly, in *Henningsen v. Bloomfield Motors*,[63] ordinarily accepted consumer contract provisions are in-validated because they are "unconscionable." We should also note a couple of fa-mous British examples. In *Lloyd's Bank*,[64] the rules of contract were modified by Lord Denning to include the new concept of "inequality of bargaining power." In *Donohue v. Stephenson*,[65] the ancient, accepted rules of contract privity were significantly altered through the tort concept of "due care," creating liability, where none had previously existed, for manufacturers to consumers of defec-tive products. Something other than legal "rules" had to be involved here if the idea of a "rule" could be so readily manipulated and modified.

Notice how dramatic these cases become for understanding the nature of legal activity: When a court seems to hit the limit of legal clarity contained in "rules"—when we enter that "penumbra of doubt" or even the "field" in the previous diagram of Hart's approach[66]—the judge can reach out and employ another element of legal material altogether: citing a "principle" as the authority for its decision that settles or clarifies what was otherwise a legal mystery. Such thinking fully endorses the concept that judges do not simply "discover" law, they can "create" specific guidance within circumstances where once only vagueness dominated.[67] And by the same token, the definition of good lawyering is now suddenly expanded to require an appreciation for this abstract level of legal argument: understanding how to derive this extra guidance and give it content sufficient to make it useful and compelling.

Indeed, one of the most telling features of this Dworkinian idea of principles was the way they altered the most basic assumptions about the nature of the legal landscape. To use another analogy, the usual image of the law is that of a jigsaw puzzle, with all the pieces neatly fitting together to create a smooth, interlocking surface—much like Flatlaw. This would mean that a change in the "shape" of one legal rule (puzzle piece) would require the carving out of a space—an exception—in another rule (piece), to allow the levelness of the law to be maintained. Abstract principles, however, have the disconcerting ability to *overlap* each other—to clash and compete in a particular case and yet remain intact to clash and compete all over again in another case. In other words, the principle of "unconscionability" of certain nasty contract terms might prevail over the equally fundamental principle of freedom of contract in one case, and yet in a different case the opposite might be the outcome. The "losing" principle in one case would not have been thought discredited regarding its use in all other cases; it would instead sit in the background waiting to arise again in a later one. This overlapping of principles is thus like adding "depth" to legal thinking, as in transcending Flatlaw.

How, then, were these contests at this abstract level to be resolved? Principles also had another important feature seemingly absent from Hartian rules—the dimension of weight.[68] While in the jigsaw puzzle analogy all rules seem to possess a kind of equality among themselves in that they are all just pieces, principles seem to have varying power to affect the legal landscape in different cases and circumstances. Sometimes a principle seems more compelling in one case than it did in others. Legal reasoning, then, is certainly becoming more complex and, perhaps, troubling.

d. The Functions of Principles within the Legal System

That is precisely the point we need now to explore further. If we accept that there is an important distinction between legal rules and legal principles, the fact that they are both *legal*—they are both present in the "wall" of the law and will both influence, if not control, legal outcomes—then what, more precisely, is their analytic relationship?

Principles would seem to perform four important functions within the processes of legal reasoning:

(1)   Developing legal "doctrine." Given that the law, whatever else it might be or involve, certainly has a core function of directing the behavior of people within its purview, the question is whether rules and principles operate *differently* in providing this guidance. Both, it would seem, establish "standards" for behavior, and both create those standards for both ordinary citizens and officials, like judges. The former are trying to determine the range of their acceptable actions, while the latter must evaluate the appropriateness of those citizen actions. The only significant distinction between rules and principles, then, seems to go back to the early diagram—abstract principles provide contextual perspective on the concrete, specific behaviors that are involved. Rather than viewing legal actions in isolation, they are grouped. Positivists would have no trouble with this proposition, for legal rules are regularly combined to form legal "doctrines" that are merely more inclusive descriptions of areas of law (like contracts, torts, property, and so on—the shapes of Flatlaw, you will recall). But questions always remain concerning how and why these doctrines—these legal combinations (these shapes)—develop. The concept of principles as a separate kind of connective tissue helps make sense of this natural legal clumping.

(2)   Allowing contextual flexibility. Principles, then, are an important perspective on the law as a *system*. To function meaningfully for both citizens and officials, the law's guidance needs to be simultaneously certain *and* flexible. Events and developments cannot be predicted with accuracy, so the law must be able to operate at different levels of specificity. For example, as we will see later in Chapter Six, how do you determine whether a particular fact is critical to a case—whether the case's key feature is that it involves a particular model of automobile, or more generally, movable machinery, or even more generally, man-made artifacts? It is fanciful to imagine that legal "rules" can *by themselves* perform this mental gymnastics of choosing their proper context. Something else must be at work to allow these variations to be assessed meaningfully.

(3)   Developing "new" legal material. These different "levels" of thinking then translate into quite familiar categories of logical analysis: inductive and deductive reasoning. If the law does have two elements (abstract principles and more concrete rules) which dominates the "direction" of our thinking? Do par-

ticular rules (either singly or in combination) tell us (inductively) what the principles are, or do the principles (deductively) establish what the discrete rules are?

Note Figure 3.4's simple picture of the situation of law's data:

Figure 3.4

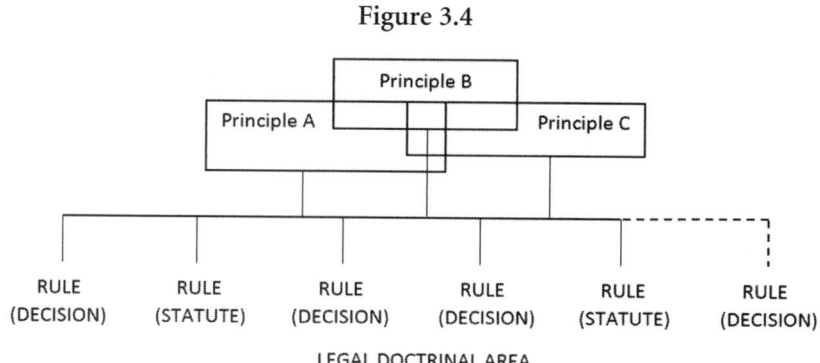

The assumption here is that principles and rules somehow interact and interconnect, so the question for legal reasoning becomes this: Do lawyers start their thinking with "big" ideas (principles) and work "down" to smaller propositions (rules), or do they let the smaller ideas tell them what the legitimate big ideas are? The answer need not be one or the other, of course: Dworkin's example cases seem to reflect different judicial directions.

For example, in the diagram above, imagine that the "rule (decision)" at the far right where dashed lines appear is the *Donohue* decision, which extended for the first time the concept of "due care" in tort law to product manufacturers. The reasoning that created it, according to Dworkin, is that the bits of rule material to the left were examined by the judge, who then realized that embedded within that data (floating above it all in the diagram) was a principle (or perhaps a gaggle of them) called the concept of "due care." It was in effect simply waiting to be discovered. Having now been identified, that principle could then be the basis for the (new) *Donohue* decision. Due care had been *induced*, and *Donohue* was the result.

In contrast, now imagine that the case to the right in the diagram is *Riggs*, which involved the heir killing the unlucky ancestor in order to inherit. Rather than looking to other existing similar cases for support (because none existed), the court invoked the big equity concept of "not profiting from your own wrong" (call it Principle A in the diagram), which seemed to descend from the ether into the legal landscape to alter the underlying data. The court *deduced* a new bit of legal material (the *Riggs* decision) that had heretofore been missing. *Riggs* thus becomes a new bit of legal data *not* because other existing "rules" presaged it necessarily, but instead because an abstract idea dictated that this new rule *should* be added.

Clearly these distinctive versions of legal reasoning cannot be attributed to a single kind of legal element—"rules"—and its manipulation. Instead, a separate player is the only reasonable way to understand these legal events.

On the basis of the three characteristics of principles thus far identified, we can get a useful impression of how legal reasoning is being transformed and expanded: Dworkin himself discusses at length how we should now appreciate legal analysis in three basic contexts[69]—constitutional law, statutory analysis, and the common law. The first can now be seen as the study of a document's announcement *not* of a bunch of rules, but of a host of abstract principles (interstate commerce, due process, freedom of speech, etc.), and we should therefore not be surprised or upset by their frequent disconcerting clashes. The task regarding statutes is to examine the details of a legislative document to determine what "larger" ideas (principles) lay behind it (and perhaps similar or related legislative actions) that might make its rule-announcements more meaningful. And the common law involves the inductive/deductive interplay described above between and among rules and principles that fills legal gaps and creates new legal data.

(4)   Privileging normativity. But it is one thing to perceive that there is an interaction between rules and principles producing complex legal reasoning, quite another to determine whether one or the other method—induction or deduction—should be considered the *norm* among legal actors like lawyers and judges. Which *should* control or dominate? Do we even have to resolve this question?

Indeed we do, but that will not be because we simply accept the idea that rules and principles are indeed separate elements in the mental exercise of legal reasoning. That conclusion would be little more than an improved descriptive, positivist explanation of the legal system. Hart, in other words, could agree to nearly everything said so far without too much pain: Principles are just big rules that have generated an equivalent internal point of view in a society. Instead, the reason the dominance relationship between rules and principles must be examined is because of the second feature Dworkin attributes to principles that make them much more than just the mortar in law's brick wall.

e. Principles as the Normative Conscience of the Law

Glue is one thing. Superglue that tells things to stick to it is another. Principles for Dworkin become not just simple magnets that attract and hold legal matter together, they become complex discriminating magnets that dictate *which* ideas are permitted to be attached. They do not simply help describe how judges in fact decide difficult cases; they become mechanisms for telling judges how they *ought* to decide cases. The first and second questions of legal theory (listed at the beginning of this Chapter)—identifying law and legal systems—become intimately bound up in the third—what should the content of that legal institution be?

Not satisfied, then, to make his name by identifying a new legal element, Dworkin sought as well to give this particle normative heft. Principles were not simply a more abstract version of a rule, they had the quality of "weight" because they carried the message of social values. Without that additional feature, the picture of legal reasoning would remain incomplete.

This is the realm of Dworkin's work usually referred to as his "rights thesis."[70] It has two components, one quite relevant here, the other requiring a different book. Our focus will be on the simple *fact*, as Dworkin asserts it, that legal reasoning must take account of normative elements, rather than try to avoid them, as Hart suggested. We will put aside the actual normative content Prof. Dworkin argues we should attribute to these principles[71]—his political, rather than legal, philosophy, as it were.

The reason that the idea of principles-as-rights matters to legal reasoning is because Dworkin asserts that rights are inherently *individual* in character and application.[72] They are about values that individual claimants can argue must be associated with their treatment by the law and legal system. Principles, then, are uniquely about what *courts* do, for only the judiciary has its authority invoked to resolve *individuated* disputes between and among litigants seeking redress. In contrast, values you would attribute to society as a whole, which you would address to a legislature, would be something different, requiring a different label: Dworkin called them "policies."[73] Your reasoning in court should therefore be dominated by individuated, singular concerns like human dignity and fundamental fairness; your arguments to a legislature can be about social goals, like economic efficiency. An example: If your opponent in court argues to the judge that a decision for her client would improve this country's international balance of payments, you could appropriately respond: "What the other side has argued to you, your honor, is all very interesting, but it is not a *legal* [meaning rights-based] argument that is relevant for this tribunal. It is instead an argument about a broad social policy appropriate for hearings before a legislative committee."

Dworkin has much to say about this distinction between principles (which are part of the law for a court) and policies (which are not) and particularly about the proper content to be given to legal argumentation (his *grundnorm* is usually summarized as "equal concern and respect").[74] But that possible substance, and the many controversies it naturally generates, we will put aside. All we care about here is the idea, which this book accepts, that to study and appreciate legal reasoning you cannot attempt to make that effort value-free. Norms *always* matter to the legal mind, even if those values are quite controversial. The issue here, then, is not whether values matter, but *how*. As a very practical matter, the challenge is to be able to listen to your opponent's argument carefully enough to discover its underlying normative foundation so you can respond effectively, and not be victimized or blind-sided.

To see this, return to the Martians and Nazis. Dworkin would not permit the inquiry into whether there was "law" in either context to be limited to the "data" of pronouncements and directives. You would necessarily be required to examine the moral substance of the legal system being studied. For him, "[t]he rule of law is a nobler ideal than the rule of legal texts."[75] The former exists in a society if and only if its system recognizes and honors arguments based in individuated citizen rights.[76] A value-free analysis, like Prof. Hart's, would be an empty, and inaccurate, exercise.

We will accept here, for purposes of identifying the full range of thinking that can be attributed to "legal reasoning," this Dworkinian perspective. Normativity as a *general* proposition will therefore be a necessary *psychological* element to build into whatever model emerges. But specific values *themselves* can remain just as controversial as ever, for we will do no choosing among them.

3. Final Lessons: Denying Dworkin's "Right Answer" Thesis

From this rather lengthy review of the debate between Professors Hart and Dworkin, what lessons can we learn that might guide us in improving our understanding of legal reasoning?

The most critical and fundamental bottom line for this book's project is that both these eminent scholars readily acknowledge the fact of legal *doubt*—ambiguity, controversy—that good legal reasoning can help us confront and try to transcend, but can never eradicate.

But what causes the doubt? As the debate demonstrates, positivist-type legal data—cases, statutes, and so on—certainly matter. This material must be examined carefully and thoroughly to determine the baselines established by the existing, traditional legal system. Yet that data, even for the positivist, varies in preciseness of direction. "Open texture" starts with the inherent vagueness of language itself, but quickly extends to the facts themselves in any legal matter, which can range in breadth from narrow to broad.

That lack of precision is then compounded by the fact that the legal data itself includes more than just the standard statements in rulebooks. Doubt certainly is generated by the normativity of general, but fundamental, legal principles connected to that data: We always question *why* a particular piece of legal material (a rule), rather than another, ought to be considered compelling, and that conclusion cannot be reached by considering only the competing rules (or possibly relevant facts) themselves. To make matters even more challenging, the values manifested in these principles also vary. If we accept that normativity is included in our legal analytic psychology, then *which* values should be chosen? Why? How do these concepts then interact with rules to generate our legal conclusions?

Prof. Dworkin's invocation of principles also raises doubt about *who* should be doing this sifting of facts, values, and so on. Are some questions appropriate for courts rather than legislatures, and vice versa? Or do both these institutions consider the entire range of possible, and varying, legal material? If so, does the distinction between them collapse?

One troubling implication of all this doubt is the possibility that the discretion of judges and others to reach legal decisions in particular cases or questions of governance may simply be unbounded as a practical matter—which would mean, sadly, that any effort to be rigorous about studying legal reasoning is largely a waste of time. For some, the conclusion is that judges indeed pick the facts and values they prefer *personally*, and then dishonestly present what might appear (to the uninformed) to be a legitimate assessment of that material. That is simply a possibility this book, or any work on legal reasoning, must accept. The Preface noted that the analysis here is focused not on the *actual* reasoning of anyone—people can be disingenuous. But the point here remains that any analysis of something as slippery as "thinking"—and how to influence that psychological process—cannot avoid acknowledging discretion and doubt. Understanding the structure of legal reasoning should at least be able to reveal the points of danger to legal legitimacy that require special attention.

This danger of excessive judicial discretion was in fact one that worried Prof. Dworkin significantly, prompting him to develop within his legal theory a bold claim to judicial *certainty* to eliminate it. We will acknowledge that proposition here briefly, but not accept it, for it is largely misunderstood. Dworkin argued that if we adopt his theory, and include value-filled legal principles into the reasoning mix, then if a court worked hard enough determining which values (rights) were involved or embedded within the legal matter at stake, then—even in the most intractable and controversial cases — a "right answer"[77] would emerge. He asserted that the kind of "strong" (as he called it), unfettered judicial discretion that Prof. Hart seemed to accept as inevitable simply did not exist. Sufficiently thoughtful judges would always ultimately know what they should decide.

This aspect of Prof. Dworkin's work, however, is an analytic red herring and aberration that we can put aside. In Chapter Six we will note that what Dworkin had in mind was something much less dramatic: that every case would have a "right (judicial) *analysis*" (rather than right answer) that should be applied to it. He would label this appropriate form of reasoning "law as integrity," and we will see its practical implications in that Chapter. It is a concept entirely consistent with the agenda and ambition of this book.

Notes

1. Karl N. Llewellyn, Bramble Bush: On Our Law and Its Study (1881).

2. H.L.A. Hart, *Positivism and the Separation of Law and Morals*, 71 Harv. L. Rev. 593 (1958); Lon Fuller, *Positivism and Fidelity to Law: A Reply to Professor Hart*, 71 Harv. L. Rev. 630 (1958).

3. Lon L. Fuller, *The Case of the Speluncean Explorers*, 62 Harv. L. Rev. 616 (1949).

4. Henry M. Hart, Jr. & Albert M. Sacks, The Legal Process: Basic Problems in the Making and Application of Law (William N. Eskridge, Jr. & Phillip P. Frickey eds., Found. Press Inc. 1994) (1958). Another casebook-type publication that probably should be ranked alongside Hart and Sacks is William Bishin & Christopher Stone, Law, Language, and Ethics: An Introduction to Law and Legal Method (1972).

5. Edward H. Levi, An Introduction to Law and Legal Reasoning (1949).

6. Although Prof. Dworkin has discussed the work of Prof. Hart in various places, the most extended direct analysis and criticism of his work appears in TRS, *supra* ch. 1 note 16, at 14–130, where, as one of his commentary techniques, he contrasts the judicial efforts of a hypothetical judges named "Herbert" (guess what the H in H.L.A. Hart stands for), the positivist, and "Hercules," the anti-positivist. *Id.*

7. Guido Calabresi & Douglas Melamed, *Property Rules, Liability Rules, and Inalienability: One View of the Cathedral*, 85 Harv. L. Rev. 1089 (1972). I will confess here that the absence of a discussion of this work in the context of an article on legal reasoning is a significant deficit, but it is beyond the scope of what can usefully be developed here. The point of the "Property Rules" article was not simply that economic principles were relevant to legal analysis, it was more profound. The observation that these authors made was that the law in at least one substantive area — nuisance law, and tort law more generally — could be understood much more accurately and usefully if one separated the "rights" that might determine who should "win" in a given case from the "remedy" that will be employed to manifest that "win." Thus, as they demonstrated, cases were decided quite differently depending on whether a victory by one party resulted in the extreme imposition of an injunction

(which they labeled a "property rule") that stopped or imposed an action completely (like shutting down a polluting factory), or it resulted in the less painful sanction of damages (which they called a "liability rule"). As a matter of economic theory, the key to this differentiation was that the former remedy would force the loser in a case, if the loser wanted to change the outcome, to pay the winner's price, whatever that might be; the latter remedy allowed the court to set the price.

But more generally (and fundamentally) concerning legal reasoning, the separation between "rights" and "remedies" speaks directly to the decision maker's context, as the issue of a "strike" illustrates as well as any. The "remedy" of calling a pitch a "strike" could be made more or less onerous than the current rule of calling the player "out": It could be that this batter would be required to do 10 push-ups before attempting to swing at another pitch; or it could be that the batter is thrown out of the game altogether. The point is that the "rule" of the strike zone cannot really be appreciated without reference to what will happen once a decision is made—how serious, nasty, unalterable, or unreviewable the result may be. Unfortunately, we will put all of that interesting nuance aside as we compare the baseball metaphor employed by Prof. Gould and Justice Roberts.

8. Steven J. Burton, An Introduction to Law and Legal Reasoning (Aspen Pub., Inc. 2d ed. 1995).

9. From Prof. Waldron's vast output, see, e.g., Jeremy Waldron, *Arguing About Normativity of Jurisprudence: Comments on Andrei Mormor's Philosophy of Law*, 10 Jerusalem Rev. L. Stud. 81 (2014); Jeremy Waldron, *Separation of Powers in Thought and Practice* 54 B.C. L. Rev. 433 (2013); Jeremy Waldron, *Judges as Moral Reasoners*, 1 Int'l J. Const. L. 2 (2009); Jeremy Waldron, *The Concept and the Rule of Law*, 83 Ga. L. Rev. 1 (2008); Jeremy Waldron, *Positivism and Legality: Hart's Equivocal Response to Fuller* 83 N.Y.U. L. Rev. 1135 (2008).

10. *See, e.g.*, Richard A. Posner, The Problematics of Moral and Legal Theory (2002); Posner, *supra* Preface note 2.

The latter text, however, deserves more discussion here than a mere citation. Indeed, it is referenced in other parts of this book as well (in endnotes in the Preface, the Introduction, two in this Chapter, and another in Chapter Six). It merits extra attention because its title alone suggests remarkable overlap with my agenda. But that is not so, for Judge Posner's ambition is quite different.

As noted in the Introduction, this book does not attempt to unpack and describe the full panoply of psychological elements that might play a role in legal reasoning generally, or judicial reasoning in particular. I am not, and never have been, a judge, so I cannot comment meaningfully on much of what Judge Posner believes is actually percolating within judicial minds, including especially forces like group dynamics on an appellate court, the role of political bias, and so on. Discussion of such factors does indeed appear in several of the many reviews that Judge Posner's book has provoked, and within that vast literature I would note in particular the lucid and thoughtful development that appears in the essay of another federal judge, Jeffrey S. Sutton, *A Review of Richard A. Posner, How Judges Think* (2008), 108 Mich. L. Rev. 859 (2010).

But I would note as well that this book is not addressed particularly to judges. It is more directly about the elements that lawyers should consider as they develop their advocacy. Indeed, Judge Sutton notes the inevitable and appropriate overlap between what he thought as an advocate mattered to judges and what he now thinks matters to him as a judge. The two may not be identical, but there is substantial similarity.

Consequently, my focus is to develop a useful, structured description of the narrower topic of more directly "professional," if you will, qualities within legal reasoning—the analytic detail on which both advocacy and judging are most deeply based.

I have also relegated my discussion of Judge Posner's book to endnote because, as I note later in note 67 in this Chapter, I believe his analysis of judging is so similar to that of Prof. Ronald Dworkin that I can best avoid redundancy by just developing the latter in detail. *See infra* note 67.

11. Prof. Schauer's contributions are the subject of notes 23 and 24, along with the accompanying text. *See infra* notes 23, 24.

Some may complain that missing from this list is a reference to LON FULLER, THE MORAL-ITY OF LAW (1964). This is indeed an important and impressive classic as well, but its agenda is not so much the nature of legal reasoning itself, but instead the (necessary) connection between law and morality. *Id.* Nevertheless, Prof. Fuller's concern with an "inner" morality of law is certainly relevant to the discussion of "hypertext" that is developed later in this book, so I put his work aside with all due reverence. *See infra* ch. 4, at pp. 110–111; *infra* ch. 7. Other work by Prof. Fuller is much more on point, and it will be discussed later in this Chapter.

12. But now a potentially serious problem emerges. If there is no "substantive" legal truth, then analytic "process"—no matter how widely accepted—cannot somehow magically produce it. Instead, these reasoning efforts, careful and precise though they may be, will only ever create results that *seem* "legitimate" in a logical sense, but nevertheless remain morally and politically controversial. Does the emphasis on process, then, in the absence of fundamental substance, mean that the process is actually phony, and unworthy of respect?

It certainly does to a group of legal theorists who are not within the traditional camp, which has so far been our focus here. Usually labeled "critical legal scholarship," this approach to law and legal reasoning will not figure prominently in this book's analysis precisely because of its attitude toward legitimate analysis and reasoning. Although the literature associated with this school of thought is both vast and varied, one useful summary discussion appears in ROBERT HAYMAN, NANCY LEVIT & RICHARD DELGADO, JURISPRUDENCE: CLASSI-CAL AND CONTEMPORARY: FROM NATURAL LAW TO POSTMODERNISM 402–460 (2d ed. 2002).

It is always dangerous, of course, to try to summarize a form of reasoning that is this diverse. Nevertheless, I will note that one of its defining characteristics is the belief "that no distinctive mode of legal reasoning exists to be contrasted with political dialogue ... Law is not so much a rational enterprise as a vast exercise in rationalization." Allan Hutchison & Patrick Monahan, *Law, Politics, and the Critical Legal Scholars: The Unfolding Drama of American Legal Thought*, 36 STAN. L. REV. 199, 206 (1984). The classic sources being summarized in the text above emphatically disagree, distilling instead from the words and actions of legal actors like judges certain patterns of reasoning that are legitimate and appropriate for the context of the law. *Id.*

Notice the profound difference in approach to law and legal reasoning that is reflected in the critical group: Regarding the previous list of three basic points to be addressed in legal theory, traditionalists start with the first two (identifying "law" and "systems") and then (sometimes) work toward the third—asking whether this seemingly "legal" material deserves normative respect. In direct contrast, the critical group emphatically employs the opposite order: If the moral substance of legal material is not acceptable, the methods by which we got to it are empty and meaningless. And regarding that substance, they start with the premise that the law and legal systems are quite bad: little more than exercises of oppressive power of the haves over the have-nots.

This approach has then, sadly, led to a separation of the critical group from the most basic of the shared perspectives usually found within the world of legal theory. Critical scholars have the unfortunate penchant to label their opponents' thinking as infused with "false consciousness"—not rational, you see, but mere rationalization—which turns disagreement disagreeable. When one's reasoning *itself* is rejected, meaningful discussions cease.

Critical scholars are nevertheless correct, in a way, when they claim that "[l]egal doctrine can be manipulated to justify an almost infinite number of possible outcomes." *Id.* But they exaggerate the point. The classic sources on legal reasoning do not, as we have noted, emphasize the outcomes of legal matters, but rather the methods behind the results: Fundamentally, legal reasoning exists, and must be studied, not because it produces legal or social agreement, but because it is the method by which we *manage* disagreement. And the traditionalists see that management effort as benign, not malign.

A good example of both the complexity of reasoning and the changeable nature of the policy conclusions that can arise in the general sphere of critical approaches to legal theory, is the work of my Emory colleague, Prof. Martha Fineman. *See, e.g.*, MARTHA FINEMAN, THE AUTONOMY MYTH 18–22 (2005) (autonomy and "its attendant ideals of independence and self-sufficiency" are "myths"); Martha Fineman, *The Vulnerable Subject: Anchoring Equality in the Human Condition*, 20 YALE J.L. & FEMINISM (2008) (introducing the vulnerability thesis).

13. EDWARD H. LEVI, AN INTRODUCTION TO LAW AND LEGAL REASONING 3–4 (1949).

14. *See* BURTON, *supra* note 8, at 25 ("Legal reasoning takes two principal forms: One is analogical; the other is deductive"); *Id.* at 27 ("Analogical legal reasoning is not fundamentally different from analogical reasoning in familiar situations. It is, however, more formal, rigorous, and uniform in its expression."); *Id.* at 46 ("Deductive legal reasoning, like its analogical cousin, is more formal and rigorous than similar reasoning in most everyday non-legal contexts."). *See also* LEVI, *supra* note 5, at 1–2 ("The basic pattern of legal reasoning is reasoning by example. It is reasoning from case to case. It is a three-step process described by the doctrine of precedent in which a proposition descriptive of the first case is made into a rule of law and then applied to a next similar situation. The steps are these: similarity is seen between cases; next the rule of law inherent in the first case is announced; then the rule of law is made applicable in the second case").

15. On matters of language, the best sources would be COL, *supra* ch. 1 note 12, at 18-20, 124–136. *See also* BISHIN & STONE, *supra* note 4, at 403–538.

16. This approach was announced in TRS, *supra* note ch. 1 note 16, at viii, 1–13, but has been a constant theme throughout Prof. Dworkin's work. *See, e.g.*, RONALD DWORKIN, MATTER OF PRINCIPLE (1985); RONALD DWORKIN, LAW'S EMPIRE (1986); RONALD DWORKIN, JUSTICE IN ROBES (2006).

17. TRS, *supra* ch. 1 note 16, at 81–130.

18. This genre could just as easily today be labeled as "pragmatist"—the effort to connect legal results to our actual experiences and practical expectations. One classic statement

within this genre is Karl Llewellyn, *A Realist Jurisprudence—The Next Step*, 30 COLUM. L. REV. 431 (1930), but examples abound.

19. To put it in its simplest form, the basic notion within this school is that claims about "law" must be rooted in some "positive," objective background source, such as a statute or court decision, rather than more amorphous possibilities like a society's sense of "morality." The most well-known, and well-regarded statement of this approach continues to be COL, *supra* ch. 1 note 12.

20. Most directly associated with the work of Ronald Dworkin, this kind of legal theory rejects any separation (rigid or otherwise) between law and the contextual morality within which it operates. In his later work, Prof. Dworkin switched from his initial references to "antipositivism" to "interpretivism." *See, e.g.*, JUSTICE IN ROBES, *supra* note 16, at 249.

21. This label basically derives from the emphasis on the demands of formal logic—major premises entail the minor, and reasoning leads wherever this process may take you. Law therefore looks a lot like mathematics, with self-referential proofs, and very narrow understandings of the reach of "rules." An excellent discussion of this approach appears in COL, *supra* ch. 1 note 12, at 124–154.

22. As an analytic matter, this approach is the opposite of formalism—it rejects the idea that an anchoring, narrow postulate lies in the background of any rule. Instead, law is an exercise in ambiguity and vagueness, with the only certainty being the ruling of an authoritative decision maker. Hence, we are back to the realists. Hart's book is also a useful source on this topic, and its relation to formalism. *See id.*

23. *See, e.g.*, Frederick Schauer, *Exceptions*, 58 CHI. L. REV. 871 (1991); Frederick Schauer, *Precedent*, 39 STAN. L. REV. 571 (1987); Frederick Schauer, *Easy Cases*, 58 S. CAL. L. REV. 399 (1985); Frederick Schauer, *Slippery Slopes*, 99 HARV. L. REV. 361 (1985).

24. FREDERICK SCHAUER, THINKING LIKE A LAWYER: A NEW INTRODUCTION TO LEGAL REASONING (Harv. Univ. Press 2012).

25. *See, e.g., id.* at 577 (noting that "No two events are exactly alike. For a decision to be precedent for another decision does not require that the facts of the earlier and the later cases be absolutely identical. Were that required, nothing would be a precedent for anything else. We must therefore leave the realm of absolute identity. Once we do so, however, it is clear that the relevance of an earlier precedent depends upon how we characterize the facts arising in the earlier case. It is a commonplace that these characterizations are inevitably theory-laden. In order to assess what is a precedent for what, we must engage in some determination of the relevant similarities between the two events."); *Id.* at 589 ("If the best solution to today's case is identical to the best solution for tomorrow's different but assimilable facts, then there is no problem. But if what is best for today's situation might not be best for a different (but likely to be assimilated) situation, then the need to consider the future as well as the present will result in at least some immediately suboptimal decisions.").

26. Fredrick Schauer, *Precedent*, 39 STAN. L. REV. 571, 576–577 (1987).

27. *Id.* at 577.

28. *Id.*

29. *Id.* at 579.

30. *Id.*

31. *Id.* at 585.

32. *Id.*

33. SCHAUER, *supra* note 24, at 118.

34. LON L. FULLER, THE PROBLEMS OF JURISPRUDENCE 637 (1949).

35. COL, *supra* ch. 1 note 12.

36. *Id.* at 16.

37. To define this idea in its simplest form, the basic notion within this school is that claims about "law" must be rooted in some objectively identifiable "positive" authoritative background source, such as a statute or court decision, rather than in more amorphous possibilities like a society's sense of morality.

38. COL, *supra* ch. 1 note 12, at 18–25.

39. *Id.*

40. *Id.* at 56, 92.

41. *Id.* at 98 ("Under the simple regime of primary rules the internal point of view is manifested in its simplest form, in the use of those rules as the basis of criticism, and the justification of demands for conformity, social pressure, and punishment. Reference to this most elementary manifestation of the internal point of view is required for the analysis of the basic concepts of obligation and duty.").

42. *Id.* at 87–91.

43. *Id.*

44. *Id.* at 98 ("With the addition to the system of secondary rules, the range of what is said and done from the internal point of view is much extended and diversified. With this extension comes a whole set of new concepts and they demand a reference to the internal point of view for their analysis. These include the notions of legislation, jurisdiction, validity, and, generally, of legal powers, private and public").

45. *Id.* at 94–98.

46. *Id.*

47. *Id.*

48. *Id.* at 157–167.

49. *Id.* at 209.

50. *Id.* at 210.

51. The critical approach was discussed briefly earlier. *See supra* note 12.

52. COL, *supra* ch. 1 note 12, at 153.

53. Just focusing on his books, Prof. Dworkin published his first in 1977, his last in 2013.

54. COL, *supra* ch. 1 note 12, at 128.

55. H.L.A. Hart, *Positivism and the Separation of Law and Morals*, 71 HARV. L. REV. 593, 607 (1958).

56. *Id.* Hart developed these two ideas as "plain cases" or "paradigm, clear cases," on the one hand, and "uncertainty at the borderline," on the other. *See* COL, *supra* ch. 1 note 12, at 125–129.

57. COL, *supra* ch. 1 note 12, at 126–135.

58. *Id.* at 153.

59. TRS, *supra* ch. 1 note 16, at 32.

60. *Id.* at 22.

61. This point is developed throughout the first half of TAKING RIGHTS SERIOUSLY. *See* TRS, *supra* ch. 1 note 12.

62. Riggs v. Palmer, 115 N.Y. 506 (1889).

63. Henningsen v. Bloomfield Motors, Inc., 161 A.2d 69 (N.J. 1960).

64. Lloyds Bank Ltd. v. Bundy, 1974 EWCA Civ. 8.

65. Donoghue v. Stevenson, [1932] UKHL 100.

66. *See supra* pp. 83.

67. This idea that judges do indeed create law from time to time, along with the accompanying idea of an underlying distinction between narrow legal rules and broader normative principles, is quite similar to Judge Richard Posner's depiction of judicial reasoning. *See* POSNER, *supra* Preface note 2. He reviews carefully the challenging, and often controversial, connections between standard legal material, like statutes and case decisions, and, as he references them, the myriad "policy" considerations that these materials inevitably embody and reflect. *Id.* These background considerations then in turn mean that judges are necessarily political actors. *Id.* at 269, 277–78, 287, 346, 369. The important difference between Posner and Dworkin, however, is that the latter has much more philosophical (rather than descriptive) ambition: Dworkin's principles are not merely "big, abstract" ideas, or even just generally "good" ideas, the way for example "economic efficiency" might be viewed as a legitimate source of judicial perspective. Instead, Dworkin's principles—fully legitimate *legal* principles—are about the individual's rights, not society's goals. And ultimately, these rights are grounded in Dworkin's concept of "equal concern and respect." Judge Posner, on the other hand, is content to argue that the only meaningful foundation to these larger ideas is "pragmatism"—or what you might think of as his version of "practical reasonableness."

68. TRS, *supra* ch. 1 note 16, at 26.

69. *Id.* at 105–123.

70. *Id.* at 90–100.

71. *Id.*

72. *Id.* at 70-75, 91.

73. *Id.* at 22, 91.

74. *Id.* at 180-83, 272–28.

75. *Id.* at 338.

76. *Id.* ("Citizens are encouraged to suppose that each has rights and duties against other citizens, and against their common government, even though these rights and duties are not set out in black-letter codes. They are therefore encouraged to frame and test hypotheses about what these rights are, and to treat one another, and demand to be treated by the state, under the beneficial and unifying assumptions that justice is always relevant to their claims even when it is unclear what justice requires. The courts participate in this

process, by providing an occasional forum for public considerations of these controversial issues of justice, and by providing leadership whose power is rightly qualified by the force of the arguments it can command.")

77. *See, e.g.*, Ronald Dworkin, *No Right Answer?, in* LAW, MORALITY AND SOCIETY: ESSAYS IN HONOR OF H.L.A. HART 58 (Hacker & Raz eds., 1977). This idea emerges in multiple places within TRS, *supra* ch. 1 note 16.

Chapter Four

Rethinking the Analytic Tradition: Text, Context, Hypertext, and Subtext

I will not argue here that any of the several approaches noted earlier within legal theory to resolving questions about law and systems and the like is "wrong" to any significant extent.[1] Instead, my contention is that our current efforts in legal theory are unnecessarily difficult to compare to each other, and are, to one degree or another, incomplete. I seek to be both more analytic about legal analysis, and more strategic about legal strategies of argument, than others have thus far been. Consequently, much of the detail in this prior work, and the details of the disagreements among the authors, can be put aside. We will instead attempt to go "underneath" this discussion to even more basic questions about how lawyers *reason* about analogies or rules or principles or values or anything else they might claim is relevant to their contentions.[2]

A. Legal Reasoning as Rhetorical Prediction

Even though this inquiry will necessarily be at a high level of abstraction, the analytic focus will still remain on the initial and most basic conceptual hurdle confronted by all new law students concerning "legal reasoning": the structure and nature of "typical" judicial thinking, and hence of legal argumentation more generally. We want to determine whether there is anything special about that mental activity—whether the concept of "thinking like a lawyer" has any identifiable content *and predictable structure* that we could then use to our advantage in assessing the contentions thrown at us by adversaries or judges (or, for this book, other commentators on legal reasoning).

From this effort, we discover that disagreement on issues of law and public policy are in fact *inevitable* and *intractable*—not because of some sinister conspiracy, but because the process of *analyzing* the issues at stake is itself so fractured. Although some law students seem to take this observation as one of cynicism and despair, it is not. Quite the contrary, it is a message of professional *opportunity*. Although we may not be able—no matter how hard we try—to drain this swamp, we might at least be able to find some useful paths through it.

It is toward that conclusion that the remainder of this book strives.

So, we now embark on the long-promised analytic journey that will confront and resolve the limitations previously identified in the existing commentary on legal reasoning. We must, then, develop more explicitly the depth of disagreement about legal guidance between Prof. Gould and Justice Roberts; give content to the challenging and murky realm within and beyond Flatlaw; go beneath Prof. Schauer's sequence of reasoning steps; determine if Prof. Fuller's sequence can be resolved; and further integrate the theoretical perspectives of Professors Hart and Dworkin.

This trip will require a new, multifaceted model of legal reasoning that, while relying on the work that has preceded it, will produce a more detailed and more structured description and explanation of this professional phenomenon. That improvement to legal theory should yield, in turn, a more practically useful understanding of it as well. As noted often in earlier Chapters, legal reasoning and social disagreement are inextricably linked, if for no other reason than the contentious situations in which the law becomes relevant. Consequently, if we discover a structure within legal reasoning, we should be able to use it to anticipate, in broad outline, the nature of the disagreements themselves that the law is being forced to confront. In other words, a sophisticated lawyer should be able to anticipate, rather than just react to, the counterarguments that will be raised by opponents (or more neutrally, by skeptics).

B. On Thoroughness and Concepts

This book's Introduction noted that one goal here would be to present a "thorough" analysis of what legal reasoning requires in its most comprehensive form. The claim I will defend is that such an understanding of thinking through the *law* in any given situation will require attention to more elements than other situations of study involve.

For example, let's briefly consider a couple of examples like the "analyze a building" idea used earlier. Imagine that you ask an environmental scientist to give you a thorough understanding of a "river." You would probably get a discussion from her that would start with the most obvious "surface" aspects of the course of moving water, but then she would note the nature of the land that contains and defines the river's course, the varying depths and widths of the water along the course, the varying chemical composition of the water or the sediments within it, the life forms within the water, the life forms that surround and are nurtured by this water, perhaps a discourse on the economic importance of the river to the larger community near the river, and so on. Despite this impressive array of information, notice how none of it is abstract— it is all well-organized *data*.

Or imagine that you asked a psychologist to give you a thorough understanding of a "person." This might be a bit more challenging, as the discussion would quickly move from the superficial, readily observable characteristics of a "human being," such as skin and hair color, height and weight, and the like—for we are certainly more than just "flesh and bones"—to background elements of ethnicity, birthplace, age, life experiences, test results showing various aptitudes or limitations, and so on. More and more detail would produce what seems to be a "complete" picture of any human being, but again in an objective, data-based way. Any abstraction about the nature or importance or character of this person would begin to challenge the edges of the psychologist's professional context.

As developed to this point, both these categories—river and person—are essentially and largely anchored in tangibility—something identifiable and familiar. What happens, though, if the topic to be developed is itself *only* an abstraction, with at best slender connections to anything concrete? For the environmental scientist, what if the question posed were: Should we dam this river, turning part of it into a lake? Is that a "good" idea? Could an answer to that question be based solely in science? For the psychologist, what if the question becomes: What is a "reasonable" person? Or what is "personhood"? We have again moved from scientific description to *assessment*, which seems to be an important category-jump. In both situations, the engineer and the psychologist can no longer be the sole voice in the conversation.

The point of all this for this book is simply this: *Every legal concept has that category-jump element inherently embedded in it.* Certainly ideas like "river" and "person" are multi-faceted, and are "concepts" because they are mental constructs that *summarize* and embody in a word or phrase a host of constituent elements lying in the background. But the problem for *legal* concepts is that their constituent elements are *themselves* abstract concepts, creating layers of abstraction. What, for example, is "property"? What can you "own"? Do you, for example, own your body? If so, why is the right to an abortion so controversial? What is a "contract"? If it is simply an agreed-upon deal, can you sell yourself into slavery? Can you actually "agree" to that to make the contract valid and enforceable? This litany can go on forever: What is a "crime"? What is "personal jurisdiction"? What is "income"? What is a "security interest"?

The challenge of *legal* reasoning in particular—to understand *legal* concepts thoroughly—is therefore the need to handle effectively this peculiar kind of information that involves the layering of abstraction on top of abstraction. Although the analysis of *any* term—"river," "person," or anything else—will need a structure of some sort to make it comprehensible, the conceptual context of the law will require more attention to this structure than we are accustomed to developing. Even something as seemingly mundane and ordinary as a "strike," because it is a purely human construct invented for the special regulatory context of a baseball game, will be a daunting proposition to pin down, as Prof. Gould's essay so nicely demonstrates.

What, then, is the nature of this "conceptual analysis" that lies at the heart of legal reasoning?

This book has so frequently invoked analogical images, why not one more? All scholars hope to add "light" to the subjects they examine. They want to put material in a new light, or put a topic under a spotlight, or highlight certain points, or enlighten us in various ways, or any number of similar metaphors. I am no different. But I will add a twist: What I seek to do is examine the light itself, to break it up into its different constituent elements.

My metaphor is this: Imagine that legal concepts, as discussed above, are forms of information, and that this information is in turn a source of light. Light, however, as you know from high school physics, is a complex phenomenon, simultaneously both waves and particles. Regarding those waves, they are of different "lengths" which can be discovered by passing a beam of light through a prism. The result is a spectrum of colors of different wavelengths.

Figure 4.1

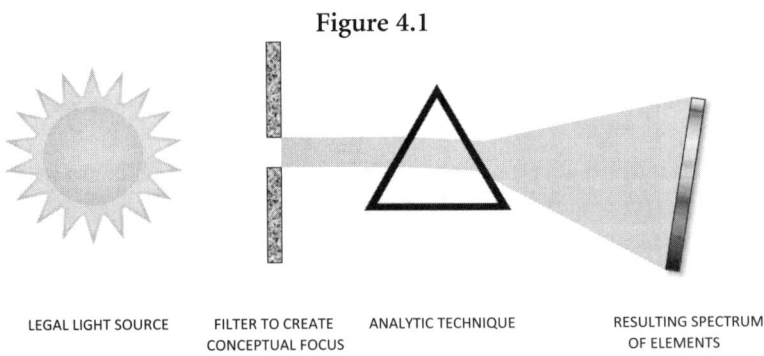

LEGAL LIGHT SOURCE   FILTER TO CREATE   ANALYTIC TECHNIQUE   RESULTING SPECTRUM
                       CONCEPTUAL FOCUS   OF ELEMENTS

Connecting legal reasoning to this image, the question becomes: What does the spectrum of conceptual legal information look like? Would we be able to separate it into segments that are otherwise not readily visible, the way different colors are contained within ordinary light? Would this allow us to study our reasoning about these concepts more systematically?

That, in a nutshell, is the ambition of the remainder of this Chapter and the book as a whole.

C. "Text" Gives Way to Context, Hypertext, and Subtext

This idea of legal information as a spectrum, is however, only a metaphor, not a claim of scientific accuracy. So the result of passing legal concepts through my "prism" of analysis will not yield the familiar linear composition of a rainbow, moving from violet to red, but instead a more complex matrix of interacting elements.

Rather than develop this book's alternative model of legal reasoning step-by-step like a detective story, it is presented here as a complete whole—to be defended thereafter sequentially.

That model has four interrelated segments, each of which contains in turn its own special internal tension of competing elements. Together, they produce a diagrammatic "map" of this special, multidimensional, and thus quite challenging, mental process.[3] As a heuristic device, Figure 4.2 uses the most obvious manifestation of the law—its words, or "text"—as the taxonomical touchstone:

Figure 4.2

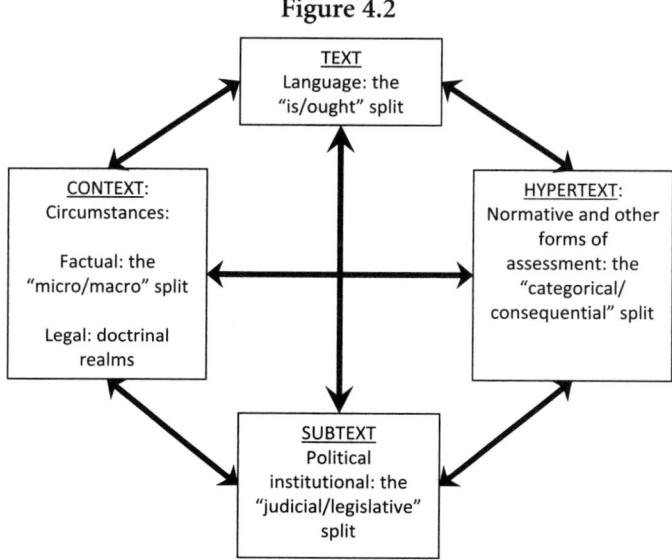

As we will see, each of these elements is fundamental to any society's effort to identify and justify the guidance that its legal system is presumed to provide, both to ordinary citizens and official decision makers, within its political context. And, as we will also see, each element is invoked in and relevant to the perspective of every scholar previously identified—Prof. Gould's essay, Prof. Schauer's analytic sequence, and the debate between Hart and Dworkin.

The vertical order of the elements depicted here is not, however, part of the analytic argument to be made. Instead, the double-pointed arrows throughout indicate that each segment of this analytic approach is simultaneously related to all the others. For example, although "text" is at the top of the diagram, it is not necessarily "first" in an analytical sense: The examination of a particular legal controversy—in a lawyer's brief or in a court's opinion—may well not begin with attention to the language used to describe or express it, but might instead emphasize immediately the human values at stake in the matter (hypertext), or the political nuances within which the matter must be appreciated (subtext).

Nevertheless, the order displayed in the diagram does acknowledge that whatever else might be relevant to analyzing a legal issue, the subtleties of the language in which it is expressed will inevitably play some role in the full consideration of that controversy. By the same token, there is no claim here that language "precedes" our moral and social values; instead, the point will be that the ways in which we attempt to capture and express our values in our language—the effort to communicate values—is intimately connected to the substance of our normativity. Language is not only the medium of philosophical exchange, it is central to understanding the exchange in the first place.

Consequently, "sequencing" within the diagram—starting here rather than there—is not directly the point. The key is instead the distinction between and among these analytical elements. Despite the fact that each segment influences all the others, they are each separate and distinct *enough* from each other to deserve explicit attention. If we appreciate each on its own terms, we can gain a more useful understanding of the craft of legal reasoning—even though, in the end, they all do mesh together.

Subsequent Chapters of this book will develop in more detail each of the pieces of the diagram, and hence each particular "split personality" generating consternation within its arena. For now, those segments can be summarized as follows:

Text: Although law and legal systems are basically about the regulation of human conduct, that effort travels, as noted, on the basis of the language used to express those regulations. Thus, any study of law must pay particular attention to the nature of language as our medium for embodying social guidance. (For any reader with any background in the academic discipline of linguistics, I urge you to remain patient. I will be invoking a much milder and more narrow sense of language analysis than you might be expecting.)

In the case of Gould's article, the disconcerting example is the single word—and critical concept—of a "strike." It is an apt illustration of that most basic of philosophical distinctions resting at the core of linguistics: the difference between the way in which a word is *in fact* used by a population, and the way in which the word *should* be used, according to some overarching criteria or normative agenda.[4] These linguistic elements in turn simply reflect the distinction that the philosopher David Hume, so long ago, urged us to make: between "is" (facts, loosely understood) and "ought" (values, largely understood).[5] It is the distinction at the core of the Hart-Dworkin debate, as we noted earlier.

Context: Language, in the form of regulation, will nevertheless be applied within shifting circumstances, and the question becomes whether this kind of contextual contingency can and *should* make a difference—to our language, to our values, or to any other aspect of our analysis of a matter. If context does seem relevant, how is this possible? How can something as basic as our language or our set of fundamental values change based on circumstances? And *how much* difference will we permit this shift in circumstance to make?

For Gould, this struggle is captured in the importance (for him) of context-based "truth" and its relationship to linguistic messiness: being in the realm of the World Series somehow causes a definitional shift. For lawyers and judges, this is the realm of "categorization" and "comparison" that Prof. Schauer emphasizes, where situations are assessed by examining possible similarities and differences. But the issue for our analysis of legal reasoning is whether these activities of labeling and relating and distinguishing regularly fall into identifiable analytic subsets. They do. The most obvious will be the two differing circumstances of, on the one hand, assessing the relative importance of different levels of generality in the "facts" involved in a matter, and, on the other, the various "legal categories" that might be considered relevant.

The intersection of these two categories is in fact something that all law students experience in the first year of law school with no one pointing it out to them. Although they note, at least subliminally, that every law school has the same set of basic courses required during that year—contracts, torts, property, and criminal law—they seldom wonder why. The answer is based in this fundamental dimension of context: The law is about regulating human behavior, and humans can interact with each other in two basic ways: consensually and non-consensually. The former is the realm of contract law, the latter, tort and criminal law. The subject matter of the vast bulk of that interacting is property law (with all its many sub-types). And students ultimately come to realize, of course, that these neat divisions can and do break down.

But we will be going much deeper than this simple observation. Regarding facts, we will focus on the fundamental, but subtle, impact on our legal thinking of the differences in the "scale," or breadth, of the facts we believe central to the inquiry. The range will vary from the "micro" (or moral) context of particular individuals in singular circumstances, to the "macro" (or political) context of larger populations in general situations.[6] This was certainly on Gould's mind: Was the key to the assessment of the pitch the specific people or teams involved or, much more grandly, the national pastime called baseball?

Concerning legal categories, you could consider this form of contextual "is" as sets of "systemic facts": the variation introduced by different doctrinal areas, like contracts, torts, property, and so on, that have their own special internal forces that influence the legal mind to appreciate a controversy in distinct ways. To use Gould's essay here, his possible thinking needs to be stretched perhaps a bit further than he would have intended: The question could be, should the rules of baseball be those of an "ordinary" game (maybe like "contract law") or those of the "special" game (maybe introducing legal concepts like "fiduciary duty")? And how and why should that contextual shift matter to the law of baseball as understood by the umpire and the players?

Hypertext: Neither text nor context, however, just "happen"—the words we decide to employ and the circumstances that somehow actually *matter* to us must be explained and justified: They become the "right" words and the "correct" social contingency to which to refer. We (meaning lawyers and judges) demand *reasons*, which in turn require reference to the *values* we believe make our choice of language and circumstances appropriate. We must, in other words, at this stage become straightforwardly interested not in "facts" by themselves, but *assessing* those facts against articulated standards—perhaps normative, philosophical judgments, as Prof. Dworkin argued, but perhaps other forms of desirability as well, like economic efficiency.

Gould makes forays into this reflective realm with his references to "justice" and "democracy," and, by unspoken implication, their relevance to concepts of community, political theory, and law. But his essay is tantalizing in part because it says so little on these critical points. We will nevertheless find in his defense of Umpire Pinelli's call an example of a fundamental distinction that legal reasoning regularly makes between two forms of worthiness: on the one hand, "categorical" (or deontological) thinking, which focuses on philosophical values (dignity, fairness, and the like) and, on the other, "consequential" (or teleological) assessments of the results that various decisions might generate (more to eat, fewer cars on the road, widespread poverty, and so on).[7]

Subtext: As a final step, to fully appreciate the relevance of Gould's essay and the Hart-Dworkin debate to the world of legal reasoning, all these factors of language and circumstances and values must be understood to intersect and integrate within a *particular* context that will put them into proper practical perspective: the political institutions—the governing system—within which efforts to regulate human conduct will take place. We must appreciate *who* makes and applies the rules, whether of baseball or the law, and the relationships between these actors. Although this topic could stretch quite far—from legislatures to court decisions prompted by litigation to private contracts creating special relationships, and beyond—this book will only have the ambition of analyzing this point in the traditional legal context of the arbitrators of disputes within situations of rule-governed activity: For Gould, the central political actor is his fabled baseball umpire. For law more generally, we will need to expand to a vision and theory of judging in the context of complex circumstances of multiple centers of regulatory authority. But Gould nevertheless supplies an interesting bridge between these two realms, I will argue, in his essay's last two words.

A final preliminary comment about the segments of the diagram: By setting aside the "critical legal" approach,[8] the list does not include a super-category that might overlay the entire exercise: "pretext." One could believe that legal reasoning is, as noted earlier, a sham—it is simply political power dressed up for public consumption. Unfortunately, those who proceed from this assumption cannot be persuaded otherwise by the legion of examples to the contrary that demonstrate, to my satisfaction at least, conscientious people doggedly pursuing what they believe to be the public good, rather than social domination.[9] (I acknowledge that a response here could be that the judges and I all *think* that decisions have reputable foundations, but we are all simply deluded.) So I will not attempt to engage in that fight. I will instead assume that the process of legal reasoning is psychologically legitimate, and the job here will be to identify its operative elements.

The resulting picture of that process will indeed be complex. This is not my fault. It is a function of the fact that none of the elements of legal reasoning exists in isolation from any other—they intersect and overlap and generally influence each other. Context, for example, can only be understood from a foundation in the language that attempts to capture it *and* an appreciation of the moral, social, and political values that shape and root it. Likewise, the values that constitute the realm of the diagram labeled as hypertext can only be appropriately understood and implemented within the legal system if they are analyzed from the perspectives of language, circumstances, and political expectations and constraints. And, in turn, those political considerations can only be appreciated suitably if one views how different governing institutions struggle with unclear language, varying circumstances, and normative disagreements.

Although the result is complicated, the most important implication of this complexity is *not* (happily) yet another academic celebration of postmodern chaos. Instead, the message here, as repeatedly emphasized, is one of quite practical *opportunity*. The point of this exercise will be to use Gould's essay, along with further attention to the work of Professors Hart and Dworkin, to demonstrate the subtle methods used by astute lawyers to listen carefully to the arguments of others, identify weak spots available for exploitation, and then perceive how to respond effectively. It is a lesson, then, in learning how to organize sophisticated arguments and counterarguments in the special world of law and public policy.

D. Predicting Disagreements: Rhetoric and Legal Reasoning

To have that kind of ambition, this book's agenda must be larger than just a response to prior academic discussions of legal material. It ought to attempt to prove its relevance as a *practical* lawyering matter by linking its new model of reasoning to the demands of the lawyer's rhetorical circumstances: What does it mean not just to think and analyze, but to *persuade*?

An important step in that practical rhetorical process consequently must be to learn how to think like those you confront—opponent, judge (or umpire), reluctant legislator, and so on. It requires not just a general understanding of and appreciation for the four-part structure to the legal reasoning process depicted above, it demands an even more practical grasp of how these segments interact to create competing points of view.

To develop this extra level of sophistication, two critically important initial steps are necessary.

The first, and most important (addressed in subpart 1 below), is to recognize that *there will always be disagreement*—that there will always be different points of view, reasonably perceived, about whatever issue is at stake. There may be, of course, disagreement about whether some concept even exists in the law at all (for example, prior to *Lawrence v. Fox*,[10] was there a doctrine of third-party beneficiary in contract law?), but in the ordinary situation of a well-recognized legal doctrine (like a right to privacy, for example, which we will use as an example in Chapter Nine) there will still *always* be differences of opinion about how to understand and apply that doctrine to specific people in specific cases. To get some perspective on this challenge we will examine below the work of the philosopher-logician Stephen Toulmin.

The second step in this analytic growth (subpart 2 below) follows from the model of legal reasoning being developed here: These unavoidable disagreements are not the product of disagreeable people, but of different ways that reasonable people *think* about the issue in the first place. Their analyses of the matter will vary in two fundamental ways: first, they will emphasize differently the relative importance of any of the four elements of text, context, hypertext, and subtext; and second, they will understand the substance of any or all of these elements differently—precisely what context, for example, means in a given case, or which hypertextual values should be applied. All of this became evident, although implicitly, in the class discussion in Chapter One of the Gould defense of Umpire Pinelli. Now we need more explicitly to depict, if we can, how these many forms of disagreement might be identified and organized. To do that, we will examine briefly one example of a legal controversy to illustrate the disagreements that perpetually plague any and all of them: the right of publicity.

So, first, Prof. Toulmin.

1. Practical Rhetoric: Toulmin Logic

Persuasion for a lawyer, of course, is not limited to litigation. Even if the task is to present an "objective" analysis of a legal situation, you must nevertheless convince your audience that your work is entitled to professional respect—particularly if the client does not like the results you are delivering. Persuasion, then, as an aspect of professional competence and confidence, is endemic to law practice.

That does not mean, however, that we must now engage in a thorough review of the vast literature of rhetoric theory. To the contrary, little of that material actually matters here because it involves psychological issues not relevant to analyzing the systemic, simultaneously data-based and value-based mental exercise of legal reasoning. To see this, recall the well-known elements of rhetoric that you probably encountered as an undergraduate, usually in the work of Aristotle:[11] *ethos* (the character or persona of the persuader); *pathos* (appeals to the emotions of an audience); *logos* (the plausible logic of the argument being made); and *axios* (the worthiness or attractiveness of the goal sought by the persuader). While the first two in this list can no doubt be studied insightfully, this kind of psychological subtlety is well beyond the scope of the effort here. And the last two, while obviously related to the concepts of assessing legal rules and principles, and certainly to the tasks of characterizing and categorizing and assimilating judicial decisions, the classic literature on these topics is too general (or in the case of logic courses in college, too formal and rigorous) to be helpful in practical (and hence messier and non-rigorous) legal circumstances.

So instead, we will focus on a modern version of rhetoric study that fits remarkably well with the professional context that is our focus. That is the work of the British philosopher and logician, Stephen Toulmin.[12] His approach to the topic of persuasion is particularly useful because the circumstance in which he puts the topic is so much closer to the reality that lawyers face: not a friendly chat among welcoming amiable cohorts who want to think through something together, but instead, a presentation to a doubtful, perhaps even hostile, audience that views the lawyer suspiciously. Here *logos* and *axios* need to be rethought.

Toulmin's theory of rhetoric confronts this uncomfortable situation by imaging a sequential argument that contentiously confronts the fussy audience's response of "Oh, yeah? Says who? Why should I care?"[13] Rather than falling into line with your reasoning, the professional legal audience is more likely probing energetically: "Why should I accept that? Prove it. But what if … ?" This means the lawyer's argument is more counter-force than brute-force—logic is not wielded like a club, but instead anticipates the reader's doubts and tries to dispose of them before they become solid obstacles.

The best way to appreciate Toulmin's emphasis on the fussy listener is to recognize that the psychological barriers here are of two kinds: The challenging audience (judge or opponent or whatever) is simultaneously *skeptical* about your claims and *risk-averse* about what you want them to conclude. These categories, however, should not be taken as rigidly separate from each other; they overlap and interact: Audiences are skeptical in part because they are risk-averse; they are risk-averse in part because they are skeptical.

To be persuaded, then, the Toulmin audience forces the arguer to go ever deeper and wider to establish adequate support, much like Dworkin's effort to reach beyond rules into abstract principles. "Deeper" support (which is my phrasing, not Toulmin's) addresses skepticism by, in Toulmin's terminology, requiring your claim to rest on accepted "grounds"[14] (relevant facts, basically) that are in turn based on official "warrants"[15] (which we would label rules) that have even more fundamental "backing"[16] (principled justification, basically à la Dworkin). "Wider" support (again my word) addresses risk-aversion by demanding attention to the breadth of the result you want: Could you perhaps make your argument seem more reasonable (less scary) by, in Toulmin's terms, "qualifying"[17] it to arise only in a narrower range of circumstances? Or agree to "exceptions"[18] to your argument, so that less comfortable situations are explicitly excluded? Or by acknowledging that "competing arguments"[19] from others may not be foolish, but are nevertheless not as compelling as yours?

Note that this emphasis on the unfriendly, rather than accommodating, audience is at the heart of this book's agenda and approach.[20] As noted from the beginning, we are interested here in "comprehensive" legal reasoning in situations where easy, simple answers are not available (or you do not like these answers, and want to make them difficult). As a consequence, the thinking we are imagining is always to some degree pushy—it is trying to move someone's mind in one directions when others may be pushing in another ("that pitch was a strike"; "no it wasn't"). The segments in Toulmin's approach therefore depict this effort to go deep and wide—to convince the skeptic that the result you seek is fully justified in facts, existing legal doctrine, and recognized legal values, and reassure the risk-averse that your argument is not unduly dangerous because it is sufficiently limited in contextual scope and addressed to the correct political decision maker.

But now turn all this on its head: The purpose of the diagrammatic elements above is not only to help you develop *your* argument, but allow you to more effectively assess your *opponent's*, identifying their potential weaknesses.

The promised example might help at this point.

2. An Example: The Right of Publicity

An important preliminary note: This example must be taken with a grain of salt, for it presents a summary depiction of a complex analytic process that takes the next four Chapters to develop fully. Much of what this discussion contains in its arrangement of interacting concepts you will have to, for the moment, take on faith. The purpose of this detour into an example is only to demonstrate that we indeed have someplace that we are actually heading. And I acknowledge that this example has been chosen more or less at random, for my claim is that the four-part analytic model depicted above applies to any legal concept you care to identify.

We will focus on the "right of publicity,"[21] which permits famous people to exploit their name and image for profit, and to prevent others from doing so. We will assume that it is the subject of a claim by a celebrity in litigation who is upset with another's use of her professional image (although the lawyering situation could just as easily be a legislative hearing where this doctrine is being examined for statutory modification). We will assume further that this right has been recognized in your jurisdiction as a general proposition. The legal question that has now arisen, however, is: How far should this right stretch? Will it successfully resolve the issue in this matter in our client's favor? As we advise our client about her legal situation, what possible approaches to, and attitudes concerning (favorable and unfavorable), this right might we anticipate arising? That is, what arguments can *we* make, and what arguments can we predict the *other side* will make?

We will make this example a real one: In a well-known case in this area,[22] Vanna White, the co-host of the *Wheel of Fortune* television program, was upset by a commercial that depicted a robot, which seemed to look and move like her, revealing letters in a word puzzle much as she does on her program. Ms. White was not consulted or compensated for this use of her famous image for this knock-off. Should she be able to enjoin this exploitation, or perhaps demand some portion of the profits reaped by the creators of the commercial, or, in contrast, should the creators be protected in their artistic re-interpretation of her image?

The analytic model here would produce the following sequence of considerations. We would probably start, quite traditionally, with "text"—the words used to embody the issue at stake. For our case it is most easily and obviously captured in the term "publicity," although that word will of course be in tension with other concepts like "artistic freedom" and the like. To make this example less complicated for present summary purposes, we will simply embed the other concepts within our attention to this "right of publicity"—both its existence and scope.

Text's split between "is" and "ought" now begets context and hypertext: What are the appropriate circumstances within which this doctrine should be invoked? And is the use of this doctrine appropriately justified by normative values? As we will see, these two inquiries are themselves split between competing perspectives, so the sequences become those shown in Figure 4.3.

Combining these two streams into a single analytic picture produces a familiar four-part box—but bear in mind that this depiction applies *both* to Ms. White's arguments *and* her opponents, which we will note below. For now, however, just focus on the range of arguments Ms. White, as your client, could make to ground and organize her attack on the parody-makers as shown in Figure 4.4.

And then note three important implications flowing from this depiction:

Figure 4.3

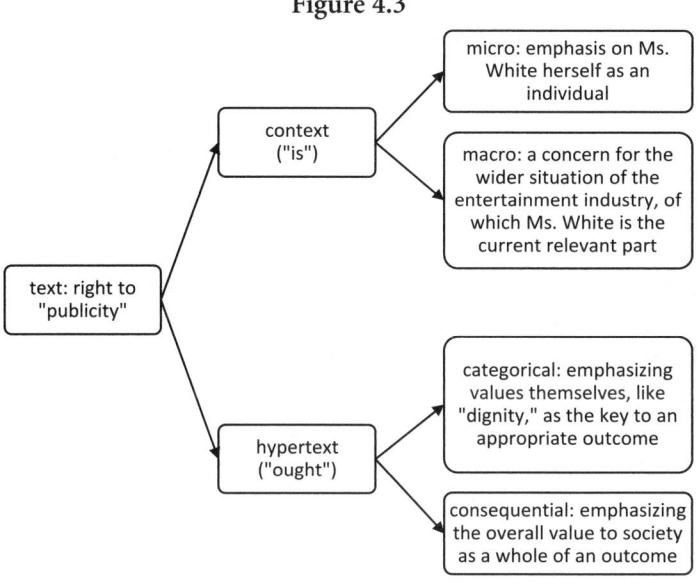

Figure 4.4

	BOX 1	BOX 2
Micro (a focus on Ms. White herself)	Ms. White's individual dignity, whether or not she is a famous entertainer, is the key to the legitimacy of her claim	Ms. White's economic interests will suffer unreasonably unless she is entitled to recover
CONTEXT	BOX 3	BOX 4
Macro (a concern more generally for famous people)	Ms. White's membership in the club of victimized celebrities is the key to justifying her recovery; she should not be forced to suffer humiliation and embarrassment just because of her fame	Ms. White should recover because otherwise celebrities would have less incentive to produce work that the public craves
	Categorical (an emphasis on the appropriateness of the right of publicity as a matter of human dignity)	Consequential (an emphasis on the appropriate social outcome produced by recognizing the right of publicity)

HYPERTEXT

First, a good advocate would not argue *one* of these positions (unless forced to do so for some reason extrinsic to this example), but *all* of them—although one or more might be emphasized more than others, depending upon your sense of the circumstances in the matter.

Second, if instead you represent the producer of the commercial, you would substitute in each box your client's name for Ms. White's and argue the opposite position. For example, regarding Box 4, the approach would be something like "Ms. White deserves no compensation because to force the producer to get her prior approval and/or pay her means that creative parodies of famous people will no longer be safe to make, which would violate the producer's (and indeed more generally, the public's) right of freedom of speech."

Third, the four-part box demonstrates that the analytic technique here does not produce a singular "correct" *answer*, or even a single "correct" *approach*, to the issue. It instead identifies the range of possibilities that sophisticated, comprehensive legal reasoning can concoct, and thus be included within an advocate's preparation in a case. All of these possible perspectives must be addressed, even if only to criticize the ones you, as an advocate, do not like.

The next step beyond this four-part box diagram is probably obvious to the discerning reader: The categories of analysis depicted here do not seem to be dramatically distinct from each other, the way the lines separating the compartments suggest. Instead, there would seem to be no "hard edges" or rigid divisions involved at all. For example, where, precisely, is the division between thinking micro versus macro? If that boundary is hazy, is this effort to identify different rhetorical strategies basically phony?

Not at all. As discussed in later Chapters with different examples, imagine the sides of these diagrams not as creating two truly distinct elements, but instead as variables with gradual differences moving from one end to the other. For example, the "context" of Ms. White's claim could be a sliding scale that moves between two extreme approaches, shown in Figure 4.5:

Figure 4.5

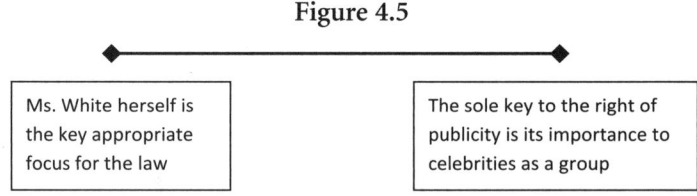

If you employ this extra analytic step, the boxes in the diagram become areas within a graphic representation, and those areas (within the concave spaces associated with each curve) can and do overlap, as you would probably imagine. See the overlaps as illustrated by Figure 4.6:

Figure 4.6

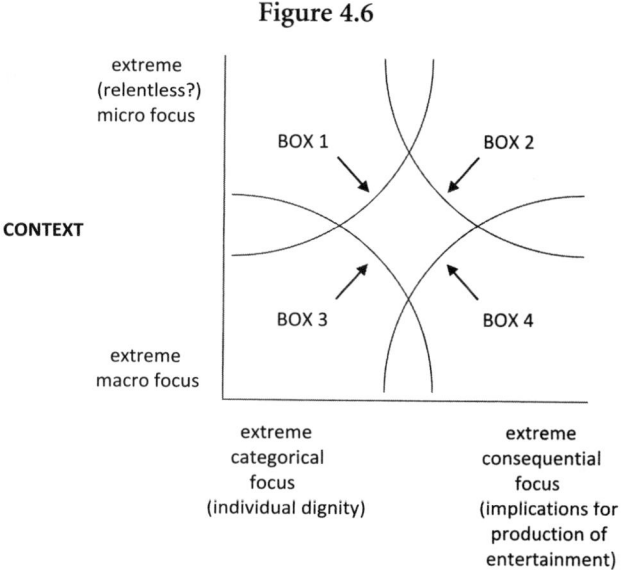

This analytic development may be greeted by a number of readers with open hostility because, I have discovered, many law students comment that they came to law school, as opposed to pursuing other professional or educational paths, because they struggled with things mathematical. Graphs, I am told, are hence more intimidating and confusing than helpful. I can only urge patience at this point.

Notes

1. As discussed in the notes to the previous Chapter, even the critical legal approach is not so much incorrect as exaggerated. *See supra* ch. 3.

2. The issue for us is not the fact that analogies are used, or that inductive or deductive reasoning is displayed, but *how* those analogies work, and *which* generalities or particulars are the beginning points for the thought process, and *why*: Do the analogies and other forms of reasoning depend on texts or on values or on references to practical circumstances or what?

3. Anyone familiar with the literature on legal reasoning will note, of course, that the analysis here is a structured approach to the concept of "narrative" that has become so im-

portant to discussions of the nature of precedent. Prof. Robert Cover was particularly poetic in his summary of the phenomenon: "Narratives are models through which we study and experience transformations that result when a given simplified state of affairs is made to pass through the force field of a similarly simplified set of norms." Robert Cover, *The Supreme Court, 1982 Term—Forward: Nomos and Narrative*, 97 HARV. L. REV. 4, 10 (1983). For him, law and narrative were "inseparably related." *Id.* at 5.

4. The point is *not*, of course, that these two elements are separate and distinct—instead, they certainly interact with and influence each other. For example:

> If I attempt to tell a funny story which I heard, the story as I tell it will be the product of two forces: (1) the story as I heard it, the story *as it is* at the time of its first telling; (2) my conception of the point of the story, in other words, my notion of the story *as it ought to be*. As I retell the story I make no attempt to estimate exactly the pressure of these two forces, though it is clear that their respective influences may vary. If the story as I heard it was, in my opinion, badly told, I am guided largely by my conception of the story as it ought to be, though through inertia or imperfect insight I shall probably repeat turns of phrase which have stuck in my memory from the former telling. On the other hand, if I had the story from the master raconteur, I may exert myself to reproduce his exact words, though my own conception of the way the story ought to be told will have to fill in the gaps left by my faulty memory. These two factors, then, supplement one another in shaping the story as I tell it. It is a product of the *is* and the *ought* working together.

LON FULLER, THE LAW IN QUEST OF ITSELF 8 (1940).

5. DAVID HUME, A TREATISE OF HUMAN NATURE: BEING (2000). ("In every system of morality, which I have hitherto met with, I have always remark'd, that the author proceeds for some time in the ordinary ways of reasoning, and establishes the being of a God or makes observations concerning human affairs; when all of a sudden I am surpriz'd to find, that instead of the usual copulations of propositions, *is*, and *is not*, I meet with no proposition that is not connected with an *ought*, or an *ought not*. This change is imperceptible; but is however, of the last consequence. For as this *ought*, or *ought not*, expresses some new relation or affirmation, 'tis necessary that it shou'd be observ'd and explain'd; and at the same time that a reason should be given; for what seems altogether inconceivable, how this new relation can be a deduction from others, which are entirely different from it.")

6. For another discussion of these elements, see Timothy P. Terrell, *Turmoil at the Normative Core of Lawyering: Uncomfortable Lessons from the "Metaethics" of Legal Ethics*, 49 EMORY L.J. 87, 100–110 (2000).

7. *Id.*

8. The "critical" approach to legal theory was discussed briefly in Chapter Three. *See supra* ch. 3 note 12.

9. Of the many responses to and assessments of the Critical Legal Studies movement, a few interesting examples would include: Jerry L. Anderson, *Law School Enters the Matrix: Teaching Critical Legal Studies*, 54 L. LEGAL EDUC. 201, 202 (2004) ("worthless concepts"); Jonathan Turley, *The Hitchhiker's Guide to CLS, Unger, and Deep Thought*, 81 NW. U. L. REV. 593 (1987) (wide-ranging review); Daniel Farber & Suzanna Sherry, *Telling Stories Out of School: An Essay on Legal Narratives*, 45 STAN. L. REV. 807 (1993) (criticism aimed primarily at the CLS technique of attacking legal doctrine through micro-stories).

10. Lawrence v. Fox, 20 N.Y. 268 (1859).

11. Aristotle, The Nichomachean Ethics (F. H. Peters trans., 5th ed. 1893).

12. Stephen E. Toulmin, The Uses of Argument (Cambridge Univ. Press 2003).

13. *Id.* at 12.

14. *Id.* at 104–105.

15. *Id.* at 91.

16. *Id.* at 96.

17. *Id.* at 83–84.

18. *Id.* at 93–94.

19. *Id.* at 14–15.

20. One quick summary source on all these elements appears in Stephen V. Armstrong & Timothy P. Terrell, *Teaching Law Students Practical Advocacy*, 20 Perspectives 160 (Winter-Spring 2012). Extending that discussion, and organizing it more directly around the elements of legal reasoning being developed in this book, I offer Figure 4.7:

Skepticism: Establishing that You Have a Credible Argument

TOULMIN ELEMENT	REASONING RELEVANCE	AUDIENCE'S IMPLICIT QUESTIONS
1) Context/Issue	Legal Issue	What is the problem here? Why should I care?
2) Claim	Result you seek	What are you arguing for?
3) Grounds/Data	Factual support	Why should I believe you and respond?
4) Warrant	"Rule" support	Why does your data matter to me?
5) Backing	"Principle" / justification support	What is the foundation for your warrant?

Risk-Aversion: Demonstrate that the Action You Request Is Reasonable and Safe

6) Qualifier	Limiting the Claim and Grounds (facts)	Is your request an absolute, or is it "usually" or "probably"?
7) Exception	Limiting the Warrant (the rule)	Does your rule always apply?
8) Competing Arguments	Acknowledging Other Warrants (rules) and Backing (principles)	Does the other side have points that should be considered?

****

9) Consequences	Implications of the Backing (the principles)	Is there a safer, less radical action I could take?
10) Competing Institutions	Nature of your Backing	Am I the appropriate decision maker? Is your "principle" actually a "policy"?

21. The background and elements of this right are developed in (among many sources) Timothy P. Terrell & Jane S. Smith, *Publicity, Liberty, and Intellectual Property: A Conceptual and Economic Analysis of the Inheritability Issue*, 34 EMORY L.J. 1 (1985).

22. White v. Samsung Electronics America, Inc. 971 F.2d 1395 (9th Cir. 1992).

Part III

Adding Depth to Each Dimension

The four Chapters in Part III now add considerable detail and nuance to the alternative analytic model of legal reasoning described in Chapter Four. The goal will be to gain not only a more academically satisfying sense of "the law," but a more practical appreciation for creative and sophisticated lawyering.

Chapter Five

The Challenge of Text: The Relationship of "Is," "Ought," and Focal Meaning

The previous two Chapters contained two important observations about language, one that must now be confronted, the other that must be expanded.

In Chapter Three we noted Prof. Fred Schauer's comment on the general mysteriousness of language, and its consequent uselessness as an organizing analytic element: the "rules of language," he concluded, are "a series of practices not substantially reducible to specifics." To the contrary, this Chapter will contend that any useful understanding of legal guidance depends upon an appreciation of the way words take on meaning—the kind of specifics, however, that are more akin to abstract Dworkinian principles than narrow rules in much the same way that precedents and statutes actually work.

In Chapter Four, however, this ambitious claim was tempered. Despite language's obvious relevance to the law, we start with that element here *not* because it is, in and of itself, the "most important" or definitive (so to speak) aspect of legal substance or legal reasoning. It is instead, as we will see in this Chapter, the most useful starting point for any fundamental, structured understanding of these topics because it channels, rather than determines, the legal analytic process. It has therefore become the traditional point of departure into the nature and content of legal guidance. But it is perfectly possible for any lawyer to begin his or her assessment of the law from any of the other three perspectives Figure 4.2 identified.

The thesis of this Chapter is twofold. The first, and most obvious (given earlier introductions), is to set up the next two Chapters. Concepts, especially all legal ones, consist of two interlocking parts—their fact-based definition (common usage) and their valued-based theories (why we care about whatever the term is expressing). One is descriptive, the other prescriptive, and both deserve independent attention, which we will certainly give them.

The second message, though, is much more subtle. Even if you accept the is-ought union beneath the words we use, the *way* these elements interact is interesting in and of itself. It is a story that frequently involves tension rather than happy marriages. This is why "text" is given its own box in Figure 4.2, rather than just being forgotten in the rush to its constituent elements.

The separate attention language will get here, however, will not be a treatise on linguistics. The agenda is more modest, but more practical—to develop a serviceable understanding of the ways words carry not just "information," but, as noted above, *meaning* to a consumer of legal material. This mental nourishment will be more than mere sustenance but less than scholarly gluttonous satiation. One important example of my divergence from academic linguistic parlance, on which I will expand briefly below, is my use of the term "prescription" in this discussion of legal words. Linguists view this element as internal to the language system being studied;[1] I, on the other hand, will view it as referring to social values external to the language in which they are being expressed.

The method to be employed here to unpack legal language has a respected history, and then use, in analytic jurisprudence, but that background will be assumed rather than developed. Its relevance is demonstrated in work in legal theory as disparate as H.L.A. Hart's positivist "open texture" and John Finnis's approach to natural law.[2] It is at the very core of careful professional reasoning. It is ordinarily the place where struggles with the law start, but never where they end, except in the most superficial discussions.

A. Language and Set Theory

Nothing is more basic to the game of baseball than the "balls" and "strikes" that constitute the competitive relationship between pitcher and batter from which everything else in the game flows. But what does Prof. Gould consider a strike to be? Clearly it includes any pitch that he *wants* to be a strike for some personal reason. But less arbitrarily, how does he "know" this pitch was a strike? On what, besides his own agenda, does he base his assertion that Don Larsen's pitch was "a strike, high and outside"?

As an initial matter, Gould must be congratulated for acknowledging that the fabled final pitch was indeed a bad one. Strong evidence—more than just Dale Mitchell's grumbling—establishes the point. Every year at World Series time a film of that pitch taken from a camera above and behind home plate is telecast as part of the usual ritual of anticipation. The purpose of the repeated showing is not, of course, to reexamine the moment critically, but to join in the Yankees' celebration of that unique, historic perfect game. Nevertheless, the film quite clearly shows that the pitch was well outside the "technical" strike zone, as Gould refers to it. But somehow, despite that evidence and Gould's apparent acceptance of it, the pitch was for him a legitimate strike. How can the term "strike" be so easily and egregiously manipulated?

One conclusion—very widely accepted in our postmodern world, in which everything is considered contingent and foundationless[3]—could simply be that language is a human construct meant to be used in human ways, whatever those may be. So Gould is doing nothing more in his essay than what anyone does when confronted by words that get in the way of desired results: Let the results define the words. This isn't, then, "manipulation" as a pejorative; it is a well-recognized form of normativity: The ends justify the (linguistic) means.

Two serious problems attend this approach. The first and most obvious is that Gould himself certainly does not understand his argument about the concept of a strike to be so crass. He clearly thinks his, and Umpire Pinelli's, use of the word is not merely instrumental, it is fully *legitimate*. It is a use, in other words, that ought to be accepted and honored not just by gleeful Yankee fans, but by disappointed Dodger fans as well. The values of *both* camps, he would argue, are here vindicated, which should cause *all* of us to *praise* Pinelli's call rather than criticize it. This is an ambitious contention to which we will continue to return in this and subsequent Chapters.

The other difficulty for the understanding of language as infinitely flexible and simply self-serving is that language does not, and cannot, work that way. If words can be made to mean anything, then they will mean nothing. Of all the information that is out there that people want to communicate, words, to be able to accomplish the task of information transfer, must designate some identifiable piece of that vast range, not any and all of it. "Baseball" cannot include the game of "basketball," nor can it include the noodles called "spaghetti" or the vehicle called "airplane." If it could, then I would have little idea what you might be talking about if our conversation turned to "baseball." Language can only be effective—meaningful—if it *excludes* as it includes.

A straightforward way to deal with these two linguistic challenges—claiming legitimacy and avoiding non-arbitrariness—is to borrow from mathematics the simple notion of set theory. Think of a word as denominating a set of instances or examples, each of which will be communicated when the word is used.[4] The more general the word ("dog"), the more instances follow; the more specific ("poodle"), the fewer. Scientists and similar professionals are of course constantly trying to make their words as specific and narrow as possible to make their linguistic references as precise as they can be. Lawyers and judges, on the other hand, are—ironically and, to many, disconcertingly—engaged in a rather different analytical exercise.

As any competent lawyer can tell you, and as all law students learn very quickly, the law, based as it is in language, is anything but precise, clear, and unwavering. It is instead slippery and malleable and uncertain. Lawyers would be among the first to embrace philosophy's postmodernism, with its rejection of objective truth or singular perspectives on meaning. Yet lawyers, and certainly judges, do not then extend this thinking so far as to reject the idea of meaning altogether. There is—there must be—some reasonable sense of truth, some practical accuracy, out there toward which we are imperfectly striving: Without this assumption, the entire legal enterprise is pointless, and worse, deceptive. Postmodernism is fine, in other words, up to a point. How then to reconcile these twin urges to accept ambiguity while simultaneously acting as if there is clarity? How, in the context of Gould's essay, can a pitch be *both* a "strike" *and* "high and outside"?

The trick to doing this with a straight face is to return to the concept of set theory and add some additional steps. The key for present purposes is to recognize—as we did as far back as Chapter One, and several times thereafter— that language reflects a basic philosophical divide between "is" and "ought": between the (relatively) objective "facts" that are captured by the use of a word and the quite subjective "values" that are being furthered or vindicated by the use of the word. The former is about dictionaries—a chronicle of how a particular population most often "in fact" uses a given term. The latter, however, is about agendas—how the word can be used to accomplish some "good" or "end." The former is descriptive and sociological; the latter is prescriptive and philosophical. Only together—never alone—do these elements produce the full "meaning" of a term in its social and legal context.

To generate practical, linguistic meaning, then, we must make three analytic steps: first (Section B below), determine the "is" definition of the term; then (Section C) consider the "ought" justification for the term's existence; and then (Section D) combine them using a series of examples. The end result will be, I will argue, not certainty, but inevitable ambiguity and vagueness; but this uncertainty will not be chaotic. It will have a structure or order to it that comes from the conventional use of the term within a population. All legal terms, then, reflect this quality of "structured ambiguity."

B. On Definitional Technique: Meaning as Structured Ambiguity

So we start with "is." The development of definitions has become something of a jurisprudential art form. A variety of elegant mental constructs has been suggested to help us understand the language we use to develop rules that govern our behavior. This book will not discuss all the possible variations on this theme. Rather, it will concentrate on one technique that appears to be the most useful synthesis, for legal purposes, of much of the learning in this area. That technique is the conceptual tool made famous primarily by the work of H.L.A. Hart—the idea of a "central" or "typical" case of the thing to be defined[5]—or, as John Finnis describes it, the "focal meaning" of that thing.[6]

1. Focal Meaning

The central case definition of any concept is perhaps best understood using what might seem a superficial mental exercise: When I say a word, identify the first actual, existing example of that word that pops into your head. Start with something mundane: As you read this, assuming you are sitting down as you do so, are you sitting in a "chair"?[7] How do you know? Note that the way you know is to compare the thing you are sitting on to some "quintessential" chair—not the "most frequently occurring" example of a chair, but the example that you would expect everyone thinking about "chairs" would agree "yes, that's a chair." Now examine the characteristics of that example. It will have, I think we would agree, the essential basic characteristics of four legs and some support for your back (three or four legs and no back would make the thing a stool); the seat would be for one person (more than one would make it a love seat or a sofa); it would not have wheels on the bottom of the legs (that would make it more of an office chair or something more specialized); and so on. A number of other possible characteristics would not matter—color, material from which the chair is constructed, the manufacturer's name, and so on. The characteristics that *do* seem to matter will encompass the necessary elements of that anchoring example of this thing in your mind.

This example then becomes the "focal meaning" of a chair—"focal" in the sense that all other examples of things that might get the label "chair" will be assessed by whether they possess or lack one or more of these central elements. The more core elements an object possesses, the more typical it is of that thing;

the more it lacks, the more peripheral an example it becomes, until at some point it can no longer be considered an example of the thing being examined.

The result can be depicted as illustrated in Figure 5.1:

Figure 5.1

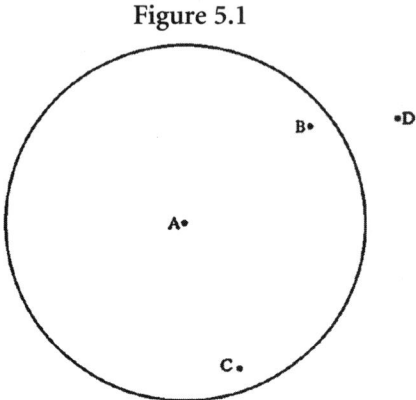

Point A represents the instance that best exemplifies the thing examined. It contains all the features that are characteristic of that thing and thus is the *focus* of our use of a particular word. Points B and C are similar things that lack one or more of the appropriate characteristics. Although they may not be quintessential examples, they are close enough to merit the same label given to the central case. On the other hand, Point D, although possibly having a few of the characteristics of the central case, has too few to be placed in the same set. (Is a beanbag a chair?) Figure 5.1 might be redrawn with the added detail of concentric circles, each corresponding to the number of characteristics the peripheral case has in common with the central case, as shown in Figure 5.2:

Figure 5.2

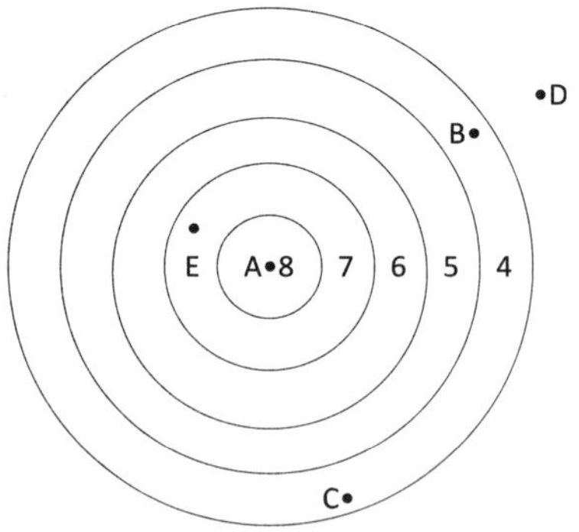

For illustrative purposes, let us assume that Point A, and the small area around it, depicts a legal concept that can be described using, say, eight key core characteristics. Figure 5.2 shows Point E as being one step away from this central case, perhaps in a simple situation corresponding to the lack of one of the core elements. In contrast, Points B and C each lack four of these core elements. All three points, however, have a sufficient number of elements in common with the central case to be placed within the outer boundary that encompasses those objects entitled to the use of the label in question. Point D, on the other hand, lacks, for purposes of this figure, five or more of the core elements, and is thus related too tenuously to the paradigm case to merit the label.

As just noted, the "central case" or "focal meaning" of a concept need not be so exacting as to be a "point" of great singularity. It could be considered the entire small circle in the middle of Figure 5.2 above surrounding the point labeled A—a recognition of a kind of small group at the core that anchors our conversations about the concept. So it would be with the idea of "chair": We would not have to have *one* extremely precise example in our heads to discuss the idea of a chair. To illustrate using another easy example: What is a "dog"? Dogness can be readily discussed without every conversation having Lassie as its anchor, just the general characteristics of four legs, fur, tail, carnivorous, a strong sense of smell, a certain level of animal intelligence, a general sense of movement capability, and so on. If you then add qualities like temperament and domestication, you can see how discussions of "dogs" and "wolves" can diverge, although be related to each other.

2. Definition and Early Legal Education

All of the discussion to this point may seem—particularly to a law student—mind-numbingly abstruse and uninteresting, because it feels very far removed from any identifiable professional (as opposed to academic) relevance. So before we proceed into ever more challenging linguistic detail, we should correct that misimpression by connecting this idea of focal meaning to a foundational educational experience that all law students encounter: their seemingly desperate need to seek out, and cling to, canned outlines for their courses (*Gilbert's*, *Emmanuel's*, and the like).

The cause, I would argue, is a typical conundrum confronted by first-year law students when a professor carefully dissects in class two judicial decisions—let's say in the contracts course. One case involves a set of facts establishing for that judge enough foundation to perceive an agreement between two parties, which in turn leads the court to conclude that this situation yields an enforceable contract. We'll call that decision Point B in the diagram above. It is not an obvious instance of such an agreement, but it seems to deserve the label "contract." But in the other decision, facts almost identical to those in the initial case produce the contrary conclusion—no contract. We could label it Point D. This is disconcerting, because the narrowness of the difference between the two decisions seems to challenge whether either decision is really appropriately grounded. Are these judges actually "treating like cases alike," or are they acting more arbitrarily in reaching such dramatically different legal results—one is a contract, the other is not—on the basis of very slender factual differences?

That worry captures the analytic mistake so characteristic of law school. The comparison that should be made in this situation is *not* B→D, but B→A and D→A. To "compare" two decisions, to return to Prof. Schauer's terminology, you should not relate them to each other, but to the central case that anchors, and hence interconnects, the entire legal set involved. When you do so, it is much easier to see why legal analysis produces at some point the response "enough is enough": You have pushed things too far; you have taken away too many core characteristics; your last step simply makes your connection to the focal meaning of "contract" too tenuous. Yes, your two cases (points B and D) are very similar to the untrained eye (and mind), but our conclusions (contract in one case, none in the other) are not at all arbitrary.

When law students finally realize the analytic game being played in class—where the Socratic technique allows the professor to vary facts in small increments to explore (usually frustratingly) the edges of legal concepts—they learn two important pedagogical lessons: (a) the importance of all those "Point A's" out there in the law organizing so much of the practical conversation, and (b) where to find that information: the canned course outlines. These texts perform the mental magic that is so often hidden or obscured in law school casebooks, which present pictures of courts struggling at the law's margins. This image is apparently intended to encourage students to, in response, work backward toward the central ideas that make the margins relevant. But the outlines are sought out because they present comforting analytical consensus, putting the academic chaos into professional context.

A related law student conundrum is represented by the effort to compare Points B and C in the diagram above. Careful analysis of two cases might produce the surprising observation that, although both judges reach the same conclusion—again, say, that an interaction has created a contract—the two nevertheless otherwise have nothing in common. (This is not as far-fetched as it might sound, if you compare in contracts law cases based on "reliance" rather than "agreement.") But how can this be consistent with "treating like cases alike"? The same analytic mistake has been made, where an apple has been compared to an orange, rather than the two being connected as "fruit." Return to Figure 5.2 with the numbers indicating layers of common elements. If the paradigm case at Point A has eight definitional elements, then Point B might have elements 1, 3, 5, and 7, while Point C has 2, 4, 6, and 8. Thus, the application of a particular label does not depend upon the characteristics that are shared by all members of the class, but instead depends upon identifying a set of characteristics that are shared *enough* by the members, even though in varying ways and to varying degrees.

The usefulness of this definitional enterprise depends, then, upon two factors: the adequacy of the description of the central case, and the location of the outer perimeter. The first factor establishes the set of characteristics for which one must search. The second enables one to determine that Point B is located inside the set and that Point D is not.

3. The Inadequacies of Definitions for Legal Theory

It does not take much effort, however, to realize that the picture of legal reasoning so far developed using this definitional technique leaves a host of questions and doubts that must be resolved. We will start that process of re-examination by connecting this technique to its most well-known user: the legal positivist. Chapter Three applied this label to a lawyer or scholar who is dedicated to analyzing law without any necessary reference to moral or political values. For this group, the task is, first, through careful observation, determine how a legal term is *in fact* used within a population, and then second, also through observation of facts, establish the characteristics of the central case and the perimeter around that anchor that create the range of appropriate uses of the term. Everything about this legal conceptual set would be grounded in identifiable past and present social experience, and future applications of the term would be judged according to that objective background.

A simple and straightforward example of this approach is H.L.A. Hart's effort to define, and then study, "punishment."[8] He posited, after review and consideration of the usual uses of that term, that the central case of this concept consisted of five core elements:

(i) It must involve pain or other consequences normally considered unpleasant.

(ii) It must be for an offence against legal rules.

(iii) It must be of an actual or supposed offender for his offence.

(iv) It must be intentionally administered by human beings other than the offender.

(v) It must be imposed and administered by an authority constituted by a legal system against which the offence is committed.[9]

We need not quibble here with the accuracy or adequacy of this list—we simply want to note how this version of focal meaning nicely sets up subsequent debates about the use of the term: For example, it is simply an ironic sense of that word to claim that one was "punished" by something pleasant ("her smile made me ache like the worst punishment"). And it is poetic license that allows us to say that violent weather "punished" the landscape. By the same token, the National Science Foundation would not fund a grant application of someone who intends to study how God is "punishing" evildoers. If any of these uses of the term are thought to be within the linguistic set anchored by Hart's elements, they would be at its farthest edges. On the other hand, an instance in which only one of the elements is missing—where, for example, a person is whipped for violating a moral or religious precept, rather than a classically narrow "legal" one—would certainly be thought within the punishment set. It would simply not be an anchoring *central* example of the concept.

The consequence of these simple observations is nevertheless somewhat disconcerting. Even in its simplest, non-scientific, seat-of-the-pants, most "objective" sociological, observational form, the "meaning" of a word will be a slippery phenomenon, subject to inconsistencies and disagreements even among reasonable, non-contentious people just trying to gather semantic data. But the situation is actually much worse. Important psychological factors involved in this effort have thus far been overlooked.

An astute reader will have noted that the relentlessly fact-based approach to language use seems not to address some aspects of legal reality, thus causing the entire enterprise to be called into question. The solutions to these challenges will reveal that linguistic description *alone* is inevitably inadequate as an aspect of legal reasoning.

What is missing is the additional dimension of prescription, or normative values, in our discussion of linguistic meaning, which I will develop in more detail below. But a preliminary caveat is important here, because there are two different ways in which such values can be made relevant to language use. One is "internal" to the discipline of linguistics itself, the other is "external" to that academic context. The former is concerned with the psychology of a linguistic community, and the question is whether the use of words is deemed right or wrong within that group.[10] A famous example was the short-lived program to use street slang in school classrooms as a bridge to teaching standard English—it was heavily criticized as inappropriate within an English-speaking community. The latter, however—which is the form in which I am using "pre-scriptive"—is the way words have larger *social* norms embedded within them as part of our communicative process, regardless of whether a *language's* in-ternal norms are being observed.

This additional element of normativity manifests itself quite straightfor-wardly in three ways associated with the set theory thus far developed. Two infect all the instances contained in the set, all the way to the central case that anchors the entire effort, and one lurks at the set's perimeter that makes the limits of the grouping not only hazy but potentially arbitrary.

a. Concepts as Cheese: Of Cheddar and Swiss

Ambiguity in a term's meaning seems to run deeper than just moving "out" from a concept's focal meaning to peripheral instances. There is also some-thing unstable, and therefore troubling, about even the most central of a con-cept's examples. For instance, return to Prof. Hart's straightforward unpacking of "punishment." Now, however, attach that word to his problem with the Nazis—or more currently, to the disturbing practices of the so-called Islamic State. Would anyone label as "punishment" the senselessness of concentration camps or the barbarity of beheadings—even if carried out "officially" by these regimes in response to "offenses" they have identified? Don't you have the sense that these examples are not simply at the furthest edge of this linguistic set, but indeed *not in the set at all*? But how can that be if all the features of the cen-tral case seem to be present? That is, even if the Nazis or members of the Is-lamic State believe that *their own linguistic system* establishes their practices as "punishment," would not everyone else in the world reject this conclusion? If so, what, beyond sociological observation, is operating here?

Constantly implicit in the background of the labeling effort establishing a term's definition is the idea that there are "exceptions" of one kind or another that must be acknowledged for the term to make practical sense. But this is the key: These exceptions do not seem to arise as a matter of sociological "fact," but as a function of *philosophical values*. These disturbing potential examples of a term are eliminated from discussion simply because they "ought" to be, not because standard language use automatically excludes them. Concerning pun-ishment, there is a sense that, if the term is to be used in meaningful policy de-bates, some possibilities are already off the table. The word, in other words (so to speak), even at its very core, seems to have "holes" in it.

What is missing in the initial descriptive linguistic effort is therefore a sec-ond step that can be depicted as follows. Return to the circular diagrams used earlier in this Chapter and now imagine that the instances within the set can be removed and subjected to individual examination, as demonstrated in Figure 5.3:

Figure 5.3

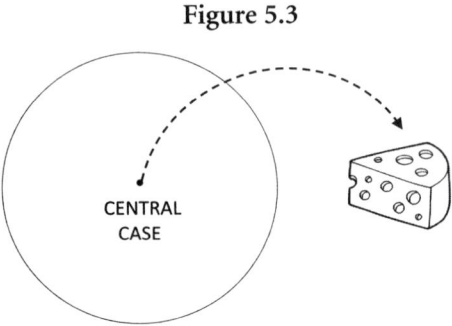

CENTRAL
CASE

What we find is that, even the focal meaning of any concept is more akin to Swiss cheese than Cheddar. Rather than being a comfortable "solid," every use of a term is perforated with background qualifications and exclusions that may not be obvious on the face of the term itself. Although we will discover this phenomenon in some examples later in this Chapter, note our current one of punishment. When used "appropriately" in discussions of legal policy, that word simply does not carry with it the use of power by the state to inflict certain kinds of responses to citizen behavior. Hart himself recognized this additional analytical element, calling it punishment's "General Justifying Aim"[11] (his capitals)—that is, the inquiry into why we actually *care* whether something is punishment or not (which we will return to in a moment). Indeed, this extra step has been made explicit in American law, rather being allowed to remain implicit, through the U.S. Constitution's prohibition of "cruel and unusual"[12] punishment. But these extra words in that document are actually quite unusual—we will note later in this Chapter that most concepts are not modified with additional adjectives to make the exceptional cases clear. Instead, the "holes" are simply implicitly present from the very beginning. Thus, as you move from the core of a term to its perimeter, the holes keep accumulating, until there is not enough remaining "cheese" to deserve the linguistic label.

The point of these observations is then this: If linguistics is an element within legal *reasoning*, then the psychology involved is richer than just piling up instances of a term's use by a population. Simultaneous with the accumulation of data is the *assessment* of that data—judgments about the worthiness of what rigorous description might produce. Although facts (the "is") are certainly necessary to a word's meaning, they *alone* are never sufficient. Hence, the analysis of text, for a careful lawyer, must always move beyond concrete "context" to include the abstract "ought"—what this book will call hypertext.

b. The Set's "Layers"

We also have the problem of reaching conclusions about the layers that the earlier diagrams have employed. What exactly is their foundation and location? How do we know that movement away from focal meaning is meaning-*ful*? Relying on conscientious accumulation of data seems like respectable common sense—the data of actual human activity will determine how the data should be depicted—but this has the ring of circularity. For example, can we really understand why one particular definitional element might be considered crucial to inclusion in a set, while others are not, simply by compiling data? The diagrams in Figure 5.4 suggest alternative ways in which a term's set could be structured, the first showing that each of five elements is absolutely critical to inclusion, and the second assuming that one element is vital, while others are not so singular:

Figure 5.4

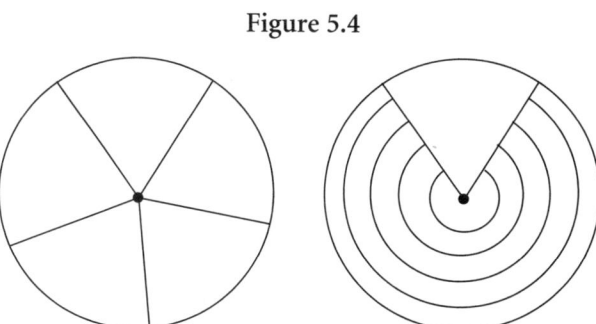

The issue is whether the data by itself can generate these semantic pictures, or whether something else is at play. The model of legal reasoning developed here argues for the second conclusion.

c. Of Wavy Perimeters

A third descriptive linguistic challenge is at the other end of this exercise. Imagine a trust fund established by a deceased philanthropist who stated that the fund's purpose would be to assist those "punished" by poverty or various environmental calamities. Would the trust be meaningless because its use of this crucial term is too metaphorical to be within the descriptive linguistic set? Would the trustees, then, be precluded from using the trust's assets to create treatment facilities for sufferers of Ebola infections? To the contrary, do you not have a sense that the term "punishment" should not stand as an obstacle to accomplishing a very worthy social goal?

Again, the problem here is the incompleteness of a purely data-driven definitional technique. Careful attention to the use of important terms might generate an urge for a kind of analytic neatness to emerge, much like the nice circles depicted earlier. But that model is simply convenient rather than necessary or accurate. Instead, attention to actual uses of a term will reveal something much less perfect. It is still a "set," but it would look like Figure 5.5:

Figure 5.5

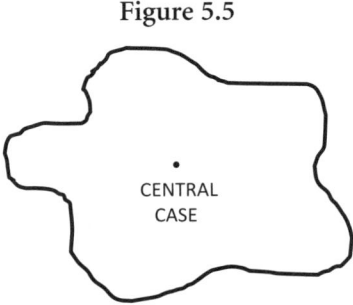

CENTRAL
CASE

The outer perimeter of this grouping will be disconcertingly distended as examples arise that we believe "should" be included (or excluded) for one reason or another. These instances of use of the term will certainly be "facts," but note that this reasoning is not based on the usual, traditional psychology of simply comparing instances so that "like cases are treated alike." The idea of likeness *itself* has a new dimension not captured by the existing data alone. Our reasoning necessarily includes, then, a normative element—hypertext—that combines with ordinary language use to produce a concept's "full" meaning.

C. On Theory: Justifying Meaning

That missing semantic element—a word's "theory"—must now be acknowledged. We consciously shift from how a term is *in fact* being used to how a term *ought* to be used—not because this community's sense of its *language* demands it, but because of normative propositions attached to an agenda *outside* the language itself. The task of Chapter Seven will be to put some substance into this daunting additional analytic step. For now, all that is at stake is demonstrating how normativity figures into the psychology of legal reasoning.

The concept of punishment is as good an example as any for this purpose. To use Hart's phrase, when one moves from the data of language use to punishment's General Justifying Aim, the concept could have lurking beneath it one or more of several theories or justifications: retribution, rehabilitation, deterrence, or simple incapacitation (isolation or warehousing for purposes of public safety).[13] The first is said to be "backward-looking," responding to past behavior, while the other three are "forward-looking," in the sense of being most interested in future behavior. But the nature and details of these theories do not matter here—this is not a book about punishment. Instead, the point is simply that they are all justifications for the infliction of state-sanctioned nastiness. Whether you favor or disfavor any of these theories also does not currently matter. Instead, we are focused on a semantic point: the impact that any and all of these justifications necessarily have on the "meaning" of the word punishment to the person using it and the person hearing it.

This part of the language exercise then fills in the gaps, noted above, that arise in the purely data-driven efforts to establish definitions. Concerning punishment, as the analysis shifts to whether any particular instance of state behavior "deserves" to be included within this label, semantic conclusions can be influenced, and new questions arise, that must be acknowledged:

- *The elements of the central case*: Could a theory of punishment determine which characteristics will form the focal meaning itself of the term, the instance to which all others will be compared? For example, if your normative focus is simply public safety, then you might not even care much about the other definitional elements that Hart identifies, like whether the government is responding to "an offense against legal rules." If all you seek is safety, then who cares what produces or enhances it? Or in the opposite direction: Perhaps your theory of punishment is focused primarily on appropriate *government* behavior, in which case you would find it distressing that Hart's list of definitional elements fails to include procedural limitations (due process) on the government's exercise of its punishment authority. In other words, possible "holes" in the instances that constitute all the data in the set may or may not be relevant to you.

- *The relative weight of the definitional elements*: Could a theory of punishment tell you how important various elements are as compared to others? For example, if your General Justifying Aim is retribution, wouldn't that mean that you would emphasize the unpleasantness of the government's impositions? Indeed, might that approach make you want to add to your focal meaning other elements of detail like suffering or mortification or confiscation of property?

- *The placement of the set's perimeter.* Could a theory of punishment permit us to manipulate the perimeter of the definitional set so that we could add to or subtract from the instances given the label "punishment" *not* through the means of objectively comparing an instance of possible punishment to the central case, but by subjectively and normatively concluding that we simply think it *legitimate* to do this adding or subtracting? Two examples: First, recall the trust fund for victims of natural phenomena. If we had no information about the benefactor's actual intent or understanding of the term "punishment," would the absence of that data bother us? I doubt it. We would know what he or she meant normatively. Second, if the "data" you examine of people's actual use of the term "punishment" demonstrates that "group therapy sessions" for convicted criminals are not considered in this society as within that term's definitional ("is") set, could you not decide anyway that such sessions *ought* to be included in the set? Here is how this might play out practically: In your jurisdiction, the protections of procedural due process only apply to instances of punishment, but the definitional exercise in which you have engaged establishes that people do not consider group therapy sessions as within this set. Yet your *theory* of punishment stresses worry about arbitrary exercises of government power. This could lead you to conclude that, to avoid permitting officials to force convicts into group therapy at whim, group therapy *ought* to be considered punishment regardless of the ordinary social use of that term.

The normative result you deem most appropriate, then, determines to some important degree the relevant "text" from which you will work to accomplish that goal. Words become not just conduits, but weapons.

These two analytic exercises comprising the reasoning element of text—description and justification—are clearly, then, not hermetically (or hermeneutically, for that matter) sealed and isolated one from the other. They necessarily interact. Each generates its own form of ambiguity to our language, but both do so in ways that can be identified, assessed, and ultimately *structured* so that words do not devolve into chaos. We can therefore have a meaningful conversation about "punishment"—even though we approach that concept quite differently—as long as we appreciate the bases of that underlying disagreement. That is the essential message of appreciating the dimensions of legal reasoning.

D. Illustrations From Our Ultimate Text: Of the Constitution's "Majestic Generalities"

Perhaps the most dramatic examples of this inevitable interplay of a concept's definition and its theory appear within the language of the United States Constitution. That document is famous for its workmanlike and remarkably thorough expressions of the most fundamental aspects of American governmental structure, ranging from foundational political authority to more specific government requirements, directions, and limitations, to listings of individual rights. And behind each of its words lurks the problem—and promise—of ambiguity. The actual, practical meanings of ideas like "speech," "religion," "property," and so on, will necessarily be developed over time through our political (and judicial) experience. That experience will, in turn, inevitably involve the intersection of "is"—observations of popular (at least legally popular) uses of a given concept—and "ought"—an appreciation of the political theories beneath all that use. This challenging overlap is captured wonderfully in Justice Robert Jackson's famous description of the Constitution's language being suffused with "majestic generalities."[14] Note his insight: not just "generalities," because language always has that characteristic to one degree or another, but *majestic* generalities—words that necessarily connote *norms* that demand not just judicial efforts at consistency or clarity, but *respect*.

Examples abound of the Supreme Court's efforts to unpack the words that govern us using both definition and theory—or, in the jargon developing in this book, context and hypertext. We shall only note a few here, although enough, I hope, to make the limited point of this Chapter. Subsequent Chapters will be devoted entirely to further nuances within the two dimensions of reasoning identified here: Chapter Six (is/context) and Chapter Seven (ought/hypertext).

1. Speech

The content of the First Amendment's guarantee of "freedom of speech" is particularly entertaining. Quite literally, for we have now reached the point that this phrase has been stretched to include, according to courts and commentators, nude dancing.[15] How did we get here?

On its face, "speech" would, as a matter of ordinary language use, seem to be focused on (indeed perhaps even limited to) things you *say*, that you actually enunciate orally. And, even more narrowly, because the word appears in a fundamentally political document that is establishing the relationship between citizen and government, things you say on *political* matters. But if that might be the word's original sense in 1789, courts long ago abandoned any serious effort to confine this right to instances either oral or political. In fact, today, you seldom encounter a legal commentator who purports to analyze our freedom of "speech"—the topic has become instead freedom of *expression*. Again, how did this happen?

Start with definition: What is the central case, the focal meaning, of speech, particularly as that word is used in the Constitution? The quintessential example that would probably leap into almost anyone's mind, even today, is a speaker standing on a soap box on Hyde Park Corner in London railing about some government policy, urging passersby to heed his analysis and warning. If so, the "is" elements of this central case would include: (1) a person—no doubt an adult as opposed to a child; (2) who is apparently sane—rather than a raving lunatic; (3) in a public—rather than private—place; (4) orally—rather than merely gesturing; (5) exhorting—rather than simply reciting; (6) others—not just him or herself; (7) in the immediate proximity—rather than some distant, imagined audience; to (8) hear and understand—rather than ignore; (9) an important—as opposed to trivial; (10) political—rather than purely private; (11) message—not just some greeting or the like.

But if that is our anchoring image, what about a child in her bedroom dancing and singing in Chinese, while no one takes note, a song that acknowledges her poor behavior while with her parents on a recent family vacation? If this is not "speech," can the government prohibit YouTube from sending out a video of this incident? Your probable response is "no," but why? And if you are sympathetic toward the broadcast of this video, does that mean, by easy extension, that you would similarly protect nude dancing in a private club?

What has happened, of course, is that no matter what the traditional central case of First Amendment "speech" might be, the set of instances given this constitutional label has been stretched as a *normative* matter to include all manner of "expressive" activity. Our concern is not so much with what we want people to be able (or encouraged) to do, but rather what we want government *not* to be able to do. It is a matter of fundamental *constitutional theory*. What that theory might be does not really matter for present purposes—it could be about generating useful ideas, or about honoring individual autonomy, or a host of others.[16] What all of them demonstrate, however, is that we (and by extension the Constitution) have come to realize that the term "speech" is not really an objectively "defined" word, but instead a consciously ambiguous *metaphor*, intended all along to cover a range of human communicative activities. So we readily accept that a group of high school students protesting the Vietnam War not by *speaking*, but by *wearing* black armbands to class is indeed an easy, not challenging, instance of protected speech.[17] And those kinds of expressive gestures lead rather easily toward endorsing bodily movement whose purpose is solely entertainment that challenges social norms of decorum (nude dancing). There are many ways to generate robust discussion of public matters, many ways to have and express our opinions, and thus many ways to "speak."

But the most dramatic example of the importance of normativity to the linguistic set called speech comes from the opposite direction. If you return to the list of elements of the focal meaning of speech, you should note that a speaker spewing pornographic statements meets every criteria of that central case, except perhaps for (9) and (10) that are being stretched a bit. A similar observation could be made about the famous example of shouting "fire!" in a crowded theater simply as a prank. Despite substantial commonality to the set's anchor, both these instances of supposed "speech" have been determined by courts *to not be speech at all*[18]—and thus readily both regulated and prohibited without concern for any constitutional protections. And this result is quite obviously *not* based on some data-driven comparison of one "speech" case to another, but on the conclusion that these activities do not *deserve* the label, and the protections, in the first place. Pornography and the like simply "ought not" be speech.

I do not mean to suggest or endorse the idea that normativity now justifies or makes possible either limitless expansion or arbitrary contraction of the term "speech." As noted earlier, if a term can mean anything you want, then it will mean nothing, as a practical matter. So I fully acknowledge that a serious and important debate can rage concerning the outer limits of and "holes" within this term's meaning. All I want to emphasize is that that debate is not simply about how far we can stretch or manipulate the "facts" of the use of the term. It is instead about the *interaction* of our effort to understand these facts of actual usage *with* justifications for the existence of the concept. Together these forces then produce the perpetually controversial legal doctrine of freedom of speech.

2. Religion

The concept of religion as referenced in the Constitution may be an even easier example of the inevitable interplay of is and ought—of facts that anchor a legal term and values that animate it. The First Amendment guarantees both "free exercise" of religion and, nevertheless, no "establishment" of religion by the government as a prerequisite to any of its authority or benefits.[19] But as straightforward as these pronouncements might seem, the problem is always determining what counts as a "religion" that can be exercised but not imposed.

For example, can drug use constitute a religion whose "exercise" cannot be legitimately curtailed by government's anti-drug policies? Not if you simply assert this proposition this baldly and generally, but it might well be endorsed if you are a Native American using peyote.[20] Note how (like for the concept of speech) the twin analytic pulls are evident: *Is* drug use a religious exercise? *Should* drug use be given this constitutional protection? These are two different, although related, issues.

Again, it is usually easier to start with the more familiar and more comfortably objective effort to define religion by examining the way the term is actually used—not necessarily by the entire population, but by judges charged with the responsibility of applying the term in actual cases. This turns out to be a rather useful enterprise because it seems quite evident, after reviewing enough cases, that the Supreme Court has always had a definitional anchor— a central case—in its mind when considering any claim to constitutional protection or prohibition concerning religion. That starting point, the one focal set of examples that the Court accepts on its face as deserving the label of "religion" without much additional thought, is the assortment of activities traditionally associated with standard, mainline churches, synagogues, and mosques: As Prof. Harold Berman[21] noted in a very useful summary many years ago, all religions with which members of the Court would be favorably familiar would have the characteristics of: (1) *ritual*—ceremonial procedures and formalities, (2) *traditions* of practice and language passed on from one generation to the next, (3) *authority* in the form of reliance on written or spoken sources that have binding power, and (4) *universality* of direction for an entire group's beliefs and actions. To this list should be added the necessary underlying prerequisites to all these qualities that they (5) are associated with a *group* (i.e., a congregation) rather than isolated individuals, (6) have as a central focus the effort to understand the *meaning of life* and its relation to the eternal, and (7) have an ultimate foundation in a *faith-based belief in a "supreme being"* of some kind that transcends ordinary human understanding or reasoning.[22]

But, as with speech, this central, multi-part image only establishes the obvious, most unarguable instances of religion that need no further justification for constitutional purposes. In effect, examples exhibiting all these characteristics are so accepted as a matter of social fact (context) that we tend to forget that we even need a "theory" of religion—a philosophical foundation (hypertext)—for granting them privileged constitutional status.

Yet, of course, we do. The problem for courts, and hence for legal reasoning, is that constitutional problems arise because of all those non-central cases out there: specifically, cases in which a court must assess (a) activities outside the traditional confines of a typical religious service, and (b) claims to religious status where various traditional (central) qualities are absent.

Concerning (a), caselaw[23] reveals rather clearly that the application of the First Amendment's religion clauses, even for the most straightforwardly recognizable church congregations, nevertheless varies directly with the "centrality" of the religious *activity* involved. That hierarchy is captured by Figure 5.6:

Figure 5.6

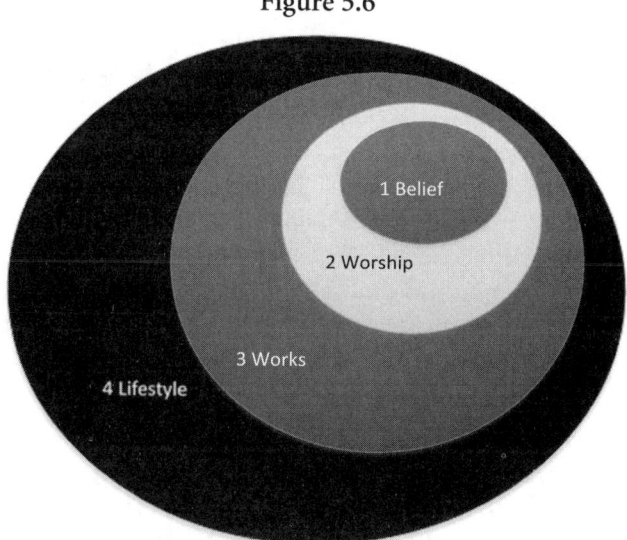

At the "core" of the meaning of religion for constitutional purposes is (1) "belief" itself: Quite obviously, no one, and certainly no government, should be able to dictate or even influence what goes on within our heads based on scripture or testimony so central to the nature of the individual himself or herself. We can think whatever we please, including even, for example, that there is no God and thus no legitimacy to "religion rights" at all, or that religion can legitimately include human sacrifice, and so on. But the moment we move beyond thought to action (2-4), the non-religious interests of the state (like public safety) play an ever-increasing role in determining the range of constitutional meaning.

For example, few exercises of (2) "worship" are restricted, because they are usually so directly related to belief—like reciting the Lord's Prayer or singing hymns or reading from the Torah and so on. But extremes, like human sacrifice or refusing to afford medical treatment to a minor child, can arise that we have little trouble restricting.[24] (But why? More on that in a moment.) Similarly, the use of otherwise illegal drugs might be viewed sympathetically if it is actually part-and-parcel of a recognizable religious ceremony (again, why?) but not at all sympathetically if not so connected.

One step further removed from pure belief, religious groups are not often limited in the kinds of (3) "works" they can perform in the name of their religion outside their traditional sanctuaries, like operating a food bank or counseling services or the like. But these actions can also push the limits of social and constitutional acceptability, like protests staged at military funerals against the "sin" of homosexuality.[25] Note, then, how actions like these, including proselytizing in many intrusive forms, are argued by the actors to be acts of religious "worship" rather than mere religious "works," in an effort to improve their chances of being given constitutional protection.

Most vulnerable of all to state regulation and limitation are manifestations of what might be termed religious (4) "lifestyle"—the many ways in which religious group members choose to live their lives generally and interact with others. Here the state tolerates such behavior only when it is benign, like the ways certain religious communities choose to dress (e.g., the Amish or Orthodox Jews). But even these seemingly innocuous actions can conflict with, and hence be overcome by, asserted state interests, like uniformity of appearance of military personnel,[26] or worry about bombs hidden under certain kinds of clothing.

This effort at categorizing religious activities does not, of course, resolve tough cases. It merely organizes them so that the arguments about the underlying concepts (like religion) become a bit clearer. Controversy is never magically eliminated by an "is," definitional exercise, no matter how sophisticated it might claim to be. For example, is a refusal by a person to work on Saturdays, based on religious precepts, an instance of "belief," and hence at the very core of our sense of protected religious activities, or is it merely an individual's "lifestyle" choice, and thus deserving of no particular social sympathy, particularly because granting protection will impose costs on society in general through unemployment benefits? The Supreme Court decided long ago that this claim was much closer to belief than lifestyle, and hence would be protected and subsidized.[27] By the same token, under the auspices of the Anti-Establishment Clause, the Court determined that the refusal of an atheist public school student to engage in state-required Bible readings was akin to imposing "beliefs" on the student, even though the student was required to do no more than just read.[28]

The same kind of range of case results exists regarding (b) above as well— when someone claims the protections of religion even though his or her beliefs or practices lack a foundation in the qualities of the central, accepted instances of the set labeled "religion." The most famous cases in this area (other than the "I use drugs for the individual transcendent experience" group) are probably those involving the struggle to determine whether a particular military draftee could claim the status of "conscientious objector" to military service, and hence avoid combat, and perhaps military service altogether.[29] The not-uncommon issue has been this: Could a person legitimately claim that his or her personal anti-war beliefs were just as sacrosanct as any traditional *religious* belief *even though* he or she: was *not* a member of any congregation, and thus engaged in *no* rituals, had *no* particular source (like a supreme being or holy text) for his or her beliefs, considered his or her beliefs to be entirely *individual* and idiosyncratic rather than universal, consequently engaged in *no* identifiable religious practices or works, and indeed did *not* believe in the evil of all wars, just the current one?

Note how such hard cases almost inevitably involve a combination of variance along both the dimensions of (a) and (b) above. You could reasonably think, I believe, that such remarkably "peripheral" cases of claims to religious status would not get much judicial sympathy, yet instead, the Supreme Court struggled mightily, and disagreed internally, regarding just such cases. The fact that these were not "simple" cases, but instead reflected analytic angst, demonstrates that something other than simplistic fact-based "comparing" of one case with another in a descriptive, definitional sense has been at work here: Perhaps the "central case" of religion itself is being rethought, or the relative importance of various definitional elements is being reassessed, or the placement of the outer perimeter of the "religion" set is being repositioned. Whatever might be happening, all of these analytic phenomena are functions, as we noted earlier, not of *what* might be religion in some socially accepted sense, but *why* these cases deserve to be analyzed carefully rather than dismissed quickly. This latter approach is ought-thinking, theoretical pondering, why-we-care contemplation. These difficult cases are, consequently being *justified* into or out of the set deserving constitutional protection.

The very difficult question now at stake, then, is what is that deep, philosophical justification for the appearance of the word "religion" in the Constitution in the first place? This, I readily confess, is a daunting analytical soup, for the answer will require both a theory of religion and a theory of legitimate government regulatory authority. To return to earlier examples, *why* is refusing to work on Saturdays a compensable religious belief? *Why* is schoolroom Bible reading religious establishment? *Why* isn't drug use always simply a matter of lifestyle choice, and hence readily regulable? What makes any of these instances constitutionally special? Although I have tried my hand at some very abstract aspects of this conundrum,[30] that work is well beyond the modest scope of the present task. This Chapter simply seeks to demonstrate the unavoidable relevance to analyzing any "text" of *both* the factual context of the words and the normative hypertext they implicate.

3. Property

The concept of property is particularly instructive concerning the usefulness of the initial effort in legal reasoning to be sensitive to text, for two reasons. First, both its definition and theory have been subjected to careful scrutiny by various scholars. Second, the results of that work have demonstrated the remarkable importance of creative legal reasoning to our constitutional jurisprudence.

As with the term "speech," perhaps it will be useful to start with an example that will lie constantly in the background—not one, unfortunately, as dramatic as nude dancing, but one nevertheless just as conceptually challenging: whether welfare benefits can be considered within the set labeled "property."[31] The answer can be critical to a recipient of such government subsidies: If these payments are *not* property, then neither the Due Process Clause[32] nor the Takings Clause[33] of the Constitution will apply to them. That is, these benefits could be revoked by the government with no apology—either procedurally (no notice) or substantively (no alternative payments). Thus, we need to know if these government payments fall within the range of this word.

We will focus here entirely on the Due Process issue, and the analysis will track both elements developed earlier. The "is" of language-use facts will entail careful examination of the background legal development of "ownership" in our society. And the "ought" of property theory will be reflected in various philosophical efforts to justify the institution of private ownership.

The single most useful venture into defining the concept of property is, I believe, an article written many years ago by Prof. Anthony Honore on "Ownership."[34] In the tradition of British analytical jurisprudence, he sought to unpack the detail of this social phenomenon by carefully reviewing the vast caselaw and literature on the topic, and determine whether there were at its foundation certain regularly occurring elements. Indeed there were, and his article developed a wonderful example of a central case of ownership to which all other instances could then be compared.

His analysis produced a complex, multi-part archetype with several dimensions, two of which he noted specifically and two others that are either implicit in or directly derivative of the initial two.[35] We will review here some, but by no means all, of this detail, for the concept's complexity is relevant to the example issue we have identified of owning welfare benefits.

Honore's descriptive, definitional elements included:

(a) a comprehensive list of the *rights and limitations*[36] associated with a clear case of ownership, like a "right to possess" the thing physically, the "right to exclude others" from the item, the "right to income" generated by the thing, the "right to destroy" the thing if one so desired, and so on;

(b) the different categories of *things* that might be owned, such as tangible, physical things, intangible claims of various kinds (stocks and bonds, patents, trademarks, and so on);

(c) (an addition to Honore's analysis) *special limitations* on ownership rights caused by individuals in the population at large who might have particular rights to invade or use the thing involved, such as easement holders, future interest holders, and so on; and

(d) the particular *social context*—the time, place, and cultural subtleties—within which the claim of ownership is being assessed (for example, differences in perspective between 1760 and 1960).

Hence, his focal meaning of ownership was an instance in which each of these elements is, in a sense, maximized:

- The person claiming ownership enjoys the full range of attendant rights (and respects the inherent limitations) associated with owning.
- The item that is claimed is tangible and obvious, rather than abstract.
- There are no others with any special, recognized interests in the item.
- The relevant society within which this claim is being made understands and accepts the ownership claim with no significant hesitation.

The quintessential "central case" of ownership, then, would be a claim to a plot of land or a physical item in the claimant's hands.

What Honore did not discuss directly and separately in his article was any underlying "theory" or justification for claims of ownership, or any particular element within such claims. That issue—for example, is private ownership accepted and honored in our society because of its relationship to individual dignity, or fairness, or economic efficiency—was not directly a part of his descriptive, definitional exercise. It simply was not relevant to his sifting of existing legal data that constituted the study of the concept of ownership. Any deeper reason for the existence of any of this detail was not as important as the detail itself. Although the element of "social context" might suggest some element of normativity in Honore's analysis, it actually did not. His perspective was that of the linguistic approach noted earlier in this Chapter, in which one engages in "prescription" (as opposed to description) when one examines sociologically whether a given community would find a linguistic practice "proper." Thus, Honore's "social context" was similarly simply an acknowledgement that linguistic propriety would vary over time and from place to place.

But now bring all this definitional effort together around the issue of welfare benefits. For the recipient — actually the lawyer for the recipient — one critical point in establishing a viable legal claim to the benefit will be to have a court label the payments as "property," for then the benefit cannot be cut off by government without "due process of law." If the benefits do *not* get this label, government could simply stop sending checks with no explanation. But the recipient's lawyer faces a serious problem: If one were to conduct the definitional exercise described earlier, comparing the welfare benefit to the central case of traditional legal relationships to land and similar tangible things, the connection will be tenuous indeed: The welfare recipient has virtually no rights to future payments by government at all — no right to possess them, destroy them, sell them, whatever. And the "thing" involved is quite abstract rather than tangible — before the payment becomes an actual check delivered to the recipient, it is just a vague demand for assistance. And it would seem that the public, in the form of the government, has all sorts of "prior" or competing claims to the dollars represented by these subsidies. The only possible slim reed on which to cling might be the modern social context in which government subsidies for the poor have become a recognized function of government.[37]

No matter how you look at it, welfare benefits *as property interests* are "Swiss cheese" with a vengeance. They are so far removed from the focal meaning of ownership that there just may be no cheese there at all. They may well be at point D.

To the rescue, as a constitutional matter, came philosophical property *theory*, rather than definition. In the now famous and much-discussed decision by the Supreme Court in *Goldberg v. Kelly*,[38] a majority concluded that welfare benefits were indeed "property" for purposes of the Constitution's Due Process Clause. Recipients therefore had at least some rights to notice and perhaps to be heard to some extent before these subsidies could be terminated. *Not* because these payments *are* (factually) like land and other "owned" things, but because these payments *should* be within the set called property to guarantee some procedural protection for the beleaguered recipients of society's largesse. The background absence of traditional legal data, like judicial decisions and such, that would ordinarily be necessary to cite to support this conclusion, just did not really matter. What swayed the Court was the emerging general social recognition of the vulnerable circumstances of these welfare beneficiaries. These people simply needed, and as a matter of their innate human dignity, deserved, procedural protections in the face of vast and sometimes impenetrable government power.

Note, then, how this reasoning is consistent with the much messier "set" picture presented earlier that has a perimeter that waves in and out rather than being comfortably circular. *Goldberg* would seem to be a wonderful example of a court simply extending the existing, traditional perimeter line (based on prior legal data) of the "property" set to now include what would otherwise have been excluded. The set simply expands, amoeba-like, to include welfare benefits (Point D). But most important for the purposes of this book, note as well the implications for good lawyering before the Court reached this decision: The responsibility of thorough and creative legal reasoning would be to perceive this opportunity to transcend the existing legal data (is/context) by invoking deeper values (ought/hypertext) to produce the challenging result sought.

4. *Due Process*

The final term to note in this quick list of "majestic generalities" follows directly from the previous discussion. I noted above that *Goldberg* involved not only whether welfare benefits were property, but also the implication that now the requirements of the Due Process Clause would apply to limit (and direct) government activity. So now we have a new term to explore: What does "due process" *mean*?

The answer is anything but obvious because both words in this phrase present challenges: Process can involve a remarkable array of possible procedures, and what you are due from government can be assessed very differently from various political perspectives. For example, at one extreme, I had an academic colleague who took the position that this constitutional clause simply meant that you were entitled to only those procedures that government actually gave you—that, in effect the Clause had no independent content itself, but was only a statement of current conventional political reality. That would mean, of course, that the fact that a court, like in *Goldberg*, determined that welfare benefits were *property* would be meaningless, for no matter what label you might give these subsidies, "due process" would not help you: Government could deal with recipients as it saw fit. If you don't like that result, then elect a new government.

If, on the other hand, you take the position that the word "due" connotes some deeper responsibility on government procedural behavior, what would that mean? Without trying to trace here the enormous literature devoted to that question, we should more modestly note that you could respond in either of the two ways discussed in this Chapter: Descriptively, you could focus on the mountain of judicial decisions in which the adequacy of procedural requirements were assessed, and try to compare your new situation to this data. Or, normatively, you could try to extract from this data, and wider philosophical inquiry, what normative values might be at work motivating courts to conclude as they do.[39]

Both of these analytic elements can be seen at work in innumerable cases, but for convenience we can stick with our particular example of *Goldberg v. Kelly*. Having concluded that welfare benefits were indeed within the ambit of the Due Process Clause, the Court did *not* then decide that recipients were consequently entitled to, for example, a jury trial every time government questioned eligibility or subsidy amounts. The "process" that was constitutionally "due" was only enough to prevent these recipients from being arbitrarily victimized by powerful bureaucratic functionaries. The Court held that if government established a program of largesse, then the Constitution required that a kind of balance between the payor (government) and the payee (recipient) had to be established and respected.

The details of what that balance might entail is itself an interesting issue, for it is apparently quite circumstance-specific: The amount of procedural protection to which one is entitled seems to be related to the "centrality" of your property claim: The more traditionally acceptable your ownership interest, the more process you are "due." So, not surprisingly, welfare recipients, with claims at the very edge of the property set, are likewise entitled to the meager procedural protections at the edge of the due process set, such as advance warnings and perhaps a statement of reasons, but not judicial hearings before payments are stopped. Owners of land, in contrast, are entitled to a range of procedural requirements before government can strip them of ownership rights.

The point of this analysis for our purposes is again not the holding in any particular case, but the implications of these decisions for an understanding of legal reasoning. Each of the terms examined in this Chapter illustrate that professional thinking about legal concepts has, and always will, require going beneath the words involved to discover the ways in which linguistic meaning is generated. Recognizing the distinction between, but inevitable interaction of, is and ought—of describing and justifying—is an important initial step. Now we must go further into unpacking each of these dimensions.

Notes

1. *See* STEVEN PINKER, THE LANGUAGE INSTINCT 383–418 (Harper Perennial Modern Classics 2007).

2. Hart's development of this technique has been noted previously. Prof. Finnis employed it in John Finnis, Natural Law and Natural Rights 6 (2d ed. 2011) (1980).

3. A useful summary of the basic premises that characterize postmodernism can be found in Peter C. Schanck, *Understanding Postmodern Thought and Its Implications for Statutory Interpretation*, 65 S. Cal. L. Rev. 2505, 2508–09 (1992).

4. For further development of this approach, see Timothy P. Terrell, *"Property," "Due Process," and the Distinction Between Definition and Theory in Legal Analysis*, 70 Geo. L.J. 861 (1982) (hereinafter referred to as *"Property," "Due Process"*).

5. COL, *supra* ch. 1 note 12, at 4, 16.

6. *See* Finnis, *supra* note 2, at 6, 9–11. Max Weber used a somewhat similar analytic concept, the "ideal type," whose function as a normative "average" was to provide an objective comparison with the actual conduct of individuals. By determining the disparities between the ideal course of action and that actually taken by the individuals involved, the historian or sociologist might discover a "concrete causal explanation" of certain events. *See* Max Weber, The Theory of Social and Economic Organization 88–126 (Talcott Parsons ed., 1947). *See generally* Max Weber, Economy and Society (Guenther Roth & Claus Wittich eds., 1968); Max Weber, The Interpretation of Social Reality (J. Eldridge ed., 1971).

7. This observation is closely related to the concept of "family relationships" developed by Ludwig Wittgenstein. *See* Ludwig Wittgenstein, Philosophiical Investigations 2–41 (G. Anscombe trans., 1953). In discussing language and definition, Wittgenstein focused his analysis at one point on "games"—"board games, card games, ball games, Olympic games"—and asserted that the reader would find nothing that was common to all "but similarities, [and] relationships." *Id.* at 31. He thus concluded that "'games' form a family." *Id.* at 32. Wittgenstein's inquiry, however, departs from the analysis here because he saw no necessity for a paradigm case. Instead, the "set" to which an object might belong could be represented as a series of overlapping subsets, each subset sharing with its neighbor one linking characteristic only. *See id.* A string of overlapping circles, rather like links in a chain, would be an apt representation of this connectivity. *Id.*

8. H.L.A. Hart, Punishment and Responsibility 4–5 (1968).

9. *Id.* at 5.

10. *See* Pinker, *supra* note 1, at 383 ("The rules people learn … in school are called *prescriptive* rules, prescribing how one 'ought' to talk. Scientists studying language propose *descriptive* rules, describing how people *do* talk.").

11. COL, *supra* ch. 1 note 12, at 4.

12. U.S. Const. amend. VIII.

13. *See, e.g.*, Nora V. Demleitner, *Types of Punishment, in* Oxford Handbook of Criminal Law 944 (Markus D. Dubber & Tajana Hornle eds., 2014).

14. Board of Education v. Barnette, 319 U.S. 624, 639 (1943).

15. The saga of nude dancing decisions at the Supreme Court can perhaps be traced initially to a hint of possible constitutional protection by Justice Rehnquist in *Doran v. Salem Inn, Inc.*, 422 U.S. 922 (1975), to more robust protection in *Schad v. Borough of Mount Ephraim*, 452 U.S. 61 (1981), and then *Barnes v. Glen Theatre, Inc.*, 501 U.S. 560 (1991).

16. Explanations and justifications for freedom of speech are legion. *See, e.g.,* Zechariah Chafee, Free Speech in the United States, 18–20 (1941); Alexander Meiklejohn, Free Speech and Its Relation to Self-Government (1948); Thomas Emerson, The System of Freedom of Expression 7 (1970); William T. Mayton, *Libel and the Lost Guarantee of a Freedom of Speech,* 84 Colum. L. Rev. 91 (1984); Stanley Ingber, *The Marketplace of Ideas: A Legitimizing Myth,* 1984 Duke L.J. 1; Robert H. Bork, *Neutral Principles and Some First Amendment Problems,* 47 Ind. L.J. 1 (1971); Thomas Scanlon, *A Theory of Freedom of Expression,* 1 Phil. & Pub. Aff. 204 (1972); Vincent Blasi, *The Checking Value in First Amendment Theory,* 1977 Am. Bar Found. Res. J. 521.

17. Tinker v. Des Moines Indep. Cmty. Sch. Dist., 393 U.S. 503 (1969).

18. On the topic of pornography, a good recent general source is Caroline West, *Pornography and Censorship, in* Stanford Encyclopedia of Philosophy (Fall 2013 ed.). On shouting fire, this example appeared in *Schenk v. United States,* 249 U.S. 47, 52 (1919) ("The most stringent protection of free speech would not protect a man in falsely shouting fire in a theatre and causing a panic.").

19. U.S. Const. amend. I.

20. Employment Division v. Smith, 494 U.S. 872 (1990).

21. Harold S. Berman, The Interaction of Law and Religion (1974).

22. *Id.*

23. Regarding these levels or layers, see, e.g., Employment Division v. Smith, 494 U.S. 872 (1990); Church of Lukumi Babalu Aye, Inc. v. Hialeah, 508 U.S. 520 (1993).

24. Church of Lukumi Babalu Aye, Inc. v. Hialeah, 508 U.S. 520 (1993) (animal sacrifice); Cruzan v. Director, Missouri Dept. of Health, 497 U.S. 261 (1990) (refusing medical treatment to a child).

25. Snyder v. Phelps, 562 U.S. 443 (2011).

26. Goldman v. Weinberger, 475 U.S. 503 (1986).

27. Sherbert v. Verner, 374 U.S. 398 (1963).

28. Abington Sch. Dist. v. Schempp, 374 U.S. 203 (1963).

29. United States v. Seeger, 380 U.S. 163 (1965); Gillette v. United States, 401 U.S. 437 (1971).

30. *See* Terrell, *supra* Introduction note 3, at 310–342.

31. An extensive discussion of the concept of property appears in *"Property," "Due Process," supra* note 4, at 865–878.

Other examples of similar forms of analysis, and disagreements among its users, include Professor Frank Snare's central case of property which involves six necessary features divided into two basic groups: first, "rights" of use, exclusion, and transfer; and, second, "rules" of punishment and damage for interference with these rights, and of liability for the use of one's property that interferes with the rights of others. Frank Snare, *The Concept of Property,* 9 Am. Phil. Q. 200, 202–04 (1972). On the other hand, Professor Bruce Ackerman, in discussing the concept of property he believes to be held by the ordinary, unsophisticated person, criticizes this list as overinclusive and redundant. Bruce Ackerman, Private Property and the Constitution 100, n. 11 (1977). He argues that the first two rights in Snare's list are alone the necessary and sufficient conditions of property. *Id.* The right to transfer he views as merely a special case of the right to use, and the last three rules in Snare's list he believes can be dismissed as features of *any* system of rights, not just property rights. *Id.*

Ackerman's conclusions, however, demonstrate that his concept of a central case is unrelated to the descriptive exercise in which Snare is engaged. Even if the right to transfer could be considered a subcategory of a broadly conceived right to use, this does not mean that the former should be subsumed within the latter because, as Snare correctly notes, the right to transfer is missing from some types of property. *See* Snare, *supra* note 31, at 203–204. Indeed, the absence of this feature becomes an important part of the description one would make of some items of property. The point of the central case exercise is not reduction of descriptive features to less meaningful generalities, but meticulous expansion of the number of distinct characteristics that distinguish the various kinds of property that we recognize. By the same token, Ackerman's dismissal of the last three of Snare's rules is difficult to understand. If these features are part of the description of the social institution of property, eliminating the reference to these characteristics simply because other social institutions also include them would make no sense.

32. U.S. CONST. amend. V.

33. *Id.*

34. A.M. Honore, *Ownership, in* OXFORD ESSAYS IN JURISPRUDENCE 107 (A. Guest ed., 1961). Professor Roscoe Pound, in discussing the Roman or civil law concept of property, which he believed to be "tied up with liberty in [a] theory of state enforcement of social functions," posited six rights very similar to the controls described in Honore's list: rights of possessing, excluding others, disposing, using, enjoying the fruits and profits, and destroying or injuring. Roscoe Pound, *The Law of Property and Recent Juristic Thought,* A.B.A. J. 993, 996–97 (1939). These rights were tempered, however, by the argument that "'the possessor of wealth ... has a social function to perform.'" *Id.* at 997 (quoting Duguit). Honore's account of ownership is considered in some detail in LAWRENCE C. BECKER, PROPERTY RIGHTS: PHILOSOPHICAL FOUNDATIONS 18–22 (1977). But Becker's analysis of Honore's work is rather different from that presented here. For example, Becker concludes that whereas the core elements in Honore's description of ownership might be "standard," there is nevertheless "no single definition of ownership in a given legal system," because the precise substance of each of the elements is subject to variation. *Id.* at 20. This leads Becker to observe that there might be a number of subsets of ownership made up of permutations and combinations of certain key elements in Honore's list. *Id.* at 20–21. In contrast, this book's implicit contention is that Honore's analysis of ownership does indeed come close to establishing *the* definition of that term in the sense of establishing its focal meaning, the meaning to which *all* variations will then be compared. Actual comparison then creates the set of instances of ownership which might, as a matter of careful observation, be composed of the subsets identified by Becker. Another contrast between Becker's discussion of Honore and that presented here is that Becker does not consider the implications of Honore's discussion of the "social context" for a full understanding of ownership.

35. *See "Property," "Due Process," supra* note 4, at 868–874.

36. *Id.*

37. On this point, the *"Property," "Due Process"* article discusses the famous and groundbreaking article by Prof. Charles Reich. *See id.* at 882–884; Charles Reich, *The New Property*, 73 YALE L.J. 733 (1964).

38. Goldberg v. Kelly, 397 U.S. 254 (1970).

39. *See "Property," "Due Process," supra* note 4, at 898–940.

Chapter Six

The Challenge of Context: What "Is" Means in Both Facts and Law

At the heart of Gould's defense of Umpire Pinelli is his assertion that "Context matters. Truth is a circumstance, not a spot." Truth is not, apparently, a single house, but an entire neighborhood. The pitch was a strike because it found itself in this magical circumstantial *vicinity* of a strike.[1] How did it get there? And what is this "there"?

The relevance of context to an argument about social guidance—whether baseball rules or legal rules—is an application and expansion of the basic descriptive "is" lying in the linguistic background. But whatever that element might be, one unfortunate implication of the previous Chapter is that this inquiry might not be at all interesting or relevant: Normative values, which seem able to pull and stretch linguistic categories as they please, appear to be the dominant player within legal reasoning. Consequently, "treating like cases alike" seems driven by desired results rather than careful, objective comparison.

That attitude is, however, premature. Contextual circumstances *do* matter—just like words, they are *not* infinitely manipulable, but instead help structure the legal controversy at stake, putting it in appropriate perspective. But to appreciate the role of context in the process of legal reasoning, one must understand carefully how it operates.

If we put normative values aside for the moment, comparing the similarity of two cases can be based, as it turns out, on two obvious factors: facts and law. The former is a quite familiar form of "is": the details of human interaction that have created the controversy at stake. But the latter—the legal categories, like contract law, tort law, trademark law, and so on, into which these circumstances are placed—is *also* a kind of "is." It is based on preexisting doctrinal areas within the legal system that carry their own weight. That is, cases in one doctrinal area will be surrounded by different principles than those in another area. Hence, the expectations formed within these fields will organize and emphasize facts in different ways.

Our organizing theme in this Chapter, then, starts with the simple division between facts and law, but within each we discover competing perspectives that play a fundamental part in making legal reasoning both fascinating and unavoidably controversial.

A. Context and Facts: Horizontal and Vertical Categories

None of the following discussion should be surprising to anyone with any amount of legal education, because playing games with facts is central to the first weeks of law school. Mr. Brown and Ms. Green can be compared for "likeness" in any number of ways: They might both be employed as teachers, or be brother and sister; they might both be the owners of a particular kind of automobile; they might both have been born on the same day; they might both be residents of a particular city; they might both be the victims of identity theft.[2] The key to assessing their legal circumstances could therefore be that they are both high school teachers, but one is in San Francisco and the other is in Chicago.

What this simple litany indicates is that factual similarities and differences can manifest themselves in two ways—one you could call horizontal, the other vertical.

The former is about the standard categories into which stories generally divide themselves. As journalists are trained, a "complete" story will include reference to the basic patterns or divisions into which facts most naturally fall: the who, what, when, where, and why/how "sets" of informational detail that comprise the situation.[3] In other words, the circumstances that may relate or distinguish two cases could be a focus or emphasis on any one or more of the following:

> *Who*: the key individuals in the situation—for example, the identity of the parties (a corporation, a grieving widow, etc.), or of important participants (the police, a board of directors, etc.), or of witnesses (an examining doctor, an eyewitness, etc.)
>
> *What*: the materials, documents, things, or issues that are of particular interest (the empty shell casings, the meeting's minutes, etc.)
>
> *When*: the sequence of events that has produced the situation (one doctor visit leading to another, an insult leading to a fight leading to revenge, etc.)

Where: the location or other geographical context in which an incident should be placed (the nature of a highway intersection, the neighborhood next to the airport, etc.)

Why/how: the explanation for or motive underlying events (racial animus, greed, alcohol, wet roads, gravity, etc.)

But simply putting facts into familiar bundles across the horizontal, if you will, plane of a story is only a small piece of the dynamic force that facts can impart in developing a compelling *legal* story. Prof. Gould's essay is a particularly fine example of weaving together a seamless narrative of surprising significance: He gives us the "what" of not just a baseball game, but a World Series game, and the subtle "when" of being at the very end of that game. The "who" is not just a bunch of players and spectators, but individuals with names: the key professionals, including Pinelli and Larsen and so on, and the key observers, including Gould himself, his classmate, and their teachers. It is not just a story, but a dramatic one. And most dramatically, these elements then ineluctably combine to support the reasonable conclusion that the pitch was a strike, not because of bias or cheating or other inappropriate attitude, but because the circumstances somehow dictated that it *had* to be.

Gould achieves this descriptive magic not by appealing directly to normative values embedded in the circumstances—remember, we have put that dimension aside for now—but by making the circumstances *themselves* make certain values inevitably more relevant than others. Somehow we just know how this particular story will, and *must*, come out. To have this seemingly innocent depiction of the baseball story produce such influence, something else regarding these facts must be at work.

That, I would argue, is the vertical sense of the facts in his story. This involves what could be variously labeled as the breadth, scale, scope, or range of the facts being considered—any of these labels means basically the same thing. The issue captured here is how "wide" the implications of any particular decision are: Will the holding be relevant to a significant swath of potential future cases or be limited to its narrow, unique circumstances?

Thus, rather than categories of facts like who and what, the analytical element here is varying levels of generality or specificity. One way to organize this for law students is to suggest a rather familiar "fact pyramid,"[4] (illustrated in Figure 6.1) where the top is the narrowest understanding of the relevance of a particular case and the base (which, by including all the levels above it) is the most general:

Figure 6.1

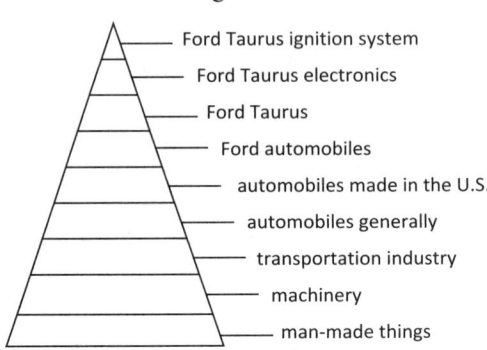

Here, the underlying factual "is" that is most important in a given case could be that it involves a very specific element in a Ford Taurus automobile, or instead, Ford automobiles generally, or instead, man-made, as opposed to naturally occurring, things. The issue for legal reasoning, then, is determining the *precedential* "meaning" of this opinion—to what kinds of cases will it be relevant in the future?

Prof. Gould's essay is once again a terrific example of attention to this analytic detail. On this point of breadth, Gould is quite consistent, and emphatic: He is relentlessly "micro." The Pinelli call did not involve merely "a baseball game," like some generic and ordinary fish plucked from the ocean. No, this involved a *big* fish, perilously caught: Much more specifically and specially, this call occurred in an enormously significant World Series game. Correspondingly, this "special game" context means that, for Gould, the "human context" is just as narrow and specific: The participants here are not just a pitcher and a batter but, much more personally, Don Larsen—by name—the "competent, but otherwise undistinguished Yankee pitcher," and Dale Mitchell—again, by name—a mere pinch hitter. This very focused attention is not an accident, nor is it merely an effort to give his argument a "homey" or "human" touch. It is a deliberate effort on Gould's part to push our consideration of appropriate values in the right direction: If we are concerned about baseball as a general proposition, we might worry about those values most relevant to protecting or enhancing the game as a whole; but if we care about "*significant baseball events,*" we will focus on values relevant to celebrating that special moment. And if we are concerned about simply the care and feeding of baseball players generally, we may fret about Pinelli's call as it might be imposed on that generic lot; but if we see the situation personally, as involving Larsen and Mitchell individually in a magical, unique circumstance, we may worry a great deal less about the "technical" inaccuracy of Pinelli's call, and honor instead the supposed "baseball values" that legitimize the call.

The critical point here is that we do not simply apply values to a situation—we worry quite explicitly about the "scale" at which those values are going to be applied. Indeed, as Gould well illustrates, the decision about scale can be part and parcel of the normative inquiry—we find particular values to be critical *because* of the scale at which we choose to view the situation. If this is so, it becomes difficult to determine which—normative values or descriptive scale—is truly dominant in the analysis.

This challenge of matching factual breadth with corresponding normativity (are we concerned with the individual actors in a drama or the drama itself as a whole?) is daunting enough to merit two additional observations, one outside of Gould's essay, and one hidden within it.

The first is this. A faculty colleague once observed to me that he had an aunt who amused him with a fundamental contradiction in her thinking and behavior. On the one hand, if she came upon a destitute person lying on a sidewalk, she would not hesitate to offer assistance, believing such actions to be at the very core of her Christian moral responsibility. On the other, she was a fierce opponent of government welfare programs of any kind, believing them primarily to encourage sloth and other bad habits. The faculty member was amused by her analytic inconsistency. But as a matter of reasoning, there is no contradiction here at all. His aunt would perceive very little *contextual* connection between the two situations. The first would, to her, be about helping a person whose desperate circumstances were immediately and clearly before her, to which she could respond in ways that could have a direct impact on the situation. The motivation to act would simply be the demands inherent in the individual dignity of the destitute person and the individual directive to her from her Christian faith to help. The other situation would be about "assisting" people she did not see or know, and assisting them with aggregate, impersonal responses in which she would participate only tangentially and involuntarily. This would be about government, not her. One context would therefore be, to her, "micro," while the other would be "macro." Although some people might believe that the two should be handled identically, she had determined that one should be emphasized to the exclusion of the other.[5]

The point of this example is therefore simply this: In the absence of a discussion of the values to be applied to these two situations—which we have *not* yet developed—there is nothing faulty in the aunt's *reasoning process* that should cause consternation. Not only is she perfectly sane, but her bifurcated approach to the contextual circumstance is in fact reflected constantly in, and is particularly relevant to, the law. Courts are always faced with precisely this dichotomy: Is the judge supposed to focus on the litigants themselves in resolving the case, or is she to take into consideration (either as well or instead) the wider social implications of a decision in favor of one side or the other? Much as any judge would like to believe that the two perspectives always perfectly coincide, they do not. For example, a judge might impose a harsher sentence than usual on a criminal defendant for a particular crime for the larger purpose of calming an outraged community (consider cases involving controversial police killings of unarmed citizens). Legal reasoning itself, then, will make decisional angst an inevitable part of the judicial job.

And this angst can actually be tied directly back to the discussion of language itself, which becomes the element of scale "hidden" within Prof. Gould's essay. It is interesting to note that we have two different words that summarize our normative assessment of events that occur within the two different contextual views—macro and micro—of a case. If our perspective is large-scale, being concerned primarily with the overall social circumstances, then we ordinarily say that "justice" or "injustice" has occurred. If, on the other hand, our view is small-scale, focused on particularized events and people, then we characterize an event as "fair" or "unfair." For example, children, who by definition see the world around them as focused on them quite specially, will label a disappointment in their expectations as "unfair," not "unjust." Justice, then, is about a societal "us," while fairness is about you and me.

Yet despite this conceptual separation, it is interesting to note that Gould actually pays no attention to it. Instead, he establishes, on the one hand, a relentless micro focus on the individual players involved in a singular moment in baseball history, suggesting that the appropriate resolution of the controversy should be based in what would be *fair* to these people thrown together there. But, on the other hand, he only refers to "justice." This is not altogether surprising, because most people do not actually perceive a difference between the two terms.[6] Gould is apparently in this camp. He does not seem to have any particular philosophical agenda in mind as he praises Pinelli's call, so this appropriate umpiring decision can be labeled anything normatively positive.

Nevertheless, I would note further that his assumption in this regard actually has some interesting philosophical support. Gould has, in effect, made the same analytic move performed with admirable aplomb by another former Harvard professor, John Rawls, in his much-admired work, *A Theory of Justice*:[7] Rawls also connects the two concepts of justice and fairness intimately, but does so explicitly, arguing that the latter leads naturally to the former: "justice as fairness,"[8] as he put it. His contention is that if you can understand the demands of fairness, it will tell you all you need to know to achieve justice as well. Likewise, Gould is contending (without saying so directly, of course) that the obvious "fairness" of calling a strike in the precise circumstances of this particular game meant automatically that the call was consistent with "justice" as well.

If you are dubious about this bit of Rawlsian mental gymnastics, however, you have me as company. Any reasoning that attempts to conflate small and large scales of assessment is problematic, which any lawyer or judge would recognize quite quickly. We noted above the different judicial perspectives between a focus on litigants versus the community, and likewise lawyers are continuously confronted with the challenge of operating professionally at both ends of the fact pyramid, above—often, indeed, simultaneously: Lawyers must necessarily attend to the micro, which is the client paying the bill (or, less pejoratively, individuals who need their professional assistance). But simultaneously, that assistance involves the macro—guiding a client through the maze of the legal system, which is itself a part of our larger social and cultural setting. What, then, is the lawyer's "proper" perspective: the client or the legal system?[9] Every lawyer always hopes that micro and macro perspectives consistently dovetail into convenient and comfortable advice. But every lawyer will also tell you that they certainly can and do diverge—that helping a client can lead to questionable legal or social results, and conversely, worrying about society's interests can compromise the legal advice given to the client.

Note the connection again to Gould's essay. His wonderful sleight-of-hand is to personalize the story as much as possible, emphasizing individual people in a special one-of-a-kind setting, but then globalize his observations and conclusions to the dizzying heights of all-encompassing *justice*. How did he do that?

Clearly, he would have made a terrific trial lawyer, bending the perspective of the story in his favor. But it is important to complete the advocacy picture here: Gould's opposing counsel would have the professional responsibility to perceive the form of trial strategy Gould is using, and argue for a competing perspective. Thus, for purposes of understanding comprehensive legal reasoning, the distinction between fairness and justice is critical, even if philosophers sometimes argue to the contrary.

B. Context as Legal Categories: Horizontal and Vertical Again

For any lawyer, another form of categorization also always seems immediately relevant: the traditional divisions of the law itself. Most of the time, this is not a complicated point: The case involves two parties trying to reach an agreement about something, so the *legal* context is contract law; or they have been involved in an automobile crash, so the context is torts; or they are trying to buy and sell a patent, so a combination of contract and property law will be relevant. This rather rudimentary observation is important, however, because much baggage follows from these characterizations. The traditions and expectations that are typical of these areas will color and sometimes dictate the way the matter will be handled. Thus, as an aspect of legal reasoning, any good lawyer would pay attention to this particular form of context as well.

Gould's essay is once again a useful non-legal introduction to this point, although admittedly you have to stretch the baseball-law analogy a bit. It seems that Gould's "legal" context of the Pinelli call is implicit, but no less emphatic: We are *not* to apply the rule-set of "ordinary baseball" to this pitch, but the separate and special set of "*extra*ordinary (World Series) baseball" rules. A strike may be one thing in the former, but it becomes a different thing in the latter. Although the physical facts have not changed—Gould readily concedes that the pitch was indeed "high and outside"—our understanding or appreciation of that physical fact certainly has. The key point is this: While the call may seem inconsistent with the "ordinary" rules, it is quite consistent with the "extraordinary" rules. By switching the "legal" circumstances simultaneously with his emphasis of certain factual circumstances, Gould's argument seems all the more reasonable and compelling.

The intriguing observation about the connection between facts and law is not, then, simply that the choice of facts can influence or determine the legal category that will be considered relevant—as noted earlier, that an accident puts us within tort law, and so on—but that the *opposite* may be at work: The legal category we *want* will tell us what facts we should emphasize. For example, in Gould's essay, which do you think came first—his "who" and "what" *facts*, or the special "legal" realm of extraordinary baseball *rules*? They seem to act inextricably together to compel us toward the conclusion he wants us to reach: It is because this alternative universe of pseudo-strikes exists (at least for Gould) that he can select the facts that will get us there.

But where did this parallel legal realm come from? Nothing in Gould's facts by themselves *dictates* that this separate context must exist. It is evident, then, that something more than the simple "is" of *both* factual *and* legal categories, in and of themselves, is at work. And just as evidently, that factor is the influence of hypertextual values, the element of legal reasoning we will develop in more detail in the next Chapter. But it would be premature to jump to that new topic immediately, for Gould's essay is only an analogy for, or approximation of, the professional sense of legal reasoning that is the actual subject of this book. Thus, we need a more traditionally *legal* example of this phenomenon of the outcome of a case being influenced—perhaps even determined—by the availability of alternative legal, rather than factual, contexts.

Fortunately, we have not only a fine example, but the perspective of a legal philosopher as well that will better enable us to appreciate it.

C. Creating Legal Breadth: *Javins v. First National Realty* and a Theory of Judicial "Integrity"

1. *Judge Wright's Legal Creativity*

The example is the remarkable decision by Judge J. Skelly Wright of the District of Columbia Circuit Court of Appeals in *Javins v. First National Realty Corp.*,[10] which was the first case in the country to recognize the legal doctrine in landlord-tenant law of a "warranty of habitability."[11] Under this new concept, tenants are given a right to withhold rent payments when the premises they have leased become "uninhabitable," and nevertheless remain in the premises as they await repairs. Prior to this decision, the tradition in this area of law—specifically, this area of *property* law—had always been the opposite on both counts.[12] First, the responsibility to pay rent was considered independent of the condition of the premises. In effect, tenants were imagined to be like their agrarian forebears who were, by necessity, jacks-of-all-trades, able to make repairs themselves. Rent simply represented the grant of permission by the landlord for the tenant to be on the premises—what those premises were like and what the tenant did there were largely up to the tenant. Second, if rented premises did become really bad, and the tenant was not at fault for this deterioration, the tenant could claim "constructive eviction"[13] by the landlord, relieving the tenant from the lease's rental obligation. The problem with this remedy, unfortunately, was (and still is) that to make this claim, the tenant had to vacate the premises, and search for a new place to live. The innovative question posed by the *Javins* litigation was whether the tenant could *both* refuse to pay rent because of the bad conditions of the premises, *and* nevertheless stay in those premises while awaiting appropriate improvements.

Judge Wright's opinion is famous, in part, for its fundamental rethinking of this entire legal context. Rather than accept and apply the traditional common law property doctrine of landlord-tenant law, he reexamined it critically, concluding that its foundational assumptions were inaccurate and antiquated. Tenants today, he concluded, desire—and indeed expect—much more than just access to particular premises. They are not farmers anymore, but—particularly in Judge Wright's context of Washington, D.C.—city dwellers, many of whom would be, like Ms. Javins, of very modest financial means. Such persons pay rent, he found, to obtain "shelter" for themselves and their families adequate to maintain some modicum of health and happiness.[14] Tenants assume, Judge Wright decided on their behalf, that they will receive in exchange for their rent payments premises that are at least "habitable." He therefore held that all residential leases within his jurisdiction would have implied into them a new clause—a "warranty of habitability"—that embodied and vindicated the tenant's expectations. Tenants should be able, under this implied landlord promise, to complain about conditions, pay no rent, and maintain occupancy.

But, reasonable as the outcome of this case appears to be to modern eyes, it was quite a legal stretch at the time. Judge Wright's problem was that he had no (or very little and distinguishable) precedent *in the area of landlord-tenant law* on which to base his conclusion. So he didn't try to do so. Instead, he reached out to another area of law to find support: contract law, and its rapidly developing, and widely accepted, concept of "warranties of fitness."[15] Within that setting, he noted, were plenty of judicial decisions imposing on sellers of goods the requirement—even if not explicitly stated in the sale contract—that the item exchanged would be fit or appropriate for the purpose for which it was purchased. Rental premises, he reasoned, were just "like" this: They were a kind of commodity—more accurately, a bundle of services that Judge Wright labeled "shelter"—that had been purchased by the tenant with a rather clear purpose in mind: to obtain a place where one could "live," in a larger sense than merely "exist."

Armed with this extra weapon of contract law precedent, Judge Wright had no difficulty in concluding—now from the safety of existing legal support— that every residential lease in the District of Columbia had within it a "warranty of habitability," even though no lease document itself actually contained any such provision. Most powerfully, as a legal, conceptual matter, this warranty was a lease provision that Ms. Javins was "legitimately"[16] *entitled* to expect, even though she had almost certainly never *actually* thought about it.[17] The key here, then, is this: Legal legitimacy for this conclusion came *not* from the area of law traditionally applied in this landlord-tenant context—property, with its focus on the "things" being traded in a market. While this would certainly have been the expectation of Ms. Javins' *landlord*, that did not matter to this Court. Instead, Judge Wright was focused on "relationships"—the human connection between Ms. Javins and her landlord, the reasons that brought them together to create this lease. That perspective allowed him to tap the resources of a parallel doctrinal universe—contract and sales law, with their emphasis on "meetings of minds" and "expectations." The judicial result of an implied warranty—indeed, a *nonnegotiable* warranty[18]—thus seemed quite reasonable and unsurprising, rather than remarkably creative.

This masterful bit of legal reasoning also enjoys powerful scholarly support as well, although it was developed many years later and without attention to this particular case or area of law.

2. Prof. Dworkin's Legal "Integrity"

In his book *Law's Empire,*[19] Prof. Ronald Dworkin reconsiders (my characterization, not his) his previous efforts to develop a comprehensive theory of adjudication, and produces an elegant and impressive new vision he labels "law as integrity."[20] It is a theory both descriptive and normative, capturing the method by which he believes judges do and should analyze challenging cases so as to reach decisions that are both intellectually and morally appropriate. It is a complex picture, but it reduces to two basic elements. One is directly relevant to a decision's "context," and thus of primary interest here, while the other is about the decision's reference to "hypertext," and hence to be discussed further in Chapter 7.

The two pieces constituting reasoning with "integrity," according to Dworkin, are:

- first, a judge must carefully analyze a decision's "fit"[21]—the way the current decision integrates into the existing legal material it must now join. This is a descriptive, contextual exercise, much like Prof. Schauer's ideas of comparison and assimilation.

- second, combine that assessment with an effort to put the law in its "best light"[22]—trying to make the law and legal system normatively impressive to the public. This is obviously a prescriptive, hypertextual exercise based in social and political values.

In other words, judges must honor *both* a sense of consistency (connectedness with the past) *and*, simultaneously, a substantive concern with "justice" and "fairness" (giving normative heft to that past and the present decision).

The key to understanding Prof. Dworkin's message is to realize that neither of these analytic elements of fit and best light is a simple, uncontroversial label that you could simply apply to a mental activity—as in "you have achieved fit," or "that is indeed law in its best light." If these abstract characteristics were simple singularities of this sort—mere "points" of data as in the Flatlaw analysis—then you could easily (and miraculously) combine the two to produce in every case a perfect, also singular, judicial decision, as in "a point of law." To the contrary, however, both these factors are actually *variables*—that is, lines, rather than points, representing a *range* of possible amounts of fit and best-ness. Hence, the appropriate way to understand judicial integrity is to realize that every decision a judge must make will require consideration of different "degrees" of both consistency and normative goodness that can be attributed to possible outcomes, and those amounts will vary, from high to low. Thus, one convenient way to imagine this interaction is with the graphic representation shown in Figure 6.2 (which I again emphasize is *my* depiction of Dworkin's reasoning):[23]

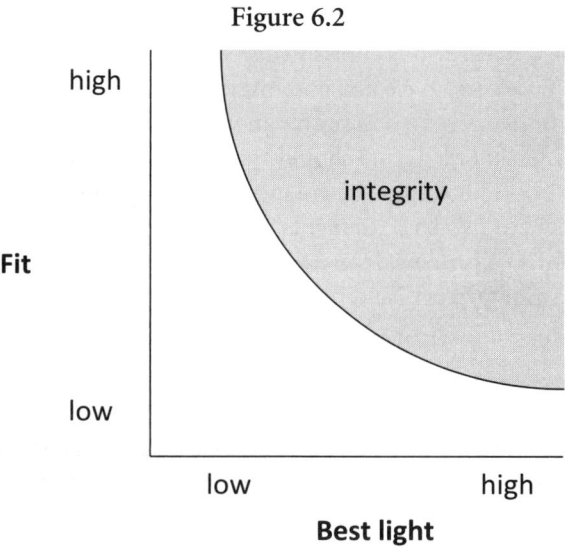

Figure 6.2

The area of integrity in the graph is therefore the range of possible opinions that a court could reach in a particular case that would at least have been produced by means of what Dworkin would call a *legitimate judicial reasoning process*. A case does not, therefore, have one unique appropriate outcome, but it does have one unique *route* by which the result should be achieved.

The relevance of Prof. Dworkin's analysis to this book is therefore at multiple levels. As noted at the beginning of this Chapter, Prof. Gould's paradoxical contention that "Truth is a circumstance, not a spot" is confirmed. Legal reasoning, no matter how thorough and exacting, produces an area of *many* legitimate results. And legal data in the form of judicial decisions is far more complex than the dots of Flatlaw, producing instead shapes and forms of legal doctrine. All this follows from the analytical thesis at work in this Chapter and the next: Legal material is always a combination of context—both factual and legal "fit"—and hypertext, the normative values of "best light" to be explored in Chapter 7. The ultimate point is that these two dimensions are indivisibly interconnected—you cannot adequately assess one without reference to the other.

3. Manipulating Context, but with Integrity Rather than "Right Answers"

But more specifically concerning our present focus on *legal* "context" and its artful manipulation in *Javins*, Prof. Dworkin's analysis is particularly interesting because he defines the concept of "fit" quite creatively, and in just the way Judge Wright seems to understand it as well. Rather than simply "counting up" cases that are directly "on point," Dworkin argues that the relationships within the supporting data should be seen in a series of "concentric circles,"[24] with the most similar precedents being given extra weight through a sense of "local priority"[25]—weight, however, that can nevertheless be overcome by stronger principles emanating from other areas of the law. Using the example of a tort case involving emotional injury, he argues that the good judge (Hercules, again) would proceed in a series of analytic steps:

> He asks which interpretation [of prior law] on his initial list fit emotional injury cases, then which ones fit cases of accidental damage to the person more generally, then which fit damage to economic interests, and so on into areas each further and further from the original ... issue. This procedure gives a kind of local priority to what we might call "departments" of law.[26]

Thus, if there aren't enough tort cases, for example, available to meet the dimension of "fit" adequately, the judge can reach out to, say, contract cases to examine their relevant principles, and then perhaps to property cases, and so on, to build support within existing authoritative sources. Quite evidently, the dimensions of "fit" and making the law its "best" are not at all starkly separate from each other, as the graph above illustrates.

Specifically in the context of the *Javins* case, it is important to note that Judge Wright expands the concept of "fit" in two ways. One returns us to the topic examined earlier of factual breadth or scope, which indicates that Prof. Dworkin's ideas of "local [legal] priority" and "departments of law" could be depicted as shown in Figure 6.3.

Figure 6.3

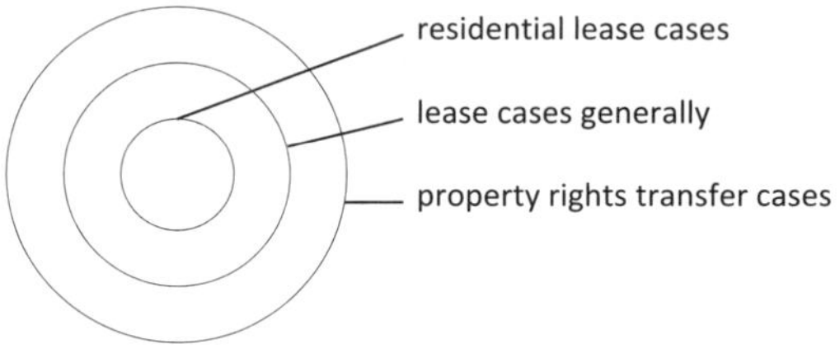

residential lease cases

lease cases generally

property rights transfer cases

Note how the similarity—the "likeness"—of two cases can be perceived quite differently: Are cases involving "leases" meaningfully related to cases involving "sales" of real estate? If so, how? Is the general factual category of property-related transactions enough, or should the scope of the analysis be narrowed? The wider your breadth, quite obviously, the more legal data you may be able to identify to claim adequate "fit"—the more limited the range, the less data you have to search for support.

But Judge Wright's second strategy concerning "fit" is more dramatic, because it is an exercise in broadening *legal*, rather than factual, comparison. It, too, was suggested by Prof. Dworkin in his analysis of judicial integrity. He argued that the effort to compare bits of legal data to find support for an argument (to generate appropriate fit) could be conducted in two ways, which could then be combined: "vertically"[27] and "horizontally."[28] The former is the more traditional search by a court (or lawyers more generally) for support for a decision by reviewing the existing legal material (prior opinions, say) in a given area of the law, and doing so chronologically—and hence "vertically"— over the many years that preceded the present case. For example, in the *Javins* opinion, this would be Judge Wright's search through the doctrinal context of landlord-tenant cases supporting some kind of implied warranty of fitness. On the basis of that effort alone, Judge Wright's intended conclusion—that such a warranty exists within current law—would look very shaky indeed, for very little support for that proposition could be identified.

Thus, on the basis of the element of "fit"—the vertical axis above—he would find himself toward the very bottom. This would mean, in turn, that to hold that a warranty of habitability actually exists within the law, and to reach that decision *with "integrity,"* he will have to work extraordinarily hard on the dimension of "best light" to push the normative force behind his decision as far to the right in the graph as possible—that is, to maximize that variable. That would allow him to overcome the problem of minimal caselaw "fit" and in turn allow his decision to appear to be over the "integrity" line. To return to the graph (see Figure 6.4):

Figure 6.4

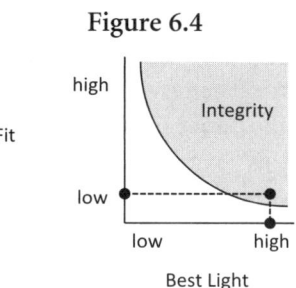

The brilliance of Judge Wright's decision, however, is his skillful *avoiding* of that pressure by making an analytic move Prof. Dworkin would heartily endorse: rethinking the dimension of "fit" by extending his search for support "horizontally" beyond the area of landlord-tenant law to include other ("parallel," in a way) doctrinal legal areas like real property sales, contracts, and torts, where the critical underlying feature of "relationships" is more important, more evident, and more developed. Thus, by searching "across" the law, by widening his legal scope, and counting the numerous decisions that appear in other lines (vertically) of cases that have imposed on sellers of goods implied warranties of fitness, Judge Wright found the "fit"—the preexisting support—he needed to make his decision concerning *landlords* all the more obvious and acceptable. The analysis could be depicted in table form, as shown in Figure 6.5:

Figure 6.5

Number of cases developing the concept of warranties of quality

		Landlord-Tenant	Property Sales	Contract	Tort
	1950's	0	4	2	1
	1960's	1	5	6	4
"vertical"	1970's	4	11	20	10
	1980's	4	16	25	15
	1990's	5	19	30	20

"horizontal"

This chart, I hasten to emphasize, uses completely hypothetical numbers just to illustrate the analytic point here. It indicates that if all one did was search for caselaw support for the *Javins* decision within the "local priority" or "department" of landlord-tenant law, the total number might seem quite low. But stretching the search horizontally to other departments that have considered the more general context of "quality" demands could yield a much higher number of cases that "fit" with the *Javins* approach.

In effect, Judge Wright could move "up" the "fit" axis of the graph, and correspondingly make his decision seem all that much more obviously to fall well within the realm of "integrity," and hence legal acceptability. His opinion, then, despite its evident boldness and creativity, and especially its controversial emphasis on the normative importance of protecting low-income tenants, could nevertheless look traditionally grounded and reasonable. The graphic representation is shown in Figure 6.6:

Figure 6.6

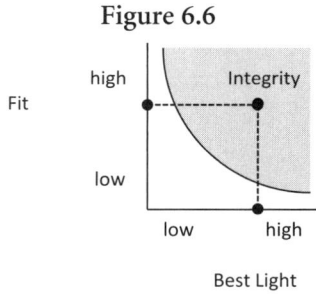

Best Light

And so it is for Umpire Pinelli as well. Prof. Gould does not want to be confined to arguing only that the called strike was correct because the "values" of baseball—its "best light"—somehow demand that result. Although he will certainly so contend, he also wants to give the call additional support by placing it within the correct "legal" context as well, where "baseball precedent" will make it look reasonable. He wants the call to "fit," in other words, within the history and traditions of baseball in a more descriptive, factual sense. He accomplishes this only by assertion, however, rather than citing particular authority: He contends that ample precedent exists for the proposition that in the circumstances of the "big game" a batter must "swing at anything close." But we can certainly see better now why he seems compelled to make that argument.

If again you are skeptical about the maneuvers of both Prof. Gould and Judge Wright to massage the breadth of their factual and legal contexts, you are not alone. But final judgment on these creative forms of analytical reasoning needs to wait until the next two elements within that process—hypertext and subtext—are included in the mix.

Before we leave this discussion of manipulating legal data, however, we must return for a moment, as promised back at the end of Chapter Three, to Prof. Dworkin's so-called "right answer" claim. You may recall that he espoused the idea that a judge who employs an appropriately rich analytic technique to decide a case (meaning, of course, what he would later label as integrity) will be able to produce a "right answer" in *every* case—an answer somehow uniquely dictated by determining the correct amount of consistency with prior decisions, the correct identification of the normative principles that animate the legal system as a whole, and the correct mix of these two elements. The image would be that the axes above would have a single spot on each of them where the "correct" degree of that element exists, and the interaction of the two of them would produce a singular "spot" or point within the graph, rather than an "area" of multiple results. This proposition has been developed by Prof. Dworkin in different places in his work.[29]

But I believe that in these discussions Prof. Dworkin was not defending (nor need he defend) the rather strange proposition that each difficult case has, lurking beneath its complexity, a singular, correct answer with which no reasonable judge (or other person more generally, for that matter) could disagree. Instead, as noted earlier, Prof. Dworkin's claim is that in reaching a decision "with integrity," a judge is at least announcing that this result is *the* unique, and uniquely appropriate, decision *for this judge.* In other words, the decision, and the process by which it was reached, are both taken by this judge very seriously, such that the judge can claim that the decision is the very best that he or she can produce. The judge is satisfied, in other words, that he or she has, in Dworkin's terms, "impose[d] order over doctrine."[30]

Consequently, for any particular judge, the graph above would indeed have a single spot on each axis where the judge fixes the amount of each variable, and their intersection will in turn identify a single spot within the graph where the "right answer" in the case resides. But different judges, as reasonable people, could fix the amount of the two variables differently, and thus if we were to plot all these possible results, we would end up with the area depicted in the text. *All* of these decisions would be able to claim legitimacy through Prof. Dworkin's *process* of integrity.[31]

Even though this elaboration of Prof. Dworkin's thesis is necessarily a limited one, two additional points must nevertheless be made about it that are directly related to the themes of this book. First, note that the difference between the "right answer" understood from the perspective of a particular judge (the "spot") and the "right answer" from the perspective of the judiciary as a whole (the "area") is a straightforward application of the "micro/macro" element within legal reasoning generally that is the focus of this portion of the book. Thus, the confusion on this point concerning Prof. Dworkin's message should not be all that surprising.

But second, and more important, the difference between the "spot" and the "area" within the graph is critical to appreciating the distinction between a theory of *law* and a theory of *lawyering*. This book is about the latter, and only by extension about the former. The key observation here is this: If the result of Prof. Dworkin's integrity thesis is the "spot" of a singular, uniquely legitimate result in every case, then every lawyer (or dissenting judge) who has argued in favor of a different position or result—*using Prof. Dworkin's own analytic technique*—is either a liar or a fool. The "right answer" takes on a mystical and mythical characteristic of ontological perfection that is both counterintuitive and unnecessary. Lawyers (and judges) who argue a losing cause do not lack integrity, under any reasonable definition of that concept. They have instead simply identified a different spot within the area of integrity that is the "right answer" *for them*.

Notes

1. The idea of "vicinity" is directly related to the "set theory" on which the approach to linguistics in this article is based. *See* Terrell, *Property, Due Process, supra* ch. 5 note 4. Another version of this idea was once related to me by a judge, who commented that his father told him, based on his experience in World War II, that ordinarily you don't have to be perfect; you just need to be "grenade close."

2. A similar example of non-obvious overlapping characteristics appears in Elements of Law, *supra* ch.2 note 9, at 172.

3. This quick summary is developed further, with examples, in Stephen V. Armstrong & Timothy P. Terrell, Thinking Like a Writer: A Lawyer's Guide to Effective Writing and Editing 111–118 (3d ed. 2008).

4. This analytic concept is certainly not confined to the law. *See, e.g.,* Glenn Wiebe, *Tip of the Week: Fact Pyramid, Because Box*, Hist. Tech (June 15, 2013), https://historytech.wordpress.com/2013/06/15/tip-of-the-week-fact-pyramid-because-box/.

5. And his aunt is certainly not alone in recognizing this important distinction between micro and macro levels in philosophical analysis. Prof. Drucilla Cornell notes in her book that Prof. Ronald Dworkin called this dichotomy the "discontinuity thesis." *See* Drucilla Cornell, At the Heart of Freedom: Feminism, Sex, and Equality 59 (1998) ("In our morally complex world we sometimes need to insist on discontinuity between what we think is good for ourselves and the people close to us and what we would allow the state to impose as the general evaluation of the good.").

6. I do not at all mean to suggest here that the use of the terms "fairness" and "justice"—by either lawyers or the public at large—consistently reflects the connection to micro and macro perspectives developed in the text. For example, some might argue that the distinction between the two terms is actually rooted in the separation of procedure from substance: A substantively "just" law can nevertheless be implemented "unfairly"; or, a "fair" election process is a necessary prerequisite to a "just" political system; and so on. But I would note two points: First, the distinction between substance and procedure is not at all at odds with the analytical distinction I am drawing between micro and macro—it is instead simply another application of it: procedures apply to particular parties in adjudicative settings; substantive laws apply to society generally. Second, whatever inconsistency one encounters in the sometimes interchangeable use of the terms "fair" and "just," this linguistic messiness does not diminish the importance of the analytic perspectives developed in the text. The words are simply an interesting manifestation—a possible bit of evidence—of our struggle with context within legal reasoning.

7. JOHN RAWLS, A THEORY OF JUSTICE (1971).

8. *Id.* at 11 ("the guiding idea is that the principles of justice for the basic structure of society are the object of the original agreement. They are the principles that free and rational persons concerned to further their own interests would accept in an initial position of equality as defining the fundamental terms of their association. These principles are to regulate all further agreements; they specify the kinds of social cooperation that can be entered into and the forms of government that can be established. This way of regarding the principles of justice I shall call justice as fairness.").

9. The American Bar Association's Model Rules of Professional Conduct (2015) begins by making every possible perspective relevant to lawyers. MODEL RULES OF PROF'L CONDUCT (AM. BAR ASS'N 1980). Its Preamble starts with this observation: "A lawyer, as a member of the legal profession, is a representative of clients, an officer of the legal system and a public citizen having special responsibility for the quality of justice." *Id.* at pmbl.

10. Javins v. First Nat'l Realty Corp., 428 F.2d 1071 (D.C. Cir. 1970).

11. The caselaw and academic literature on this doctrine is immense. A useful summary continues to be JESSE DUKEMINIER ET AL., PROPERTY 515–525 (8th ed., 2014).

12. Javins, *supra* n. 10 at 1074.

13. A good example of a modern discussion of the doctrine of constructive eviction appears in Village Commons, LLC v. Marion County Prosecutor's Office, 882 N.E.2d 210 (Ind. 2008).

14. Javins, *supra* n. 10 at 1074.

15. *Id.* at 1075.

16. *Id.* ("In order to reach results more in accord with the legitimate expectations of the parties ... courts have been gradually introducing more modern precepts of contract law in interpreting leases.").

17. We have no evidence on this one way or the other. Instead, people seem to reach conclusions about Ms. Javins' thought process based on their preconceived notions of what low-income tenants "are like."

18. *Id.* at 1081–82 ("The duties imposed by the Housing Regulations [which now include the warranty of habitability which they help create] may not be waived or shifted by agree-

ment if the Regulations specifically place the duty upon the lessor."); *Id.* at 1082 n. 58 ("Any private agreement to shift the duties would be illegal and unenforceable.").

19. RONALD DWORKIN, LAW'S EMPIRE (1986).

20. *Id.* at 225–275.

21. *Id.* at 230.

22. *Id.* at 231.

23. And I hasten to add that the depiction is also only a summary of Dworkin's discussion, for there are further, complicating steps within each of his two basic categories of fit and best light. The former has the elements of vertical and horizontal, which are discussed in the text, and the latter consists of at least two normative qualities—justice and fairness—and perhaps a third (although I never found this all that clear from Dworkin's discussion)—procedural due process. *See id.* at 243.

24. *Id.* at 250.

25. *Id.*

26. *Id.*

27. *See* Terrell, *supra* ch. 1 note 1, at 65–6.

28. *Id.* The discussion in this part of the Chapter is drawn generally from my article on the *Art of Legal Reasoning. See id.* at 64–6.

29. *See, e.g.*, Ronald Dworkin, *No Right Answer?, in* LAW, MORALITY, AND SOCIETY: ESSAYS IN HONOUR OF H.L.A. HART 58 (Hacker and Raz, eds., 1977). But the most elaborate defense of it may be the portions of LAW'S EMPIRE that precede his elaboration of the "law and integrity" technique in the chapter that bears that title, as well as in that chapter itself. *See* DWORKIN, *supra* note 19, at 45–86, 260–263.

30. *Id.* at 273.

31. I believe this "correction" to Prof. Dworkin's argument is consistent as well with Judge Richard Posner's criticism, in HOW JUDGES THINK, of any judicial effort to assert certainty regarding any decision. As he argues, there are no "right answers" to difficult legal questions, *Id.* at 9. Any effort to claim otherwise is at the heart of his condemnation of any judge who claims that he or she can, in reaching a decision, focus solely on narrow pieces of legal material without reference to the wider policy foundations from which this material springs— or as Judge Sutton discusses it, wrongheaded "legalism—a blend of originalism and textualism." *See* Sutton, *supra* note 10, at 864.

But I think that Judge Sutton is correct in his criticism of Judge Posner on a couple of points. First, Judge Posner's argument seems aimed primarily, if not exclusively, at what Prof. Dworkin called "hard cases"—where the standard, traditional legal materials do not produce a clear and straightforward conclusion. Looking at the data of judicial decision making as a whole, it would appear that there is indeed more judicial agreement than disagreement.

But even regarding the difficult cases, Judge Sutton notes that if there are no "right answers," then there can be no "mistakes" by judges. *Id.* at 862. Yet judges identify legal mistakes quite regularly. So how to square these conflicting ideas? I think Judge Posner would agree, as I have argued here, that although legal *answers* may not be purely right or wrong, nevertheless the legal decision making *process* can be imagined in more absolute terms. That is, judges can indeed disagree with each other "with integrity" as they assess differently the elements of language, circumstances, values, and institutional responsibility. But to the extent that a judge believes that one or more of these factors simply do not matter in a controversial case, and are therefore to be ignored, then he or she is indeed reaching a decision based on a "mistake."

Chapter Seven

The Challenge of Hypertext: The Struggle within "Ought" of Multiple Perspectives on Fundamental Values

At long last, after numerous promises that this analytic gap would be filled in, we now confront the legal reasoning element of hypertext. There is a reason it has been postponed for so long. It will, as you might imagine, prove to be the most challenging aspect of this topic.

Bear in mind, however, that for some who study legal theory, this move into values can be considered inappropriate altogether: Positivists, like H.L.A. Hart, contend, as we noted earlier, that legal (as opposed to moral) guidance should be limited to the data of existing, identifiable, positive legal sources, and not invoke abstract, perhaps idiosyncratic justifications for a decision. But even positivists do not argue that values be stricken entirely from the conversation. Recall Hart's effort to give the concept of justice some content by linking it to the need for social order and predictability. And certainly any judge would be permitted to consider any values that a legal source *requires* them to consider (like antitrust law's focus on markets and efficiency).

The issue here, instead, is the kind of role philosophical and other non-legal perspectives can play *implicitly* within legal thinking—that is, directing and shaping arguments and results.

We have encountered earlier several examples of the possible influence of "deeper" propositions on legal material. Prof. Gould certainly believed that the underlying values inherent within the game of baseball established why a pitch "high and outside" was nevertheless a legitimate strike. Similarly, part of the move beyond Flatlaw is the sophistication to see the data of the law (two-dimensional shapes) as incomplete larger realities (three-dimensional forms) that recognize the relevance of forces outside traditional legal material. And in the previous Chapter, within Ronald Dworkin's concept of judicial integrity, the factor of "best light" obviously requires a judge to consider the normative implications of a decision.

To develop this aspect of legal reasoning, however, we must begin with a familiar caveat: Just as the topics of the previous Chapters of this book were not, respectively, "everything about language that might be relevant" and "every possible context you might imagine," the topic here is not "everything you ever wanted to know about philosophy." Instead, the focus is again on *reasoning*, as it has been relentlessly: how we analyze, approach, and apply the abstract subject of values — how we *organize* our understanding of normativity. And more particularly, the subject under examination is not all possible forms of normative reasoning and organizing, but those efforts that seem most characteristic of the lawyer mind.

So the question now, as it was with text and context, is whether this additional element of legal reasoning is similarly *structured* in some way that can be identified and exploited. I believe it is. But as we witnessed in the previous Chapter, the divisions may be as multiple as they are esoteric. There are two challenges here. The first is to note that the general topic of "values" that might be invoked in a legal argument are not confined to the discipline of philosophy alone, even though that is the immediate reasonable assumption when thinking becomes abstract. That issue is developed in Part A below.

The second challenge is that within the (for us) most relevant discipline of philosophy there are competing perspectives that must be organized in some way if we are to make this aspect of legal reasoning accessible. That effort will be undertaken in Part B.

To try to pull this complex mosaic together, we will in Part C return to both the *Javins* decision and Prof. Gould's essay to explore the remarkable range of hypertextual approaches that *could* have been developed by the parties, by Judge Wright, and by Umpire Pinelli to defend themselves.

A. The Range of Legal Theories Within Hypertext

As noted above, Chapter Two's discussion of Flatlaw and the effort to transcend it introduced a third dimension to the depiction of legal reasoning, and that addition was composed of *any* additional perspective that made the two-dimensional data of legal pronouncements simply evidence within a larger social reality. Consequently, you could consider yourself within that realm in any number of ways — viewing law as reflecting the sweep of history, or as implementing the invisible hand of economics, or as influenced by sociological forces, or (which has been the primary assumption in previous parts of this book) as endorsing certain philosophical values, and so on. The problem presented by all this range of what you could call "theories" of law is that they should not be lumped together into a single category. The perspectives they suggest regarding the law in fact fall into two distinct groups. One is based in a contextual "is," and is therefore more closely related to the previous Chapter, while the other is a true "ought," and therefore more directly related to what Professors Gould and Dworkin had in mind.

The first of these groups of theories contains all the kinds of analysis that could be labeled "social science." Any critique they offer on the substance of the law—whether they think current legal rules are good or bad—is not actually based in a prescriptive "ought." To illustrate the problem, and resolve it, we will focus here singularly on economics,[1] but that is solely for convenience. You could just as easily substitute sociology or another similar discipline.

The conceptual conundrum that economic analysis presents is that, on the one hand, its emphasis on "efficient" use of resources sounds like an endorsement of one form of activity and a condemnation of its opposite—inefficiency. On its face it seems to be saying much the same thing as the philosophical theory of utilitarianism (which we will consider further in a moment), with its endorsement of a cost-benefit analysis. But the problem is that the costs and benefits under consideration in economic analysis do not have any *normative* content themselves *from the perspective of economics*. For example, one could argue that we have an inefficient criminal justice system because our concern with procedural rights allows too many guilty people to escape punishment, and hence we have insufficient deterrence, and then in turn we have too much criminal activity, and then in turn again we waste resources protecting ourselves from criminal activity. Assuming all that is true, would reducing our procedural rights and protections from government power be "good"? Is this a form of efficiency we would endorse? Economics cannot answer that question. It can only give you a factor you may want to consider in determining what sorts of rights we should have.

So the question becomes whether economic analysis is, in this book's effort to structure legal reasoning, a proper subject for this Chapter on hypertext, or whether it should be addressed elsewhere. It *does* belong here because the move we have made from context to hypertext is from "facts" (both micro and macro) to *assessments* of that data for policy purposes. The problem is that you can step back from a descriptive, factual set of materials, and reach conclusions about either their direction or meaning, in two very different ways: You can *justify* the picture that the data paint, or you can *explain* that image. Philosophy does the former; social science disciplines like economics and sociology do the latter.

The analytic relationships here, along with the confusion they can produce, look like this, shown in summary form in Figure 7.1:

Figure 7.1

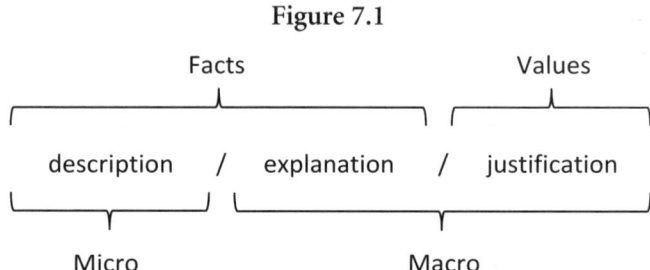

"Describing" things or concepts is inherently a "micro" mental activity because you are choosing an instance or example to capture some bit of reality. Even if you describe a group of such things—like moving from discussing your dog to discussing all dogs—you are nevertheless merely examining this set and listing characteristics (as we did in Chapter Five's exercises in linguistics). All this activity is also simply about facts, as objectively as possible, without value judgments. It is just observational.

But you can then move to observations about the *actions* or other interactive characteristics of this thing or concept. You can, in other words, "explain" the behavior of dogs, or explain the way courts approach the concept of ownership, and the like. Again, there is no value judgment involved, but you have changed an important aspect of your thinking. You have moved from a specific instance to a wider range—from the micro to the macro. To explain the behavior of your particular dog, you must compare it to dogs more generally; to explain the concept of property, you need more than one judicial decision.

But by increasing the breadth of your examination or inquiry you have *not* transcended your factual circumstances—you have instead just shifted within it. To go beyond facts—to "justify" some activity—you must move to the world of the normative. There is no objectivity here, however, but rather the subjectivity of the moral and political values you believe relevant, but about which others can disagree adamantly. The sometimes confusing connection of this aspect of analysis to that of explaining is that when you justify something, you are similarly operating at a "macro" level: Values are meaningless unless they apply generally to one degree or another, as opposed to specially and uniquely to just one example. Human dignity is a silly idea if it is only applicable or relevant to one person.

So the hypertextual analysis based in economics can be misapprehended for a couple of reasons. First, it is, on the one hand, based initially in the rational behavior of individual human beings (descriptively), but on the other, generates general observations about the behavior of human beings as a whole (macro) as we attempt to maximize our resources. It thus *explains* why humans respond to incentives based on costs and benefits; it explains what an efficient outcome in a case would appear to be, given that the decision will be a guide to people beyond just the litigants. But even though economics is delivering assessments of facts in action, it cannot *justify* any particular result beyond its own limits of observed objective data. Although it *sounds* as if, by pronouncing some outcome as "efficient," economics is saying that that outcome must necessarily also be normatively "good," that is an inappropriate category jump. Economics *is* claiming that resources are being produced or distributed in a way that can be understood as connected directly to rational human behavior generally, but that "macro" statement is still only about psychological facts, not values.

This potential confusion around the status of economic efficiency claims is in fact central to Prof. Dworkin's earlier distinction between "legal principles" and "social policies," and will therefore in turn be central to the discussion in Chapter Eight of the final legal reasoning element of political subtext. For present purposes, however, despite the potential confusion that can attend claims to an "economic theory of law," it is perfectly acceptable for us to include the assessments of economics (and other social sciences) within the general category of hypertextual perspectives on various legal arguments. We just have to be careful not to lump all these forms of judgment into one undifferentiated mass.

It is to the effort to *justify* that we now turn.

B. Justifying Legal Material

The challenge here is to determine whether within the vast universe of straightforwardly philosophical perspectives on the law there exists any structure beneath an advocate's claim that her approach is deeply, normatively justified—that an argument or decision deserves a remarkable level of respect.

1. A Return to Fairness and Justice: The Moral and the Political

One quick and easy route into organizing one's normative thinking is simply to return to the dichotomy noted in the previous Chapter on context: micro and macro. We noted there that this separation lies behind the different labels we attribute to assessments of legal and policy arguments: fairness and justice, respectively. But the distinction here goes much deeper than mere words.

Corresponding to the perspective we have thus far labeled micro, and connected to the concept of fairness, is the realm of "moral" philosophy[2]—the set of values we attach to interactions on an intimate scale: how you and I should treat each other. On the other hand, corresponding to the macro-justice perspective is the domain of "social" and, more specifically for our purposes, "political" philosophy[3]—the set of values pertaining to larger scales of interaction: how men should treat women; how the institutions of our government should be arranged and guided; how, in the most general sense, we should govern ourselves.

However, just as there is no evident break in the gradual movement from micro to macro (from one end of the contextual "fact pyramid" to another), so, too, there is no clean break between these two philosophical categories. Hence, we should not be surprised if the separation between them will be challenged (or misperceived) from time to time. That is simply one of the interesting aspects of legal reasoning that offers strategic opportunities to build rhetorical advantage. The key to note here is *why* there are differing hypertextual strategies available: Quite simply, the "facts" at the top and bottom of the pyramid, while obviously related, are *not* the same. Their comparative breadth matters, for the *values* attached to different levels of the pyramid are correspondingly not identical: The values constituting what we mean by fairness will not necessarily be the same as those we associate with justice.

This is disconcerting, because it is already challenging to appreciate, within Dworkin's requirement for analytic integrity, the difference between arguing legal "fit," on the one hand, and arguing "best light," on the other. Now we have to recognize that the variable of "best light" itself is actually far more complicated than is suggested by the simple line on the graphs in the previous Chapter. Is there any way to get a further handle on the thought process underneath this dimension?

I admit, this is not easy. But exploring this philosophical labyrinth can be both interesting and professionally useful. We shall do so in two steps. The first will be to acknowledge the dizzying range of possible philosophical perspectives that might be invoked to demonstrate that a legal argument or outcome reflects appropriate respect for relevant values. Then we will focus on the two forms of normative argument that seem most directly relevant to practical legal reasoning.

2. Some Philosophical Background

Despite the fact that normative thinking is indeed a vast, complex, and controversial topic, what is important (and quite useful) here is that this "ought" element within legal reasoning has its own fundamental dichotomy that helps organize discussions of values. And, oddly enough, that division is based in another, more abstract version of the is/ought distinction itself. What one discovers regarding *philosophical* reasoning is an extensive series of pairs of competing ideas that produce the tension we ultimately see within *legal* reasoning in particular.

The sequence to be developed here, even though it is very summary, is nevertheless long and, to anyone who lacks a background in philosophy, daunting. It is not meant, however, to intimidate, or even to educate. Its purpose more modestly is to establish that philosophical thinking, abstract though it is, nevertheless has always been presented as a series of organizable normative tensions. This push-and-pull can at least give us some insight into what philosophers are arguing about. Indeed, as we progress down this list, we get closer to the normative categories most familiar to lawyer audiences.

The list is divided between, on the one hand, values that are inherent or innate—in a sense "pure" because they transcend or precede actual human circumstances—and, on the other, values that are more connected to human activity.

Values	Values in Context
A priori: Given	*A posteriori*: Experience
Passive	Active
Static	Dynamic
Innate	Observed
Kant: Noumenal	Phenomenal
Categorical	Hypothetical
Modern: Deontological	Teleological
Right	Good
Categorical	Consequential
Legal: [Substance]	[Procedure]
Legitimate	Reasonable

One particularly fundamental dichotomy in philosophy is that between *a priori* reasoning and *a posteriori* reasoning.[4] The former, in summary form, proceeds from "givens"—postulates that precede us in some way, but from which we can derive guidance or insights as we move forward. The latter is a set of conclusions we derive from experience, from our actually acting in the world rather than just perceiving it. *A priori* is therefore normative justification (ought) in its purest form, and is passive and static, while *a posteriori* is a sense of ought tinged with a broad assumptive sense of a contextual "is" in which values are being applied, and is therefore active and dynamic. It should come as no surprise, then, that legal reasoning, with its inevitable concern with actual human behavior and governance, tends most often toward the latter.

To see why, remain at this level of abstraction for a moment. Every philosophical perspective divides its reasoning between passive and active conceptions of why and how we "matter," and hence why developing sets of values matter for us. The *a priori* element in this reasoning attempts to characterize our importance or relevance not according to any physical or mental qualities we might possess, but with reference to abstract values that unavoidably attach to each of us. For example, typical normative issues here would be: Do we assume that human beings are equal in some metaphysical sense, or do our differences actually dominate our initial sense of our essence? Do we assume, before anything gets started, that human beings all have some kind of inherent worth or dignity, so that each of us will somehow "count" in the process of developing universal values? Or do we instead see worth as something that is more earned than innate, or perhaps as a quality that some humans initially possess in greater quantity than do others?

A posteriori reasoning, on the other hand, layers the active onto this inert mold. It asks: At our essence, what kind of ability do we have to respond to our circumstances? Regardless of the presence or nature of the values of equality and dignity, do we assume, based on our actual experience, that humans are basically capable of acting rationally and sensibly, or are humans instead fundamentally flawed as they interact with each other? Do we have respect for the fundamental mental capacities of humans to react to their circumstances, or do we consider those capacities suspect, because our experience suggests that humans are far from impressive?

As dissatisfyingly abstract as these contentions may be, bear in mind that in this book there will be no attempt to resolve any of these important issues. We will merely observe their existence and relevance to legal disagreements. The point is not that any particular philosophical answer to any of these issues is "best" or "correct" — it is just *available* as a position that a lawyer may espouse on behalf of a client as arguments ascend to this level. Appreciating the nuances of legal reasoning is simply a matter of being prepared.

To continue down the earlier list, another well-known dichotomous analytic struggle in our philosophical background is associated with the work of Emmanuel Kant.[5] He developed in his metaphysics the next two entries in the lists, distinguishing between the noumenal—things "in themselves," their "actual" essences—and the phenomenal—things "as experienced," the way they are imperfectly perceived by others. Although we would never be able, as imperfect humans, to bridge this gap completely and perfectly, Kant, like Aristotle,[6] emphasized *reason* as the method to move us as closely as possible from the phenomenal toward the noumenal. A corresponding outgrowth from this separation was Kant's argument about our perception of moral values themselves. Our normative duties to one another were similarly divided between what you could call a pure form and an instrumental, or contextual, form: on the one hand, "categorical" imperatives are fundamental, uncompromising commands to act as morality demands, regardless of actual consequences; on the other, "hypothetical" imperatives, are simply means to use toward achieving some moral requirement, but they are not moral demands in and of themselves.[7]

The way these esoteric categories have translated into more modern philosophical discussions is that they become the basis for the distinction between deontology[8] and teleology,[9] and their shorthand versions of "right" and "good."[10] A deontological moral theory focuses on values in and of themselves, for their own sake, regardless of teleological, actual outcomes that may transpire because of a dedication to these values. In other words, "right behavior" is privileged over "good" social and personal consequences. The most famous example of this philosophical approach is Kant's development and emphasis of his singular, most fundamental "categorical imperative"—his form of the familiar Golden Rule: "I ought never to act in such a way *that I could not also will that my maxim should become a universal law.*"[11] (what you want done to you, you must do to others). Applied rigorously, Kant acknowledged that this duty could force you to answer a question truthfully (the right thing to do) even though the result will be to reveal to bad people the location of a friend, and thereby put her in physical danger (an unfortunate not-so-good outcome). Truth (morally speaking) trumps consequences.

The classic example of a teleological political theory, on the other hand, is utilitarianism,[12] a calculus of pleasures and pains aiming to maximize the "good" in life. From this perspective, "right behavior" is in turn defined as that which moves us toward this best result. Consequences trump (moral) truth, if necessary. Our earlier discussion of economics reflects this thinking, although inappropriately: An efficient outcome will not, in and of itself, tell you what your rights should be.

A common question, then, for any political theory is whether that theory puts "good before right" or "right before good." That rather opaque distinction is captured very nicely in a hypothetical situation suggested by Ronald Dworkin, which also helps explain why this brand of normative inquiry can seem so strange and counter-intuitive to someone trying to do practical lawyering. He asks us to imagine a baking contest where the objective is to produce the "best" possible cake.[13] The odd proposition that develops here is that you must consider this contest in two very different ways, one that focuses on the cake, the other on the ingredients.

Teleological thinking (good outcomes tell you right behavior) would emphasize and reward, quite practically and reasonably, the taste and texture of the final resulting cake, with ingredients being modified and manipulated as necessary to achieve this end. Deontological reasoning (right behavior begets the acceptable social good), strangely enough, would worry instead about the ingredients themselves, for their own sakes, and let the cake have whatever taste and texture it finally happens to have. It is as if the sugar has "rights" that must be taken "seriously," no matter what the impact on the taste of the cake might be.

The latter makes no sense to anyone in the ordinary world, who would naturally assess any cake by its final resulting characteristics, not by whether the salt or sugar was given proper "respect" as the cake was being assembled. But the odd thing is that in the abstract world of values—and specifically the *legal* portion of that world—this strange kind of thinking is not only possible, it is quite relevant and respected. We will see how in the next subsection below.

A related, and also well-known, philosophical conundrum that lurks at the most basic levels of political and legal theory is simply a "chicken and egg" paradox: Which comes first, philosophically speaking: the individual or community?[14] In other words, which perspective—independence or interdependence—should be privileged in our normative thinking? Do we create our communities, or do they create us? For example, what kind of basic capability should we attribute initially to humankind—weakness or strength?[15] Do we need philosophical "help" *at all* to develop the proper substance of human rights, or can we do the job adequately on our own?

As these issues illustrate, it is difficult to imagine a political or legal theory being based wholly or exclusively on one or the other perspective. The very definition of rationality would seem to insist that both values *and* social outcomes are relevant to our thought process all the time—that "right" and "good" travel together rather than alone—although in varying combinations or proportions that will inevitably be controversial. Legal reasoning, fully understood, will certainly reflect that observation.

3. Distinguishing Categorical from Consequential

Toward the bottom of the earlier list of philosophical dichotomies, we begin to encounter the way normative distinctions are most often expressed by lawyers and policy makers to characterize their disagreements. The difference here follows directly from Kant's analysis, and correspondingly divides legal reasoning between fundamental, sometimes complementary, but sometimes competing, perspectives. One understands values as "categorical" in nature, and hence emphasizes individual rights, while the other is "consequential," emphasizing the appropriateness of social outcomes.

As the earlier list indicates, the former is deontological, determining "right" behavior by reference to pre-existing (*a priori*) so-called "first principles."[16] These are norms that are identified and imposed independent of any good "results" in society they might entail. An example would be the concept of human dignity, which is simply accepted as an appropriate normative standard. This is often what people mean, rather loosely, when they assert their "rights" to one thing or another. Their claim is meant to have some sort of immediate grounding without the need of further "proof" of appropriateness.

Consequentialism, in contrast, is correspondingly teleological, focusing for justification on the "good" *results* that are experienced from a decision or set of circumstances—like more happiness or safety or goods and services—which we know are praiseworthy because of shared human experience (*a posteriori*). This is the normative context, then, more often associated with social goals or ends, rather than individual characteristics, which in turn is conceptually closer to human "interests" rather than more substantively our "rights." Nevertheless, "rights" claims by individuals can be, and often are, based in such appeals to appropriate social outcomes—hence guaranteeing a level of confusion in all hypertextual analyses.

The question in this Chapter regarding legal reasoning is this: Which of these perspectives—pre-existing fundamental values or values derived from our experiences—will dominate the assessment of claims in a case?

To bring these observations down to earth, consider an actual legal example.

Perhaps the single easiest doctrinal illustration is the never-ending debate over the "deep," or fundamental, theory of freedom of speech:[17] Why does the Constitution guarantee this particular right? Note that you have available two immediate, but quite distinct, responses. It could be because, teleologically, freedom of speech produces a better society, all things considered: The reasoning could be that with lots of ideas out there circulating, we can compare and contrast competing propositions to determine which produce better social results and which do not, and then give legal protection to the former and deny it to the latter. Or, quite differently, we could value freedom of speech deontologically, meaning that we believe that all citizens are entitled, as a matter of individual dignity, to express themselves, whether or not what they have to say will make society better in any way or be instrumentally useful to anyone.

In turn, to make that area of law come alive, perhaps the single most celebrated actual legal controversy involving this philosophical distinction is the reasoning and result in *Smith v. Collins*.[18] The case arose from the effort by the American Nazi Party and the Ku Klux Klan to obtain a permit to hold a parade/demonstration down the main street of Skokie, Illinois—a city well-known for having a significant population of survivors of the Holocaust. What could be more offensive or socially unproductive? The officials of the city predictably rejected the application for a permit. But the Nazis and the Klan found an unlikely and rather ironic ally: the American Civil Liberties Union, which challenged the city's action, and won a significant victory for them in the federal courts. The argument by the ACLU was not that their clients had anything useful or appropriate to say; instead, it was that as citizens, they were nevertheless entitled, simply as an aspect of their citizenship within our social and political community, to the inherent human right to express themselves, even though the vast majority of the community would find their statements not just worthless, but harmful to our very sense of community in the first place. It was a courageous, relentlessly categorical/deontological, argument—that freedom of speech was based in values themselves, pure and simple, and not in any particular outcome produced by the expression. And it was an argument that cost the ACLU, in the short term, a significant chunk of its membership.[19]

Although this is a particularly dramatic example, it is by no means unusual: The constant struggle in litigation is to determine (hopefully, with the kind of "integrity" identified earlier by Prof. Dworkin) which of the contending parties possesses the requisite "rights" that will justify a ruling in its favor. The analytic question is whether this reasoning should be based on the categorical values reposed in the arguments of one party or the other, or should it be grounded in the consequences, either to these parties or to the community more generally, that will flow from one result or another? Should the "rights" possessed by Nazis prevail, or should we be most concerned with the impact on the residents of Skokie?

C. A Return to Judge Wright and Umpire Pinelli

To bring us to the end of the earlier list of philosophical tensions, and bring the analysis of hypertext within legal reasoning full circle, we return to two of this book's central examples of impressive legal reasoning: Judge Wright's decision in *Javins* and Umpire Pinelli's controversial called strike.

1. *Contrasting the Reasonable with the Legitimate*

A final set of dichotomies in the earlier lists relates the philosophical divisions to standard elements within legal reasoning. One, which we will not develop to any degree in this book (hence, the brackets around them in the lists), is the difference between substance and procedure, which is certainly well-known and often referenced, even if not always perfectly understood and clearly drawn. The doctrines or rules of "the substantive law" are often separated from their "application" in particular circumstances. We will go no further than this observation, however, because the reasoning underlying both these legal categories reflects the same elements of reasoning that are being developed in these Chapters. To return to Prof. Dworkin's observations, both will be composed of principles and rules in the kind of interrelationship we noted earlier. Both, then, will have all the legal reasoning elements of text, context, and hypertext as lawyers attempt to use them.

The other distinction, however, is quite relevant to this Chapter because it captures quite well the difference in legal analysis between categorical and consequential thinking. Here is a quick example: As we shall see in more detail in Chapter Nine on the right to privacy, a method of search conducted by the police might be prohibited simply because the context in which it is to be employed is someone's home, and the *category* of "home" will, for some legal thinkers, *by itself* trigger a range of legal protections *regardless* of any consequential benefits that the search might produce for society more generally. Or, from the opposite perspective, a possible impact on society may be considered so grave—such as an attack by terrorists—that certain freedoms ordinarily enjoyed without limitation are believed appropriately curtailed. Although not employed with perfect consistency, the usual reference in legal situations to these contrasting approaches is that the categorical argument involves a "legitimate" claim to a particular judicial result, while a consequential argument involves a "reasonable" claim.

Neither of these approaches is, however, *as a matter of legal reasoning*, necessarily to be privileged over the other. Either could have been employed in the *Javins* case, for example, to justify a result in favor of *either* party. In the circumstance of a landlord who seeks to evict, or extract money from, a tenant who has failed to pay rent (indeed, admits readily to having failed to pay rent), Judge Wright could have reasoned at this hypertextual level with Dworkinian integrity in several different ways, any of which would have been appropriate efforts at putting the law of residential leases in its best light:

- *categorical; tenant wins:* (the actual approach and result in *Javins*) emphasize the categorical rights to human dignity possessed by the tenant not to be subjected to inhumane treatment by a powerful landowner, and thus view the tenant as never having actually "agreed" to live in squalor; or

- *categorical; landlord wins:* emphasize the fundamental property rights of the landlord, which requires respect for the lease agreed to by the tenant that gave the tenant the right to be on the premises, and that document imposed on the tenant the responsibility to pay rent; or

- *consequential; tenant wins:* emphasize that a ruling for the tenant would force improvements to be made in the premises available to renters generally, thus also improving the stock of rental housing, and thus in turn improving overall social circumstances; or

- *consequential; landlord wins:* focus on the consequences to the immediate or larger community in which these parties interact, concluding that a ruling in favor of the tenants would cause rents to rise and the housing stock to shrink, while a ruling for the landlord would maintain stability in the housing market, thus benefiting the social context appropriately.[20]

Or, a court could mix elements of several or all of these approaches.

But it is important to note that this focus on Judge Wright's thinking is only a piece of the legal picture that needs to be drawn here. The larger point is that lawyers arguing before Judge Wright should have been able to identify this range of possible approaches to the dispute, and then correspondingly been able to organize their contentions in court to the best advantage of their clients, anticipating as necessary arguments that might be made by the other side.

In the *Javins* case itself, Judge Wright, in holding for the tenant and imposing the implied warranty of habitability, employed primarily the categorical perspective in the tenant's favor, although he seemed to assume that positive consequences would also follow in the local low-income housing market more generally. Very important for present analytic purposes, he stated that the lease must be interpreted with reference to the "legitimate" expectations of the parties—meaning the expectations of a person entitled to a categorical sense of human dignity—who is seeking decent shelter, rather than a farmer seeking land to plow. The key here, though, is this: Judge Wright did not need any "proof" on this fundamental point of judicial orientation. He did not need or expect testimony of any sort from Ms. Javins herself about her mental state when she signed the lease—that is, what her "actual" expectations might have been at the time. That information was now irrelevant, because he was *not* concerned with whether she, or the landlord for that matter, was acting or thinking "reasonably." Judge Wright determined that the tenant was simply *entitled* to refuse to pay rent as a matter of, quite simply, values rather than facts.

2. Combining Context and Hypertext

Now things *really* get complicated. More is going on in Judge Wright's assessment of the factual and legal situation in *Javins* than just different approaches to values that might be employed. He is evidently also, and simultaneously, applying any relevant values at different "scales" of reference: Is the key here the values to be associated with Ms. Javins herself or her particular landlord, or the values attributable to the *community more generally*— tenants as a group, or landlords as a group, or the wider community of Washington, D.C.?

This additional step obviously links us back to the preceding Chapter's focus on context: We noted there that legal reasoning could divide itself between focusing on factual distinctions or legal distinctions, and that both would be assessed by reference to different "scales" of analysis, from micro to macro. Adding hypertext to the mix, we now realize that legal reasoning can quite straightforwardly produce, for *any* case, four different analytical perspectives, as shown in Figure 7.2.

Note how daunting this picture is: *Each* of these perspectives can be the basis for a ruling in favor of *either* of the parties. The point here—to emphasize it once again—is *not* that the process of legal reasoning will generate any particular result, but that it can generate a *range* of legitimate outcomes. But most important: That range can be identified and predicted *in advance*. Appreciating that fact is the key to "sophisticated" lawyering.

The same observations can be made, although more tentatively, concerning Prof. Gould's essay, as he skillfully mixes context and hypertext to produce a desired result, and make it look eminently appropriate. Beyond the circumstances of the World Series game itself, values certainly matter critically to his defense of Pinelli's call, for he invokes nothing less than "justice" to vindicate the umpire—indeed, a sense of justice grounded in our sense of individual accomplishment, which he in turn links to our deepest Amer-

Figure 7.2

		MICRO	MACRO
CATEGORICAL		*Values* connected to the *parties* are key (e.g., Ms. Javins' "dignity; OR her landlord's right to the sanctity of contractual obligations)	*Values* associated with the *community* are key (e.g., tenants seek something more than just a place to "exist"; OR landlords have established a market based on time-honored "property rights"
	HYPERTEXT		
CONSEQUENTIAL		The *impact* on the *parties* is the key (e.g., Ms. Javins should not have to live in squalor; OR her landlord should not suddenly be forced to operate a business without cash-flow	The *impact* on the larger *community* is key (e.g., tenants will be assured that the available housing stock will not be disgusting; OR landlords will not be burdened with new responsibilities that will cause them to leave the market, and hence make the housing shortage for low-income tenants worse
		MICRO	MACRO
			CONTEXT

ican political justification of "democracy." But where did this remarkable normativity come from, and what is its nature and structure? Unfortunately, Gould only asserts these values and their relevance rather than trying to prove the point, so we will have to do some speculating and filling here to round out the argument.

Gould seems rather obviously to emphasize the categorical over the consequential. His argument is apparently that the unique circumstances of that particular game combine with the unique virtues of dignity and human struggle to produce a clearly justified outcome. The values critical to him do in fact seem to be rooted in democracy: He asserts, indeed emphasizes, that the event must be viewed from the perspective of the belief within political theory that "*single* acts of greatness are intrinsic spurs to democracy"—that is, that our most basic normative assumption is that "rule by the people" is justified in our minds by our abiding assumption (indeed, our abiding faith) that *anyone* among us is capable of a heroic act. Equality, then, upon which democracy is based, is ironically, but powerfully, rooted in the *un*equal: individual behavior worthy of praise and admiration. Thus, it is important that the pitcher of this perfect game is not a great baseball star, but an ordinary Joe called upon to produce a moment of brilliance. In this singularity of extraordinary pressure, the "law" of baseball—to be decided by the umpire, not by a jury of players or fans or anyone else—would *have* to be, would it not, that the batter must "swing at anything close." Just as Gould says, "[t]ruth is a circumstance, not a spot."

Now we can see all the factors in Prof. Gould's reasoning come into play. And it is, I freely acknowledge, unavoidably complicated:

- The definition of a strike depends upon separating the physical facts from the normative values at stake;

- those values must in turn be assessed within the proper context, which is micro in character, focusing on the extraordinary event of this particular World Series game and its final inning when the law of baseball itself may undergo a shift;

- and in this narrow and unusual circumstance, the hypertextual values that are key are therefore not consequential in nature, because the ramifications of the umpire's call will necessarily be quite limited in scope and future relevance to the game of baseball, but instead categorical, as Gould links the event to our most fundamental moral and political norms.

And by being so complicated, this result is by no means inevitable. Reasonable people could disagree at each analytical point along this journey. For example, at the final stage of invoking fundamental values, one could argue that Gould's connection between democracy and heroism is misplaced. A different approach is illustrated in Berthold Brecht's play *The Life of Galileo*,[21] in which one of Galileo's students criticizes him for succumbing to the pressure of the Catholic Church to recant his scientific findings in exchange for his life. The student laments, "Pity the land that has no heroes."[22] Galileo responds: "Pity the land in need of heroes."[23]

Perhaps this is the problem with Gould's praise of Pinelli: It misapprehends, one could say, the very nature of our civil society, which depends for its deep justification not on the occasional extraordinary act by impressive individuals, but on the vast bulk of ordinary behavior by people humble enough to expect to be treated with equal dignity no matter what the circumstances. Thus, the focus of our attention at that World Series game should not be on Don Larsen, the glorified pitcher, but Dale Mitchell, the forgotten pinch-hitter, who is entitled to just as much respect.

The point here is not, however, that Prof. Gould got it wrong, for the analysis in this book does not depend on any particular conclusion about Pinelli's call. The point instead is, as it has been from the beginning, simply the reasoning behind our assessment of the call. With careful attention to the elements of that process, one should be able to see more clearly the layers within the thinking of Prof. Gould or Judge Wright or anyone else presenting a "legal" argument. The matter at stake is therefore only indirectly the presentation of sophisticated legal *answers*; it is more directly the effort to develop the sophisticated legal *questions* that lie "under" or "before" those answers.

At its most practical and instrumental, then, this book is about listening to an opponent's contentions carefully to identify spots of weakness and strength. It is the essence of "thinking like a lawyer."

3. The Final Step: Dimensions as Variables

But as you examine the tidy, symmetrical four-part box in this Chapter, you can predict the next analytic complication, can you not? Doesn't the neatness of this depiction seem rather convenient? It is. In fact, the situation for legal reasoning is even *more* daunting.

Recall that both the dimensions that constitute this box—context and hypertext—are *variables*, not simply two-part entities. We have focused so far on the major and most obvious subdivisions within them—for context, the split between micro and macro facts; for hypertext, the separation between categorical and consequential values. But these distinctions are not either-or. For example, the "fact pyramid" depiction in Chapter Six illustrated the *gradual* move from very specific and narrow facts to much more general and inclusive circumstances. And there is similarly no requirement that one's normative thinking be *only* deontological or *only* teleological. It is not only possible but quite reasonable and predictable to imagine that people worry about both simultaneously, and to varying degrees. A well-known example comes from discussions of so-called "threshold deontology,"[24] where you have a categorical aversion and opposition to torture, but you capture a terrorist who can tell you, with a little enhanced interrogation, where a nuclear device is hidden in a major city. Extraordinary consequences might overwhelm your ordinary sense of individual rights.

Hence, the last steps in attempting to structure these elements within legal reasoning is to imagine the four segments of Figure 7.2 as revealing *not* hermetically sealed segments, but instead four areas within a larger field of *many* possible results that these elements can produce, as shown in Figure 7.3:

Figure 7.3

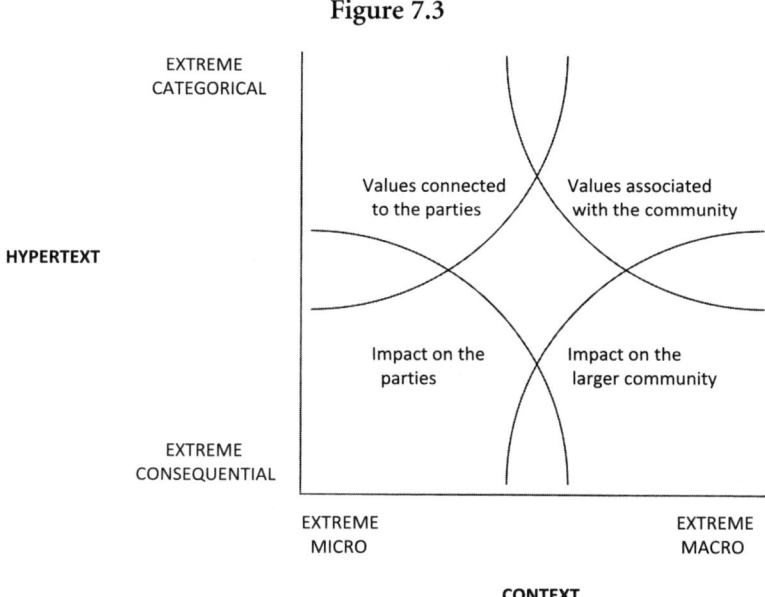

The insight here is that one's legal reasoning can, and probably does, have a kind of background anchor to it: You might have an *initial* inclination to approach a legal controversy from one of the four areas, but you then consider different mixes of perspectives to move yourself from one area within the field to others.

I would observe further that both the four-part box and this more complicated graphic depiction also illustrate the distinction that is so often noted between law practice and law teaching. For a practicing lawyer, the task is to travel around the full range of these reasoning approaches in search of the best version for vindicating a client's interests. For an academic trying to make a name for herself, one convenient way to do so is to stake out a position within the array of possibilities (and often the more extreme the better), announce to the scholarly world that yours is indeed the "correct" position, and then defend yourself constantly from others who support different perspectives. You could imagine, for example, a vast, contentious literature that might develop around Prof. Gould's essay, if scholars took it seriously. But the only way to be able to sort through and assess the various positions being espoused would be to unpack the analytic assumptions at the root of competing claims to analytic truth.

Notes

1. If you need a general reference to economics and economic theory see, e.g., N. GRE-GORY MANKIW, PRINCIPLES OF ECONOMICS (7th ed. 2015).

2. Moral philosophy is usually equated with "ethics," and both terms are often used as labels for a wide range of inquiries into values. *See generally* Kai Nielsen, *Problems of Ethics, in* 3 ENCYCLOPEDIA OF PHILOSOPHY 117, 118 (Paul Edwards ed., 1967); Raziel Abelson & Kai Nielsen, *History of Ethics, in* 3 ENCYCLOPEDIA OF PHILOSOPHY, *supra* note 2, at 81. This term has, of course, been applied much more broadly and loosely in a number of contexts. *See, e.g.,* Abelson & Nielsen, *supra* note 2, at 108–12; Nielsen, *supra* note 2, at 116–19. *See also* ETHICAL THEORY: AN ANTHOLOGY (Russ Schafer-Landau ed., 2007).

3. One useful summary of this category is as follows:

> The history of political philosophy is the succession of notions about the actual and proper organization of men into collectivities and the discussion of those notions. It is philosophical in character, because it is concerned with obedience and justice as well as with description; the persistent preoccupation of political philosophers has been the definition of justice and of the attitude and arrangements which should create and perpetuate justice.

Peter Laslett & Phillip Cummings, *History of Political Philosophy, in* 6 ENCYCLOPEDIA OF PHILOSOPHY, *supra* note 2, at 387. *See also* ARGUING ABOUT POLITICAL PHILOSOPHY (Matt Zwolinski ed., 2009).

4. On this distinction, see generally Bruce Russell, *A Priori Justification and Knowledge, in* STANFORD ENCYCLOPEDIA OF PHILOSOPHY (Edward N. Zalta ed., 2012).

5. *See generally* Michael Rohlf, *Immanuel Kant, in* STANFORD ENCYCLOPEDIA OF PHILOSOPHY, *supra* note 3.

6. *See generally* Christopher Shields, *Aristotle, in* STANFORD ENCYCLOPEDIA OF PHILOSOPHY, *supra* note 3.

7. IMMANUEL KANT, GROUNDWORK FOR THE METAPHYSICS OF MORALS 215–218 (Arnulf Zweig trans., Thomas E. Hill Jr. & Arnulf Zweig eds., Oxford Univ. Press 2002). The distinction between categorical and hypothetical has been explained thus:

> The imperatives of morality command categorically, unlike those of skill or prudence, which have only hypothetical force … A rule of skill or counsel of prudence bids us take certain steps if we wish to attain a certain end—good health or overall happiness, for example. There is no "if" about a command of morality: it bids me act in a certain way whether I want to or not, and without regard to any result the action may bring about. It represents a course of conduct as unconditionally necessary, not just necessary because it conduces to a certain end.

W.H. Walsh, *Immanuel Kant, in* 4 ENCYCLOPEDIA OF PHILOSOPHY, *supra* note 2, at 318.

8. *See* SIR W. DAVID ROSS, FOUNDATIONS OF ETHICS 114–145 (1939); SIR W. DAVID ROSS, THE RIGHT AND THE GOOD 1–15, 65–74 (1930).

9. *Id.*

10. This distinction is also developed at length in the more modern classic, JOHN RAWLS, A THEORY OF JUSTICE 28, 32, 446–48. That book is discussed at other points in this book as well.

11. KANT, *supra* note 7, at 203 (emphasis in original).

12. Utilitarianism, which understands "good" in terms of maximizing individual and aggregate "utility," or happiness, is usually associated with the work of John Stuart Mill. *See* JOHN S. MILL, ON LIBERTY (Elizabeth Rarport, ed., Hackett Publ'g Co. 1978) (1859); UTIL-ITARIANISM AND OTHER ESSAYS 272 (Alan Ryan ed., Penguin Books 1987) (1863). While the rights that constituted liberty were important to Mill, the reason they were important (and the reason that particular rights were particularly important) was ultimately a func-tion of their ability to maximize utility. *Id.*

13. Ronald Dworkin, *Why Efficiency?*, 8 HOFSTRA L. REV. 563, 564 (1980).

14. This distinction is at the heart of the different philosophical perspectives offered by liberalism, based in (and focused on) respect for individual autonomy, and non-liberalism, based in (and demanding) respect for connectedness.

15. This question is central to the growing school of philosophical thought labeled "vul-nerability." Its principal proponent is Prof. Martha Fineman, whose initial work on that topic is noted in Chapter 3. *See supra* ch. 3 note 12.

16. This idea is, of course, related to, and often identical with, the topics of metaphysics and the *a priori/a posteriori* distinction noted earlier. *See, e.g.,* F.H. Bradley, *F.H. Bradley, in* STANFORD ENCYCLOPEDIA OF PHILOSOPHY (2013); Bertrand Russell, *Russell's Metaphysics, in* INTERNET ENCYCLOPEDIA OF PHILOSOPHY, http://www.iep.utm.edu/russ-met/.

17. For various explanations and justifications for freedom of speech see *supra* ch. 5 note 16.

18. *See* PHILIPPA STRUM, WHEN THE NAZIS CAME TO SKOKIE: FREEDOM FOR SPEECH WE HATE (1999); Smith v. Collin, 439 U.S. 916 (1978) (Blackmun, J., and White, J., dis-senting) (Skokie had a population of approximately 70,000 persons, a majority of which were Jewish. Of these Jewish residents, a number were survivors of World War II persecu-tion. In March 1977 the National Socialist Party of America publicly announced plans to hold an assembly in front of the Skokie Village Hall).

19. When it decided to take on the litigation in 1977, the ACLU had 200,000 members nationwide. *See* STRUM, *supra* note 18, at 23. Toward the end of the year, as the litigation dragged on and garnered much attention in the press, the ACLU had lost about 30,000 members, or 15 percent of its membership. *Id.* at 82.

20. For a classic discussion of this range of possibilities using general tenets of economic analysis, see, *e.g.,* Bruce Ackerman, *Regulating Slum Housing Markets on Behalf of the Poor: Of Housing Codes, Housing Subsidies and Income Redistribution Policy*, 80 YALE L.J. 1093 (1971).

21. Bertold Brecht, *The Life of Galileo* (Desmond I. Vesey trans., 1960).

22. *Id.* at 107.

23. *Id.* at 108.

24. *See* Michael S. Moore, *Torture and the Balance of Evils*, 25 ISR. L. REV. 280 (1989). For a critical response, see Larry Alexander, *Deontology at the Threshold*, 37 SAN DIEGO L. REV. 893 (2000).

Chapter Eight

The Challenge of Subtext: Considering the Judiciary's Role in the "Game" of Legal Life

The final element in the schematic image of legal reasoning developed in this book is particularly interesting because, although fundamental to the lawyer's craft, it is the least recognized among non-lawyers. It most often operates below the surface of popular discussions of legal controversies, just as it has throughout much of this book. Not surprisingly, then, it occupies the spot at the bottom of the summary diagram in Chapter Four. This is not because it is the least important of all the elements in this topic. To the contrary, it is critical to the social institution of the legal system. It is the last topic in this book's sequence simply because it arises as a serious additional issue in only the most contentious, most politically charged disagreements.

In these tough situations, the ordinary impressions of lawyering are specially challenged. The vast bulk of the population readily understands that legal guidance and constraints are expressed in words that lawyers manipulate as they can; they expect consistency within those pronouncements through "like cases being treated alike"; and they would accept the idea that any legal event worthy of general attention implicates basic (although quite vague) values of good and bad, fair and unfair, dignity and indignity, justice and injustice, and so on. But in high-profile, controversial matters, another issue is added that ordinarily escapes attention: *who*—institutionally—should be reaching, pronouncing, and imposing legal decisions and issuing legal guidance?

Although people recognize that "law" exists, whatever it may be, they seldom appreciate the relevance of the multifaceted *system* that surrounds and grounds it. Legal reasoning, however, can never put this question completely aside. Appreciating the political subtext within which all the other elements are operating helps put the entire process into sharper perspective. In many ways, subtext is what we mean by, not just "the law," but the "rule of law" as a social ideal.

191

Shining a light on this issue will also reveal a limitation in this book's discussion of the topic of legal reasoning. Throughout the previous Chapters, and indeed in the bulk of this one, the assumption has been that the facts in any given legal matter have been established to the satisfaction of the lawyers and judges who will now use their legal reasoning prowess to frame contexts and invoke appropriate values to make effective arguments about proper decisional outcomes. This is the standard picture of the appellate legal process. Yet regarding this fundamental element of the facts of any matter, there is another key player to which we have given no attention: juries. The final Part of this Chapter will address this point, and give at least some explanation for its minimal coverage.

A. From Law to the Rule of Law

The reason for the institutional gap in popular attention to legal matters is quite simply the fact that the American legal system has long ago blurred its institutional lines—its divisions of authoritative responsibility. *Javins* is indeed a wonderful example: A court announces a decision based on its seat-of-the-pants sense of general social facts characterizing the landlord-tenant situation—unequal bargaining power, low-income housing shortages, and the like—all without the benefit of hearings like those conducted by legislative bodies. And it renders a legal decision about the nature of leases in this jurisdiction as profound and far-reaching as anything a legislature could enact. By the same token, legislatures and administrative agencies can grant or impose micro-level advantage and disadvantage on persons, treating them much like litigants petitioning for judicial relief. And *all* of these actors within the legal system accomplish these feats of governance using the same set of elements thus far developed here: by giving words meaning; by establishing relevant resemblances and differences; and by invoking basic values like individual dignity, alleviating social unrest, protecting natural resources, you name it.

This topic is indeed so important that it will require two Chapters to do it justice (so to speak), and even then only incompletely. This Chapter will focus on the critical, and often controversial, role of the judiciary as an independent force within the legal system—precisely what Justice Roberts was worrying about when he made his comments about "just calling the balls and strikes." The reasoning required of lawyers often must confront how best to argue to a judge not simply the meaning of words or the comparison of facts or the substance of competing values, but the nature of the judge's role *itself* in considering these points. The arguments can become, remarkably enough, something like "Judge, behave!"—meaning "behave consistently with the rule of law."

Chapter Ten will then turn to the murky relationship between courts, on the one hand, and, on the other, legislatures and administrative agencies that have addressed an issue through statutes and regulations. When these pronouncements prove to be (as they often are) sloppy or unclear to any degree, the decision makers charged with fixing the mess is the judiciary. The additional question in that Chapter will therefore be what the character and challenges of legal reasoning become in the specific legal realm of "statutory interpretation."

For purposes of the present Chapter, however, a remarkably convenient illustration of the subtle depths of institutional subtext is once again supplied by Prof. Gould's essay. The key, as noted much earlier, is the way his five paragraphs end, which, all things considered, is quite surprising. Having mounted a spirited and impressive defense of Umpire Pinelli's called third strike, Gould nevertheless acknowledges that the famed umpire returned to the locker room after the game "and cried." If, however, according to Gould, Pinelli was so "correct" in that call—having indeed reached a uniquely "truthful moment"—why would he do so? Has Gould just been kidding throughout his essay, knowing all along that Pinelli was in fact quite wrong in making that call, or is there a final twist to the story that we need to add?

B. Why Did Pinelli Cry? Psychological vs. Institutional Explanations

Returning to the example law school discussion in Chapter One, students in my class have been split on the explanation for Pinelli's emotional reaction after the game. Most seem to believe that Gould is correct in his assessment of the appropriateness of Pinelli's call, and that Pinelli knew that he had decided correctly. The explanation for the tears, they conclude, comes from the extraordinary pressure of the moment—that fabled event of the only perfect game in World Series history, and likely the only one ever to be pitched—which simply overcame him when he had a chance to pause and reflect. It was a release, pure and simple.

Others, however, believe that Pinelli broke down because he knew that, because of the pressure of the moment, he had gotten it wrong. He had called a strike not because the pitch was "in fact" a strike, but because, under intense pressure, he made the call he *wanted* to make—to give Don Larsen his perfect game—but not the call the rules of baseball directed him to make. Thus, he had failed in his responsibilities as an umpire, and indeed failed when it mattered with particular gravity.

From this perspective, his only defense, of course, would be that he believed, along with Gould, that the pitch *should* be a strike—that Larsen somehow *deserved* the strike call, and deserved it more than the batter deserved a physically accurate call. But that convenient move into hypertext isn't consistent with his tears. Perhaps, then, he recognized the thinness of this value-based façade, and was simply, and appropriately, ashamed for having made such an inaccurate call in front of the entire baseball world.

Unfortunately, neither of these competing explanations—the pressure of the moment or the acknowledgement of shame—can ever be "proven" to anyone's satisfaction, which means that the issue will forever remain frustratingly in doubt. But this is not where the matter should be left. Another perspective is possible that, while no more certain descriptively or psychologically, does provide a kind of analytic satisfaction—a version of closure, if you will—on our connection of Umpire Pinelli to the world of judicial decision-making.

Rather than attempt to explain Pinelli's tears in the limited form of either emotional catharsis or embarrassment for a specific mistake, we could (and should) connect his response to our foundations of context and hypertext—but do so by blending them into another, separate element within our topic of legal reasoning. In doing so, we will, at long last, return to, and appreciate in a new way, the remark made by Justice John Roberts, noted way back in Chapter One, about the judge's job being merely to "call the balls and strikes."

Pinelli's reaction may, for our purposes, be understood best not as a reflection of *personal* angst, but of a larger and more profound *professional* regret on his part: His tears could reflect his realization that the key importance of his call was *not* whether it was "right" or "wrong" in any sense we have thus far identified—that is, whether the pitch was a strike according to the baseball rule book (text), or because the social or cultural circumstances of the game (context) said so, or because the deeper values of the game (hypertext) justified the label. Instead, and quite differently, he may have been—and perhaps should have been—upset when he realized that the call was *institutionally* questionable, concerning *his role* in the game as an umpire. From this perspective of "subtext," the issue in his mind would not have been the narrow one of strikes and balls as such, but more profoundly the concept of *umpiring itself*—the nature of the difficult task of decision-making he was required to accomplish. Perhaps he realized that, despite the comfort offered by Prof. Gould's defense of his call, he had made an error *independent of* (perhaps even deeper than) the call itself.

What he might have regretted was his violation, as almost he alone could have perceived it, of his function as a judicial-type arbiter within baseball disputes. It was not his eyesight or his reasoning that had gone astray. Instead, it was his mishandling of his professional status as a decision-maker operating with some degree of discretion[1] that had caused him in turn to affect the game inappropriately—in fact, to *redefine* the game itself. The dislocation he may have perceived he had introduced was not, then, linguistic or circumstantial or normative—it was *political*.

To perceive this important point appropriately, we must first connect our baseball analogy directly to legal circumstances. To do so, we return to another source previously examined—H.L.A. Hart—whose work provides a convenient analytical bridge linking the difficult circumstances faced by Umpire Pinelli and those confronted by judges on a regular basis.

C. "Scorer's Discretion" and a Positivist Approach to Judging

Early in Prof. Hart's argument about the proper way to imagine how legal systems develop sociologically, he suggested an example drawn, conveniently for us, from sports.[2] Imagine a game, like baseball, that is being played "informally" by, say, a group of kids on a sandlot. It has players that can claim they are playing the game because they have a set of shared rules in their heads that define the nature of the game—what they are trying to accomplish within this competitive and cooperative environment, what actions are permitted and forbidden to the players, and so on. The game can continue as such, and be enjoyed, as long as the players simply know, and agree among themselves, what these rules and expectations are. Disputes about violations of the rules will certainly arise from time to time, but as long as the players can work things out (again simply among themselves), the game will be able to proceed.

To this familiar, uncomplicated picture Prof. Hart then adds another element, and poses a challenging question: What would happen to the game if an "official scorer"[3] of some kind became the arbiter of issues involving the game's rules and their application? Does the nature of the game itself stay the same, or does it change significantly, shifting from its original "baseball" to what Hart called "scorer's discretion"?[4] Surely it is *supposed* to remain the same game, with the same rules and expectations, but with only the addition of an improved method of resolving disputes.

Hart's point, of course, was that this common-sense observation was consistent with, and helped confirm, the positivist perspective about the nature of a society's legal system: Just as the most basic rules of—and intrinsic values within—a game develop and are accepted among the players *before* there is a referee or umpire designated to help make them behave properly, so too the most basic values characterizing a *political community* develop *before* there are any judges designated to resolve disputes. In Prof. Hart's well-known terminology noted in Chapter Three, "primary rules of obligation" (social basics like rules against murder, theft, and so on) precede the invention of "secondary rules" (rules for the legal system) that help resolve disputes about the nature and application of the primary rules—that is, the rules that guide umpires and judges as they make decisions. "Official scorers," then, do not—and should not—normatively transform the game; instead, they simply inherit whatever game they have been instructed to observe and help regulate.

Judges, by the same token, from Hart's perspective, inherit the legal system that preceded them. They do not have an independent normative foundation from which to impose improvements upon the society that has designated them as decision-makers. The moral content, or lack of such content, of any of the rules of their society should not matter to any judge doing his or her job appropriately. The rules are simply the rules, to be applied to the facts as straightforwardly as humanly possible, no matter how uncomfortable or unfortunate those directions may be from the judge's own personal perspective. Perhaps the most extreme version of this approach, not surprisingly rendered from the perspective of a statutory-based civil law system[5] (rather than caselaw-based common law), comes from Montesquieu: Judicial judgments are to be "fixed to such a degree that they are never anything but a precise text of the law."[6] Judges were "only the mouth that pronounces the words of the law, inanimate beings who can moderate neither its force or its rigor."[7] Thus judicial power becomes "invisible and null."[8]

This would seem, then, to be the perspective offered by then-Judge Roberts in his remark during his confirmation hearings: He is simply a good, old-fashioned Hartian positivist, understanding the task of judging as letting the game of life proceed as it will, making "calls" occasionally in disputed, close moments when an independent eye is necessary, but otherwise not insinuating himself into the contest. "Life," then, in all its social, political, legal, and moral complication, remains the same, basic game it was before he arrived on the scene. No independent element of discretion has been introduced to alter it meaningfully.

This would seem to be a happy, comfortable, and above all, *politically legitimate* resolution of the issue. But our questions here now become these: Is this reasoning, and positivist defense, available to *Pinelli*—and by extension, to Justice Roberts? Did Pinelli's called third strike permit baseball to remain baseball, or had he transformed it, even for just a moment, into "score's discretion"? Had he injected himself into the game as an independent force or variable that made him a "player" as well? But most important of all: If we conclude that he had indeed become a part of the game, is that necessarily *wrong*, as the positivist approach seems to maintain? Or could it have been profoundly *correct*, as Prof. Gould certainly concludes?

D. Perspectives on the Subtext of Political Institutions

At this point, you should not be surprised to learn that (at least) three possible approaches to this issue are immediately evident, each based on the analytic perspectives developed earlier: text, context and hypertext. And, as they progress as assessments of Pinelli's call from harshest to kindest, they offer different explanations for Pinelli's tears after the game. In turn, they each offer different assessments of whether the "scorer's discretion" analysis is available as a defense for then-Judge Roberts' remark.

1. Pinelli and the Supposed Primacy of Baseball's "Text"

First, perhaps Pinelli realized that he had indeed erred in a profoundly political way because, by failing to apply the rule of "strikes" in the manner contemplated by baseball's rule book, he had altered the game itself—indeed, in its most celebrated and venerated moments in a World Series game. He had, in effect, transformed the game from one of exacting, consistent expectations and demonstrated skill, to one of approximation ("close is good enough"), as well as suddenly uneven demands ("batters must swing defensively, rather than pitchers must pitch accurately"), and indeed endorsed paltry performance ("given all your earlier good pitches, I'll let you get away with a few bad ones"). From this perspective, Prof. Gould's defense of Pinelli on the basis of the supposed unwritten rule that "batters must swing at anything close in a big game" was actually nothing more than a thinly veiled rationalization for his error, and an excuse probably based in Gould's biased attitude toward the outcome of the game.

Thus, perhaps Pinelli thought the call made *him* look biased as well: Maybe he had always harbored favoritism toward the Yankees, and it emerged most evidently in that particular moment; or maybe he had, over the course of the game, developed a sympathy for Larsen personally because of the pitcher's superior performance up to that point. In either event, despite Gould's attempt at praise, Pinelli's tears of embarrassment as an official gone wrong would be both explainable and justifiable.

And, as noted above, perhaps this would be Judge, now Justice, Roberts' perspective as well. His theory of judging, at its most fundamental, could be that judges should conscientiously avoid interfering with or intruding into the social milieu they have been asked to *assess* by introducing into that contested setting elements *extrinsic* to it. They should instead focus on only the text of the rules they must apply, making that element *the* singular key to their decision-making. Admittedly, the other analytic factors of context and hypertext— of circumstances and values—may sneak into the decision-making process simply because the judge is human, and thus might consider in some background, unconscious sense whether the specialness of the game or any of the players should make any sort of difference, or whether the game has an underlying normative dimension that would justify a modification of the usual rules. But these elements would be perceived as the inappropriate interlopers they are. The analysis should instead remain focused on the consistent application of the pre-existing, announced rules of the game. The "life" of baseball, if you will, should not be altered just because umpires have been hired to call the balls and strikes.

Examining the opinions[9] of then-Judge Roberts reveals much evidence of this approach. When confronted with the problem of defining an important word or phrase in a text—a federal statute, given the Court on which he was serving—Judge Roberts never launched into the kind of creative, multi-factored analysis pursued by Judge Wright in *Javins*. To the contrary, if a text did not reveal its own meaning on its face, he regularly simply turned to another text: a dictionary. For example, to define "action for money damages"[10] and "complaint,"[11] he turned to BLACK's LAW DICTIONARY; to define "divert," he employed BLACK's and the OXFORD ENGLISH DICTIONARY.[12] The fact that dictionaries can have disagreements among themselves would not seem to matter much, because whatever differences they may have would nevertheless introduce less flexibility and controversy into the situation than a judge turning to sources as broad and unanchored as context or values.

In circumstances in which neither "plain text" nor a dictionary would (relatively) settle the matter of meaning, Judge Roberts would, in statutory interpretation circumstances, turn to the traditional limiting factor of the statute's "purpose."[13] Although this would seem to open a door to a much wider and richer inquiry, Judge Roberts never found any serious difficulty in divining Congress's direction. Even though a reference to "purpose" would necessarily send us outside the strict confines of "text"—which would suggest disconcertingly that "context" and "hypertext" would inevitably seep into the analysis—by focusing on *Congress's* supposed purpose, any circumstances or values that might be invoked to give meaning to any words would be *Congress's*, not his. No significant independent inquiry on his part would be necessary.

Similarly, Judge Roberts certainly acknowledged in a couple of cases[14] that the words of a statute could indeed be broad and ambiguous, leading to challenges in their interpretation. The explanation for this phenomenon lay again in the concept of legislative purpose, for Congress had apparently meant just that: a breadth of discretionary results: "The fact that a statute can be applied in situations not expressly anticipated by Congress does not demonstrate ambiguity, it demonstrates breadth."[15] And "The Supreme Court has consistently instructed that statutes written in broad, sweeping language should be given broad, sweeping application."[16] But in both these instances, this looseness in the law did not trouble him, for the discretion created by the statute did not apply to *him* (meaning the judiciary), but to administrative officials who would use this breadth of authority to create and apply regulations that would fill in these "gaps" in the law. Hence, *his* "call" remained easy: The question was only whether *others* had discretion and had exercised it legitimately. Perhaps *their* judgment calls would now reach out beyond text to context and hypertext, but that was equally untroubling because Congress had implicitly endorsed that approach for these non-judicial actors.

None of these examples would seem to be of much comfort to Umpire Pinelli, however. Baseball's rulebook text on strikes seems rather clear, with no discretionary breadth. Dictionaries will not add anything to the analysis. A resort to purpose (whose, exactly?) would seem disingenuous and self-serving. And there is no one to whom Pinelli could delegate the call who might be able legitimately to exercise the discretion he so much seems to want to apply. Judge Roberts' approach, then, for Pinelli would lead to nothing but the conclusion that the umpire simply got it wrong, period. Tears of professional embarrassment would indeed be appropriate.

To avoid this harsh conclusion—to supply any other, kinder explanations for Pinelli's emotional catharsis—we must therefore employ other elements of legal reasoning: We must develop more carefully the "is" and "ought" of Pinelli's *political* role in the game. Perhaps alternative perspectives are available through viewing Pinelli's role *not* as *extrinsic* to baseball—that is, as somehow outside this milieu—but as *intrinsic* to it—that is, as directly part of, and necessary to, the game itself. That will require resort to context and hypertext, either of which can nevertheless be the source of angst leading to tears.

2. *Context: Pinelli and the Ambiguity of Baseball's "Customary Law"*

As a second possibility for assessing whether Pinelli misbehaved *as an umpire*, we might become much more sympathetic to Prof. Gould's praise of the called third strike if we were able to examine much more carefully and thoroughly the *facts* of the game itself—meaning the way baseball is actually played from the sandlot to the professional ranks, and in ordinary games all the way to the World Series. We might discover (or at least conclude to our satisfaction) that Gould is correct as a psychological matter concerning the expectations of the players involved—that players do indeed anticipate in situations like that faced by Umpire Pinelli that the pitcher *does* get a break of some unknown number of inches in the strike zone. This would then allow Pinelli to root his call in what scholars of, for example, property law and international law (and indeed, what Prof. Hart would attribute as a feature of English law generally) would readily recognize as "custom:"[17] an unwritten, but nevertheless existing and legitimate, part of the "rules" of the game. The customary law of baseball might then include, just as Gould argued, this rule that "in a big game, at key moments, batters must swing at anything close."

While this certainly makes Pinelli's actions less arbitrary and more institutionally acceptable, troubling questions nevertheless linger: When does the usual definition of a strike shift? What is "close enough" to justify a strike call? Part of the job of the umpire would then seem to be to exercise the authority to decide these difficult points whenever necessary. But in the absence of widespread and articulable agreement on these points, we would seem to be back to the world of "scorer's discretion" where the game is at the mercy of the potential arbitrariness of a non-player. Baseball becomes "whatever the umpire says is baseball."

Nevertheless, this could be what the players and fans *in fact expect*: In difficult game situations, a certain amount of arbitrariness is simply unavoidable. Pinelli's call was not, then, really either right or wrong—it was just a decision he had to make where he had been given the authority to make it. The customary law of baseball, then, would be that the umpire, from time to time, would have to identify these occasional unwritten rules, perceive their relevance, and apply them at the appropriate moments.

But with such a happy defense, why would Pinelli cry after the game? Here we actually return to the favorite explanation of the law students: All the ambiguity surrounding these customs could be the basis for serious decisional angst, for difficult questions now abound. Does the supposed custom actually exist? Do players actually have this particular expectation about variations from this particular (otherwise written) rule? Did the umpire apply this variation well, and in the appropriate moment, or did he or she go too far? Or not far enough? The more that reasonable people can disagree on any of these points, the more pressure Pinelli could have felt about the weightiness of his decision—about whether he was just "calling" the game, or altering it. Emotional release in the form of tears in such a politically charged circumstance would seem quite reasonable.

In turn, that pressure could be relevant to the apparent reluctance of Justice Roberts to push his view of judging beyond the text of the rules. The search for unwritten forms of guidance is scary and dangerous, for it infuses the "official scorer" into the game in important ways that players and observers may not want or welcome. Participants may *think* they know the nature of the game they are playing (or watching), but at crucial moments, they could be wrong—and wrong in ways that they would not have been able to anticipate by reference to any rulebook. It is a matter of inadequate *notice* to the players, and therefore inappropriate.

The counterargument by a defender of Umpire Pinelli, however, would be based instead in inadequate *mindfulness*. If these players had been paying attention appropriately, they would have known about these subtle variations, and have known that they might be imposed in the blink of an eye, so nothing unfair has occurred. But it seems troubling, I think many sense, that a judge—an official *arbiter* of the rules, rather than an actual rule-*maker*—has the authority to identify, define, and apply these rules that have never otherwise been officially adopted by the relevant community.

Yet this justification for potential sudden rule-shifting—from the physical strike zone to "anything close"—does indeed seem to be inherent in Prof. Gould's assertion that baseball "truth" isn't a "spot"; it's a "circumstance." There is thus a range of truth into which Pinelli could insert himself, just as a judge can be "in the neighborhood" of justice. And an important judicial task then becomes determining the scope of that expected and accepted discretion. This exercise then becomes a good practical example of Prof. Dworkin's sense of judicial integrity, which, as depicted graphically in Chapter Six, was also an area of many decisions that a judge could claim was correctly reasoned.

If we accept this approach, then Justice Roberts' suggestion that baseball's balls and strikes are objective, clean observations, lending themselves to easy consistency, could be seen as quite disingenuous. Given our observable history of judicial struggle and frequent disagreement, it would seem quite odd for him to mean that we should simply reject the idea that judges face a range of possible decisions they could reach—that rules are rules are rules, without meaningful variation available in their application, producing singular appropriate results. It would be equally troubling if he means instead that, despite the fact that rules *can* be messy occasionally, the job of a judge is nevertheless to *pretend* that each decision is grounded in simplistic rule-book-like certainty. Both of these possible understandings of his comment would be quite inconsistent with the epistemic complexity presented in this book. Neither would seem to be a professional and political image toward which our courts should aspire. And indeed the latter approach based in phony certainty is worse, because it simply endorses judicial dishonesty.

3. Hypertext: Vindicating Pinelli Through Baseball's "Values"

A third perspective from which to determine whether Pinelli's call was an example of good or bad umpiring, in and of itself, also draws on something potentially intrinsic, rather than extrinsic, to baseball: the deeper normative values that are a constituent part of the game. Why does baseball exist, particularly at a professional level, and continue to be such an integral part of our culture? It is at least, in part, because of its celebration of athletic excellence (indeed, excellence that can be measured with the exactness of calculations to three decimal points), the individual integrity (usually) and personal investment of those who play, the teamwork that is nevertheless necessary for success, the history and continuity of the game, the strategy and intelligence that is necessary to win games at the highest levels, and so on. What is interesting here is that there seems to be an additional, subtle element that is integral—unavoidably necessary—to achieving all of these values, something beyond the players themselves, or the venues in which they play, or the fans that flock to watch: *It is the umpires.*

The key observation here is that the more "important" the game—that is, the more critical to the appreciation of the game the elements of excellence and integrity and strategy and so on become—the more the game requires an "official scorer" to become involved. Sandlot games, in other words, are one thing, while professional games are something else altogether. They are *not,* in a normative, value-laden sense, *even the same game.*

This recognition now becomes the true basis on which Pinelli's call can be either *justified* or *condemned*—not just "explained" as a rational act. The argument would be, from this hypertextual perspective, that the game of baseball itself, at this higher level, has become a game dependent on the presence, and the decision-making authority, of umpires. The values inherent in the game demand that this extra participant—even though not an actual player—be introduced to the situation. Without officials, the game cannot manifest the values it needs to remain the game we have come to respect. Thus, the game of baseball *has* become altered by the addition of "official scorers," not because the scorers have forced or remolded it into a new form of "scorer's discretion," but because, without umpires, the values of *professional* excellence and integrity and the like at this very high level of expectation cannot be adequately and appropriately appreciated and implemented.[18]

Understood in this way, umpires do, and are expected to do, much more than just "call the balls and strikes." They exist to make certain that the values that keep the game alive and well are manifested in the way the game is being played. *Part* of their responsibility would therefore obviously be to follow the narrow, technical rules of the game as articulated in the text of its official rule book—but that is *only* a part. The additional question would always be whether the particular application of any given rule in a particular context is consistent with the long-term normative health of the game, or whether a variation on the rule, widely but perhaps not perfectly perceived, would be better for the game overall.

This is apparently what Prof. Gould meant when he characterized Pinelli's call as not just respectable (as grounded in some existing "custom"), but "his finest, his most perceptive, his most truthful moment." The call was, for Gould, the vindication of the umpire's role itself. It was a reflection of an umpire carrying on the deepest, most important traditions of the game: recognizing that the key *values* of baseball could, in the right instances, determine the rules by which the game would be played. "Truth" in baseball—those normative elements that sustain it—is therefore indeed, as Gould observed, *simultaneously* a variable "circumstance" *and* unchangingly "inviolable": the former because shifting contexts matter fundamentally to the application of any value, the latter because the values remain the same even if their applications vary.

Why, then, Pinelli's tears, if he got it so right? That's precisely the problem: How would he *know*, in this pressure-packed moment, that he *had* gotten it right? With something as abstract, and undoubtedly controversial, as baseball's values at stake, how could he assure himself that he had made the correct call? Others could argue just as vociferously as Prof. Gould did that Pinelli got it exactly *wrong*: In the game's toughest moments, the job of the umpire is to apply the rules of the game as rigorously and carefully as possible. The umpire is *not* to get swept up in the emotional circumstances of the Big Game, but to remain aloof and judicious, to keep even this Game within the best traditions of the sport. The strike zone should not vary for either the pitcher or the batter, but remain relentlessly consistent, as required by baseball's values of excellence, integrity, and respect.

The tears, then, represent doubt—not about the "accuracy" of the call, but about whether it was the most appropriate, the most professional, call that could have been made. Did he have the values right, or had he done something that would hurt the game? Which values were the more important: those of the game in some general and amorphous sense, or those of treating the individual players fairly and with respect? Did others see the unique context of this World Series moment the way he did, and particularly the way that context affected the values of baseball? Would others understand and appreciate his creative, contextual, perhaps customary approach to the rule book's definition of a strike? These are difficult, worrisome issues, the kind that vindicate Soren Kierkegaard's famous, but seemingly exaggerated, observation that moments of decision are "moments of madness."[19] They are the moments when all the elements of reasoning come together—perhaps more accurately, *crash* together—simultaneously. For those who must make contested, close decisions on a regular basis, this makes for serious professional angst.

E. From Umpires to Judges: A Renewed Appreciation for Judicial Independence

Which returns us to the connection between Pinelli's plight and the debate about the nature of judging. Now the issue is fully formed, for surely this complex analysis of decision-making is controversial on several fronts when it is expanded beyond the realm of the game of baseball. It is one thing to perceive umpires as permitted—as a matter of the "political" structure of baseball—to unearth from the game they observe the values that are intrinsic and critical to it, and make judgments based thereon; it is quite another to imagine permitting judges the same range of political authority to examine society from their vantage points behind the bench to find the values that are similarly essential to civil society, and thus determine the way in which they will apply society's law to its citizens.

But this is the essential political issue: One might well argue that the role of the judiciary should be much more limited and circumspect, focused on finding facts and applying law determined by our texts. If a rule needs to be modified to handle an unusual situation more acceptably, it is up to other political actors, with more political accountability, to make that change. This is the only way to ensure that our civil life does not become a version of "scorer's discretion."

Despite the reasonable modesty of this approach to the issue, however, it fails to capture an important nuance within the debate that must be confronted. On the one hand, social life as a general proposition could certainly go on whether or not we have judges available to adjudicate disputes. As Prof. Hart observed, human interaction of all forms indeed preceded the existence of any formal judiciary. Thus, in the absence of judges, people would still buy and sell, eat and sleep, love and hate, and everything else we do. But on the other hand, could *civil life*, certainly in any modern form as we have come to understand and expect it, continue in anything like an acceptable form without the presence and participation of judicial arbiters? Would our economy still function, our interactions remain constrained, our communities continue to operate in a supportive manner, if we did not have an accepted, legitimate form of settling disputes among us? Beyond our need for police to arrest wrongdoers, do we not obviously need some guidance about the use of the police in the first place? It is hard to imagine that anyone could reasonably argue that these fundamental features of ordinary life would survive meaningfully in the absence of an established, respected, independent judiciary.[20]

The better perspective from which to view this issue of the proper judicial role is to recognize that we, as a political community, abandoned the view of a limited, myopic, super-neutral set of judicial "scorers" well over 200 years ago. The Constitution did *not* assume, as had the Articles of Confederation, that the existing, local, traditional judiciary—the kind that assisted in the assessing and settling of occasional disputes—was sufficient to address the kind of disagreements that would arise in the future. To the contrary, national-level disputes would no doubt arise, and resolving them would require a judiciary adequate to this more challenging task. Not surprisingly, then, that political entity was established by the same fundamental document as the rest of the new national government.[21]

This must mean that this country's political "game" *included* "scorers" from the very beginning—not for the purpose of imposing themselves on the game and transforming it as they pleased, but to be part and parcel of the action that would become modern life. The more challenging this game would become, the more important a thoughtful, sophisticated judiciary would be to it.

Judges, then, properly understood in their most fundamental political sense, are not simply *observers* of balls and strikes. They are instead essential to the *existence* of balls and strikes in the first place. The key proposition is therefore this: Judges do not exist as a part of modern political life to make the easy calls that make the sandlot game a bit more efficient and (perhaps) fun and satis-fying; they exist to make the frequent hard calls that our circumstances now demand for us to remain a viable civil community. The players in this game of civil life expect nothing less, for the game itself has been redefined by all of us to include the presence, and authority, of these "official scorers."

This observation, I think, gives additional perspective to the concept of ju-dicial independence[22] about which we hear from time to time—quite often from the judiciary itself. Judges are indeed not players in the drama of real life the way the rest of us are; they are referees who should be able to provide this vital function without being harassed by the players or the fans. The ability of an umpire to end a dispute by throwing a player or manager out of the game is therefore entirely appropriate and easily explained: At some point, to pre-serve the game itself, interference with the umpire's function must end, and the umpire is in fact in the best position at that moment to make that determina-tion. By the same token, judges must be able to operate from a vantage out-side the fray that produced the dispute that is before them. It is not as if they do not live in our ordinary non-judicial communities—they most certainly do. But those communities should not be able to dictate to a judge—once an issue has been brought before him or her—what the judge's assessment of the situation should be.[23]

Perhaps most daunting of all, however, is the further observation that be-cause judges are essential to the game, they are also essential to the *values* that constitute and justify the game. An important additional conclusion is there-fore unavoidable: Every judicial decision will be relevant in some way to the val-ues that are inherent in civil life, and the only question becomes whether judges acknowledge that fact or attempt to hide from it.

The fact that hypertext permeates the legal process does *not* mean, how-ever, that these values are now clear and uncontroversial and readily available for reference in every judicial decision. Quite the contrary, the only point here is that moral and political values are unavoidably intertwined with the factual contexts involved in every decision, even though those normative propositions can remain murky and in serious dispute within civil society.

Consequently, the criticism here of Justice Roberts' attempt at institutional modesty with his "balls and strikes" reference is not that his analogy was in-accurate—it was instead misleading. It suggested that the job of judging is a purely objective task of applying given facts to given legal texts, and the out-comes then determine themselves—so long as the judge has a good pair of glasses to use when considering all this material. If, instead, Justice Roberts meant that his theory of judging was that judges should not insinuate themselves *personally* and idiosyncratically into legal life to turn that game into "scorer's discretion," that would be far more acceptable. One would hope that judges have not been elected or appointed for the purpose of running amok. But if he meant that the values embedded and reflected in the legal world are simply *not relevant* to a judge—they are to be conscientiously ignored or denied—then that is something else altogether. It reflects a failure to understand the nature of judging itself, which I very much doubt he misperceives so badly. Instead, then, his "balls and strikes" remark should be attributed simply to the convenient politics of the confirmation hearing circumstance, where no one would attempt to unpack the image carefully to see the difficulties and contradictions contained within it.

F. The Jury as an Additional Issue in Subtext

As noted in this Chapter's introduction, one element of our legal system to which this book has given no serious attention is the jury. Not only is there a struggle between the legal decision-making authority of judges and legislatures, there is an equivalent tension between the provinces of the judge and the jury at the trial of any matter. The traditional understanding of the division between them is that judges are in charge of the law to be applied to the dispute while the jury will determine the facts to which that law will be relevant.[24] But that comfortable picture downplays a host of difficulties familiar to any practicing lawyer.

Is, for example, the question in a case of whether the defendant acted as a "reasonable person" an issue of fact or law? When could a judge decide that there is insufficient evidence *as a matter of law* to allow a jury to even deliberate on that element in the case, and thus prevent the jury from perhaps disagreeing and finding instead in favor of the plaintiff? Or, to return to our earlier example, why was the actual thought process of Ms. Javins—her "expectations" about the leased premises—never an issue that needed to be developed and established before Judge Wright ruled in her favor? How did her expectations become philosophical, and hence a matter of law for Judge Wright to decide, rather than more traditionally psychological, and hence a matter of fact for the jury to consider?

This is the legal world, of course, of procedure—summary judgment, directed verdicts, and the like—all remarkably important to the practice of law. But, I will contend, these lawyering situations are not as uniquely separate from or differently relevant to the subject of legal reasoning to justify further development in any detail here. The question of how facts and law interact in a trial courtroom is instead a specialized and subtle instance of all the dimensions of legal reasoning thus far identified: Obviously, because a jury is sitting in a particular case with particular parties, the contextual focus of this group will be appropriately micro. But that does not mean that larger elements of social policy, like public safety or nasty landlord behavior generally, are now irrelevant to them. And while these parties in this litigation are primarily entitled to the values inherent in fairness, larger aspects of justice will nevertheless be part of any jury's thinking, and thus may well be argued to them by the parties.

Consider once again, as an illustration, the circumstances of Umpire Pinelli's World Series call. Note that the traditional rules of baseball give sole and final authority to the umpire to make these quick decisions. Even though reasonable people might indeed disagree with a conclusion this official reaches, no one is given any standing to reverse the call. There is no jury to weigh any evidence. The decision is a matter of both fact *and* final legal result.

Until recently, however. The modern and developing "tradition" in big-time sporting events, in contrast, is to use the modern technology of instant video replays to review the decisions made on the field. There is in fact now a kind of jury to which the close situations are submitted, and the assessment by these impartial observers governs the matter no matter what the game official may have said. Why this development? It seems clear that the interest in changing this aspect of the game has underneath it all the elements we have been discussing: concern with the context of the game, the hypertextual values it embodies that we are trying to honor and vindicate, and the subtextual struggle concerning appropriate foundations for competing decision makers.

So I concede the relevance of the law-fact distinction to the subtextual issue of dividing decisional responsibility between judges and juries. But I will have nothing further to say on the topic here. I consider the development of the pieces within legal reasoning developed in this text already complicated enough to warrant *not* adding to the challenge.

Notes

1. In a return to the problem of the inherent differences between decision-making in baseball and the law first discussed in Chapter One, this idea of "discretion" actually reinforces the similarities of the two contexts. *See supra* ch. 1. Anyone who has played baseball at a significant level will recall a coach or manager yelling to a batter: "Protect the plate! Protect the plate!" (usually followed by something like "You moron!"). What the coach is acknowledging is the inherent human fallibility that will characterize the umpire's effort to call balls and

strikes: The pitches are fast and the margins are small. The batter must assume, then, that the "discretion" that will be exercised by the umpire may well be disadvantageous, and pitches at the margins will therefore have to be scrutinized carefully and defensively. By the same token, lawyers advising clients always know that a judge's discretion in contested situations may well be exercised in a direction the lawyer and client do not like, and they too will "protect the plate" in the sense of structuring their circumstances as carefully as possible to avoid these marginal situations, and litigators, of course, will always portray their positions as not marginal at all, but "straight down the middle."

2. COL, *supra* ch. 1 note 12, at 142.

3. *Id.* at 142 ("Like the changes from a regime of custom to a mature system of law, the addition to the game of secondary rules providing for the institution of a scorer whose rulings are final, brings into the system a new kind of internal statement; for unlike the player's statements as to the score, the scorer's determinations are given, by secondary rules, a status that renders them unchallengeable.").

4. *Id.* at 143 ("There might indeed be a game with such a rule, and some amusement might be found in playing it if the scorer's discretion were exercised with some regularity; but it would be a different game. We may call such a game the game of 'scorer's discretion.'"); *Id.* at 144 ("Up to a certain point, the fact that some rulings given by a scorer are plainly wrong is not inconsistent with the game continuing … The fact that isolated or exceptional official aberrations are tolerated does not mean that the game of cricket or baseball is no longer being played. On the other hand, if these aberrations are frequent, or if the scorer repudiates the scoring rule, there must come a point when the either the players no longer accept the scorer's aberrant rulings or, if they do, the game has changed. It is no longer cricket or baseball but 'scorer's discretion …'").

To truly appreciate this point, you would have to be familiar with the justly famous comic strip *Calvin and Hobbes* by Bill Watterson, in which the wildly idiosyncratic and ever-changing game of "Calvinball" is introduced.

5. The distinction between civil law and common law systems can be summarized thus: "The common law has its source in previous court decisions. The main traditional source for common law is therefore not legislation but cases … In civil law countries, cases are simply not a source of law—at least not in theory … Civil law jurists tend to see the civil code as an all-encompassing document." JANE S. GINSBURG, LEGAL METHODS 66, 69–70 (rev. 2d ed. 2004).

6. CHARLES DE SECONDAT DE MONTESQUIEU, THE SPIRIT OF THE LAWS 158 (Anne M. Cohler, Basia C. Miller & Harold S. Stone trans. & eds., 1989) (1748).

7. *Id.* at 163.

8. *Id.* at 158.

9. I noted back in this book's Introduction the very limited range of decisions by Justice Roberts that would be discussed, and the reasons for that approach. *See supra* Introduction note 17.

10. Amoco Production Co. v. Watson, 410 F.3d 722, 733 (2005).

11. *Id.*

12. PDK Laboratories Inc. v. U.S.D.E.A., 362 F.3d 786, 801 (2004) (Roberts, J., concurring in part and concurring in the decision).

13. *See, e.g.*, AT&T Corp. v. F.C.C., 394 F.3d 933, 939 (2005) (Judge Roberts notes that "The whole purpose of the tariff provision in question was to ensure that benefits could be transferred without concomitant obligations.").

14. *See also, e.g.*, In Re England, 375 F.3d 1169, 1179 (2004).

15. PGA Tour, Inc. v. Martin, 532 U.S. 661 689 (2001).

16. Consumer Elecs. Assn v. FCC, 347 F.3d 291, 298 (D.C. Cir 2003). Judge Roberts cited to both *Consumer Elecs Assn* and *PGA Tour* in *In re England* to rebut arguments for a narrow application of a federal statutory provision that were based on a plain language reading of the provision. *See* In re England, 375 F.3d at 1179.

17. For an example of the use of custom as law in the United States, see, e.g., State ex rel. Thornton v. Hay, 462 P. 2d 671, 676–79 (Ore. 1969) (English doctrine of custom used to create public rights in dry sand areas of coastal beaches). For discussions of custom in international law, see, e.g., ANTHONY A. D'AMATO, THE CONCEPT OF CUSTOM IN INTERNATIONAL LAW (1971); THE NATURE OF CUSTOMARY LAW (Amanda Perreau-Saussine & James B. Murphy eds., 2007). Indeed, Professor Hart argued that custom was a fundamental feature of English law generally. *See* COL, *supra* ch. 1 note 12, at 44–48.

18. The disconcerting circumstance of the sudden absence of experienced umpires and referees from professional sports has been discussed in the press extensively. Regarding baseball, *see, e.g.*, Dan Martin, *It's Quitting Time—MLB Umps to Resign on Sept. 2*, N.Y. POST (July 15, 1999, 4:00 A.M.), http://nypost.com/1999/07/15/its-quitting-time-mlb-umps-to-resign-on-sept-2/; Cliff Corcoran, *The Strike: Who Was Right, Who Was Wrong and How It Helped Baseball*, SPORTS ILLUSTRATED (Aug. 12, 2014), http://www.si.com/mlb/2014/08/12/1994-strike-bud-selig-orel-hershiser; Matthew Callan, *Called Out: The Forgotten Baseball Umpires Strike of 1999*, CLASSICAL (Oct. 2, 2012, 12:03 P.M.), http://theclassical.org/articles/called-out-the-forgotten-baseball-umpires-strike-of-1999. Regarding football, see, *e.g.*, Mike Garafolo, *NFL Referees and Lockout After Reaching New Labor Deal*, USA TODAY SPORTS (Sept. 27, 2012, 1:52 A.M.), http://usatoday30.usatoday.com/sports/nfl/story/2012/09/27/nfl-referees-end-lockout-after-reaching-new-labor-deal/57846906/1; Dave Jamieson, *NFL Referee Lockout: Refs Resist Pension Freeze Out, Cite League Profits*, HUFFINGTON POST (Sept. 13, 2012, 7:41 A.M.), http://www.huffingtonpost.com/2012/09/13/nfl-referee-lockout-pensions_n_1879049. html; David Vinjamuri, *The Referee Lockout is Hurting the NFL Brand*, FORBES (Sept. 25, 2012, 4:47 P.M.), http://www.forbes.com/sites/davidvinjamuri/2012/09/25/the-referee-lockout-is-hurting-the-nfl-brand/#577cdad01fc0; Judy Battista, *N.F.L. Reaches Labor Deal with Referees*, N.Y. TIMES (Sept. 26, 2012), http://www.nytimes.com/2012/09/27/sports/football/nfl-and-referees-reach-labor-deal.html?_r=0.

19. Although this phrase is often attributed to Kierkegaard by other philosophers, like Jacques Lacan and Jacques Derrida, among others, its precise location within Kierkegaard's own work is notoriously difficult to pin down. *See, e.g.*, Geoffrey Bennington, *A Moment of Madness: Derrida's Kierkegaard, in* 33 OXFORD LITERARY REV. 103 (2011). It is no doubt drawn from *Fear and Trembling*, along with Kierkegaard's equally dramatic description of the passage from ethical reasoning to religious reasoning (if it can be called that) as the "teleological suspension of the ethical." Derrida's use of Kierkegaard in Jacques Derrida, *Force of Law: The 'Mystical Foundation of Authority'*, 11 CARDOZO L. REV. 919, 967 (1990) is typical: All we get is "The instant of decision is madness, says Kierkegaard." *Id.*

20. The literature on judicial independence is immense. *See, e.g.*, THE JUDICIAL BRANCH (Kermit Hall & Kevin T. McGuire, eds., 2005); JUDICIAL INDEPENDENCE: AN ANNOTATED BIBLIOGRAPHY (Brennan Center for Justice, NYU Law School, 2004); Harry L. Carrico, C.J., *A Call to Arms: The Need to Protect the Independence of the Judiciary*, 38 U. RICH. L. REV. 575 (2004); H. Jefferson Powell, *The Three Independences*, 38 U. RICH. L. REV. 603 (2004); William H. Rehnquist, C.J., *Judicial Independence*, 38 U. RICH. L. REV. 579 (2004); Penny J. White, *An America Without Judicial Independence*, 80 JUDICATURE 174 (1997) (former state supreme court justice).

21. The U.S. Constitution's first three Articles create the three basic (perhaps as implicit co-equals, or perhaps in descending order of importance) branches of the federal government: Article I, the legislature (Congress); Article II, the executive (the President); and Article III, the judiciary (the federal court system). U.S. CONST. art I–III.

22. *See supra* note 20.

23. This does not at all mean that judges must necessarily enjoy life tenure and be insulated from the democratic processes of election. A community can, quite consistently with the analysis here, be given the political authority to remove a judge from office for unpopular (or incompetent or whatever) decisions, just as a baseball umpire can be fired for incompetence. The point is that this dramatic community response is not made *at the time of the controversial decision*—in the heat of the moment—but at regularly scheduled political (or employment) intervals.

24. Background citations on this proposition would be endless. *See, e.g.*, Walker v. N.M. & S. Pac. R.R. Co. 165 U.S. 593 (1897); Byrd v. Blue Ridge Rural Elect. Coop., 356 U.S. 525, 537 (1958).

Part IV

Bringing it All Together

As noted in the Introduction, this Part examines two challenging legal topics using the analytic method developed in all the preceding Chapters. Although both are well known and much discussed, they have something else in common that adds an extra layer of interest: Unlike many debates about legal doctrine, which include a key policy disagreement about whether the doctrine is legitimate in the first place (e.g., Should we have gun control *at all*? Should we have publicly funded education *at all*? Should medical care and research have government subsidies *at all*? Should manufacturers be liable to remote purchasers *at all*?), the two topics to be examined in this Part are universally agreed to be fundamental ingredients in our legal system: Everyone today accepts the idea that the right to privacy is a necessary, foundational element of our political and legal culture. And everyone acknowledges that courts must understand the words of a statute—words produced by a separate branch of government—well enough to apply that legislation to litigants before them. Yet both subjects provoke endless disagreement among lawyers and scholars concerning their practical detail.

Thus, while neither of these doctrines is controversial in and of itself—that is, each has a presumptively legitimate core—the disagreements they provoke are at their edges and applications. Concerning privacy, continuing controversy concerning its content raises the question whether that doctrine is in fact so sacrosanct.

Concerning statutory interpretation, multiple judicial approaches raise the similar question of why, after centuries of judicial experience with such texts, can't judges and scholars resolve the rather limited question of how courts should understand and apply the legal words used by other branches?

The point of these Chapters will be, as we have seen throughout this book, that disagreement within the law on *every* topic is, to one degree or another, inevitable. Good lawyers understand this and plan for it.

Chapter Nine

The Right (or Rights?) to Privacy (or Privacies?)

Since the claim in this book from its beginning has been that the topic of legal reasoning is at its most relevant in the most difficult and controversial cases, we should spend some time testing that thesis further. The perpetual struggle over the meaning of the right to privacy is as good an example as any, although it may prove to be *too* good. The mountain of case law and commentary it has spawned leaves very basic questions circulating: Is the right to privacy one big right, or several related rights? And is privacy itself one concept, or several related concepts? Examining it from this book's analytic perspective will *not* reveal some new, hitherto unexplored direction from which to appreciate this legal topic, and hence resolve the many debates about it. Quite the contrary, the approach here will reveal why there will *never* be a comprehensive settling of such disputes.

But that less-than-ideal result will nevertheless be useful information, for it will assist anyone caught up in a case in this area who seeks to develop arguments and counterarguments. Thus, the lesson from this Chapter will not be despair over all the disagreements acknowledged in these various judicial opinions, for their evident differences are not chaotic. Instead, they follow identifiable patterns that have been developed in this book. The message then becomes that the task for lawyers, judges, legislators, and so on, should not be to search for *the*, singular, answer in this daunting legal context, but to be better able to anticipate the range of *competing* answers—each with strong arguments in its favor—that they will confront. The goal should be the principled management of grudging situational compromise. For litigators in particular in these circumstances, the job becomes understanding this range of potential argument well enough to anticipate the challenges their clients will face.

This Chapter will not, of course, be a treatise on the immense topic of privacy. It will instead use a few examples that usefully illustrate the elements within legal reasoning that have been developed earlier. The primary focus will be on three Supreme Court cases, two from the United States and one from

Canada. The two from the United States have been chosen because they can be uniquely compared and contrasted: They were decided the same year by the same set of Justices, so the variables of time and decision makers have been eliminated. They both also involve the intersection (and hence clash) of privacy demands with modern technological developments that make invasions into personal information so much easier. Yet the factual circumstances within which the claims to privacy are asserted are quite distinct—in one, a news reporter seeking to disclose information; in the other, the police investigating possible wrongdoing. This will mean in turn that the cases will involve different legal contexts as well, as claims to privacy compete with different legal principles (freedom of the press and search and seizure).

And, not surprisingly, then, both cases reveal an array of disagreements among the Justices—not just about the appropriate results in the cases but, more important, the methods to be employed to reach the results. One point here will therefore be that all of these disagreements could have been *predicted* from the very beginning.

The Canadian decision has been included because it involves precisely the same factual circumstances as one of the U.S. decisions (police surveillance), but the reasoning and result are quite distinct. It too, however, illustrates the same analytic elements that this book has developed.

To substantiate all these points, initially a fairly detailed review of the cases will be necessary. This traditional review will lead us gradually into discussion of the elements of legal reasoning embedded within the different approaches used by various justices.

A. The U.S. Cases: Cell Phones and Heat Detection

Bartnicki v. Vopper[1] involved a privacy-based challenge to the broadcast of an illegally intercepted cell phone call; *Kyllo v. United States*[2] involved a privacy-based challenge to the search of a home by government agents using a heat detection device. Privacy could be said to have "lost" in the first case to a stronger claim based in freedom of speech, while privacy "won" in the latter, overcoming a government claim based in reasonable search and seizure. The evident doctrinal differences between these cases—one relating to the appropriate behavior of a broadcaster (albeit publicly funded), the other the appropriate behavior of the police—nevertheless obscure what is common between them, and therefore more interesting and fundamental.

Given the different results in the two cases, and given the current Court's ideological split, it is not surprising that the author of the majority opinion in one case also wrote the dissent in the other. But that is about as far as the usual assumptions about the Court will take you. The coalitions that otherwise produced the results in each case were quite different mixes from what one might ordinarily expect. As the various opinions reveal, even though all the Justices certainly agree that a constitutional right to "privacy" exists, they disagree, as we all do, on the fundamental basis of that right as it competes with other recognized rights and policies. The Justices also evidently can, and do, disagree about how technology affects privacy—whether it is through its actual invasion of some space, or an invasion of a more abstract aspect of our lives, or through the data it produces to be used against us.

1. Bartnicki: *Does Speech Define Privacy or Privacy Define Speech?*

Bartnicki involved a heated labor dispute that at one point provoked a cell phone call between two teachers' union activists angered over a school board's "intransigence" in negotiations. During the lengthy conversation, one of the activists made what sounded like threats to the property of the board members. The conversation was intercepted by someone unknown, and a tape of the conversation was delivered to the mailbox of the head of a local taxpayers' organization that had opposed the union's demands. This person in turn played the tape for the school board members and delivered it to a local radio commentator who had also been critical of the union. The commentator played the tape on the air, and the union activists heard on the tape sued both the person who received the tape and the radio commentator under both federal and state anti-wiretapping statutes.[3]

Cross motions for summary judgment were filed, which the district court denied. But it certified for interlocutory appeal the issues raised by the defendants: Were the statutes unconstitutional as applied to these defendants in the exercise of their First Amendment rights? A majority of a Third Circuit panel replied in the affirmative, reversing the district court's denial of summary judgment for the defendants. The Supreme Court, in a 6–3 decision, in an opinion by Justice Stevens, affirmed. Justices Breyer and O'Connor filed a concurrence, and Justice Rehnquist wrote a dissent in which Justices Scalia and Thomas joined.

One important aspect of this case is that the claim by the union activists was based not in some abstract, general sense of a right to privacy, but in a more precise statutory manifestation of that right. Thus, the Court understood its task as comparing this statutory right to the defendants' constitutional rights under the First Amendment.[4] To set that comparison up carefully, all the opinions assumed, as the lower courts had, certain facts concerning the recording and broadcasting that would eliminate any collateral issues: The defendants had had no involvement in the clearly illegal recording of the conversation itself; although the defendants received the recording legally, they knew or should have known that the recording was nevertheless illegal; and the conversations dealt with a matter of public concern.

The Justices disagreed most basically, however, over whose right to speak was at stake. The majority focused on the defendants—basically as surrogates for all of us—who want to have a right to speak about issues of public moment.[5] The odd point, of course, is that these defendants wanted to "speak" using other people's words. The dissent focused on the activists, in two senses: first, narrowly as individuals who, by being denied the protection of privacy, are being forced to speak publicly in a particular way against their will; and second, more generally, as people—like us all—who do not want to encounter disincentives to speaking, such as having our private conversations used against us. The odd point here, of course, is that this ostensibly private conversation was directly relevant to issues of public importance.

So which context should be dominant? Is this case a "speech case" with a privacy twist, or a "privacy case" with a speech twist? The difference is critical in orienting the analysis of the technology involved: Is the interception of cell phone conversations to be assessed within the overarching principle of public debate, or within the overarching principle of personal choice regarding when and how to enter that debate? To put this issue in terms of the model of legal reasoning, we can return to the analogy of Swiss cheese used in Chapter Five: The most fundamental question orienting this debate is which concept—privacy or speech—is the cheese and which is the holes?

In fact, all of the opinions in this case viewed speech as the cheese, with the question being the size of the potential hole privacy claims might make in that fundamental right. The majority created the smallest privacy limitation, connecting the case to the line of precedent focused on the importance of the First Amendment to maintaining a democratic society. The question became whether the interest in protecting the confidentiality of certain information outweighs the consequences of chilling the American tradition of vigorous debate. As the majority recognized, confidentiality seldom wins that contest.[6] Only the most egregious public detriment, such as interfering with a war effort, could compete with that social and political perspective. Thus, in *Bartnicki*, the activists' argument for privacy-based restrictions on news-related activities would be a tough one to sustain. The fact that new and unusual technology is causing an impact on confidentiality would not seem to make any serious legal difference.

But Justice Stevens' opinion for the Court did take the activists' arguments seriously. He noted as "considerably stronger" the government's contention in favor of the anti-wiretapping statutes that these laws "minimiz[e] the harm to persons whose conversations have been illegally intercepted."[7] Yet his conclusion was clear: Not only did his opinion hold that "privacy concerns give way when balanced against the interest in publishing matters of public importance,"[8] his reasoning made those public matters actually define the privacy concerns in such a way that they were bound to lose in this balancing. Citing the original article on the right to privacy by Warren and Brandeis, Justice Stevens noted that "[o]ne of the costs associated with participating in public affairs is an attendant loss of privacy."[9]

Hence, the initial attention paid in Justice Stevens' opinion to cases involving dangers to privacy from new technologies was really of no consequence to the result. No matter how vulnerable some new technology might make our conversations—or perhaps other personal data, for that matter—the overarching facts of public importance and debate orient the analysis away from individually focused privacy rights and toward the politically oriented First Amendment rights of speech and press. One wonders, however, how far this idea of "public interest" can be taken, particularly concerning information about public figures.[10]

Justice Breyer's concurrence[11] is significant for its effort to avoid these somewhat scary implications by trying to increase the size of the privacy limitation on speech. He criticized Justice Stevens' tendency to put this case in the context of the "strict scrutiny" given to prior restraint cases, and urged instead a straightforward, but therefore more flexible and less predictable, balancing of the public and private interests implicated in the case. Both of these elements, he contended, have constitutional relevance concerning speech within our society. Yet he concurred in the result simply because he believed the statutes involved in this case did not properly strike that balance.

But why these statutes failed is interesting. Although Justice Breyer agreed with the majority that the public quality of the issues *did* matter to analyzing the statutes' constitutionality, and he further agreed that the actual technology involved in the case did *not* matter, he differed by focusing on the actual data produced by the technology—that is, the substance of the overheard conversation itself. He noted that the balance between the public and private elements in the case was seriously affected by the nature of the activists' message: In threatening the safety of others, the activists "had little or no legitimate interest in maintaining the privacy of the particular conversation."[12] The information involved therefore became "of a special kind,"[13] and the statutes could not protect the activists. Thus, although the hole in the speech cheese was a bit bigger, the activists simply did not manage to get themselves within it.

In significant contrast, Chief Justice Rehnquist's dissent reversed the orientation entirely—making privacy the cheese, and indeed the basis of the definition of freedom of speech in this case. He took the nature of the technology at stake to be the critical, anchoring context for the constitutional question: "[T]he Court's decision diminishes, rather than enhances, the purposes of the First Amendment: chilling the speech of the millions of Americans who rely upon electronic technology to communicate each day."[14] Privacy, therefore, at least as much as the "public importance and debate" aspect of a situation, defined both the nature of the statutes at stake and the nature of protected speech itself: "This concern [in the federal anti-wiretapping statute] for privacy was inseparably bound up with the desire that personal conversations be frank and uninhibited, not cramped by fears of clandestine surveillance and purposeful disclosure."[15]

Justice Rehnquist therefore not only rejected the majority's emphasis on the "public debate" element in the case, but he rejected Justice Breyer's more explicit, but more privacy-friendly, balancing approach. For Justice Rehnquist, there simply was no balance to be struck here, no competing set of consequences that needed to be considered:

> The Constitution should not protect the involuntary broadcast of personal conversations. Even where the communications involve public figures or concern public matters, the conversations are nonetheless private and worthy of protection. Although public persons may have forgone the right to live their lives screened from public scrutiny in some areas, it does not and should not follow that they also have abandoned their right to have a private conversation without fear of it being intentionally intercepted and knowingly disclosed.[16]

The anti-wiretapping statutes, as a consequence, should be understood as perfectly appropriate, quite constitutional, efforts to protect privacy interests from "a marginal claim to speak freely."[17]

The result in *Bartnicki* is this: For the majority, the public-interest based freedoms of speech and press define an important limitation to the individual-interest based right to privacy. When anyone engages in any activity related to public affairs, that public character necessarily reduces the range of any claim to privacy. In turn, for this weakened claim to privacy, the technology involved in the invasion does not much matter. Similarly, for Justice Breyer in concurrence, there is a public-based limitation to privacy, but it is a bit less dramatic, coming into play only when the substance of the information sought to be protected threatens public safety. Thus, while it would remain difficult to justify a limitation on speech based on the content of one's expression, it is apparently, and ironically, much easier to justify a limitation on one's privacy based on what one says in private. For the dissent, the contest is more about two competing claims to free speech, with that competition being decided by one side's additional claim to privacy for its conversations. From this perspective, technology, as the means of invasion into that privacy, matters a great deal.

Thus, we end up with three opinions with quite different approaches. How can something as fundamental and accepted as a right to privacy create such legal chaos?

2. Kyllo: *Does Privacy Define Searching or Searching Define Privacy?*

Given that a clear majority of the Court in *Bartnicki* took privacy interests to be serious competitors for freedom of speech, it is not particularly surprising that a majority of the Court in *Kyllo* took privacy interests seriously enough to hold a new form of sensing technology to be an unconstitutional search. But what *is* somewhat surprising is that the reasoning and coalitions in the two cases do not match up, indicating that something else is at stake as well.

The most unusual grouping in this regard is Justices Stevens and Rehnquist, who could not have been much further apart in *Bartnicki*, but are here together in dissent. Since both *Bartnicki* and *Kyllo* involve claims to privacy in the face of new technology, the key analytic challenge becomes explaining the reasoning that brings the two of them together.

The facts in *Kyllo* were uncomplicated.[18] Police suspected that a particular residence was being used to grow marijuana. Because this would require high-intensity lamps, the police aimed a thermal-imaging device at the home to determine whether unusual heat was emanating from any portion of it. They determined that there was, and obtained a search warrant to enter the home. Based on "tips from informants, utility bills, and the thermal imaging,"[19] a federal magistrate issued the warrant, and the search revealed more than 100 growing marijuana plants. Mr. Kyllo was of course indicted, and moved, unsuccessfully, to suppress the evidence found in the search.

The Ninth Circuit initially remanded the case for more fact-finding concerning the thermal imaging technology, and when the conviction returned for review, a panel reversed the conviction. That opinion, however, was withdrawn, and a new panel affirmed the District Court's refusal to suppress the seized evidence. The defendant lost for two basic reasons: The Court con-

cluded that the homeowner lacked a *"subjective* expectation of privacy"[20]—
that is, they were not convinced that the defendant had *inside his own head*
any real expectation of privacy because he had done nothing special to insulate his dwelling from heat loss. And even if he had such an internal thought,
he still lacked an *"objectively* reasonable expectation of privacy"[21]—meaning
that, no matter what his own thinking might have been, the legal system more
generally could conclude, based on its precedents, that there was nothing particularly intrusive about the workings of the thermal-imaging device.

The Supreme Court, in a 5-4 split, reversed, suppressing the evidence of
the seized plants and overturning the homeowner's conviction. The disagreement, as in *Bartnicki*, turned primarily on whether—and how—privacy and
the nature of a new technology would be critical elements in defining a constitutional right.

The connection between *Kyllo* and its decisional predecessors is even more
direct than that for *Bartnicki*. A long line of cases has worried about the government's ever-increasing ability to gather information through new technologies, and the relationship of that ability to the Fourth Amendment's
prohibition of "unreasonable searches and seizures." The issue in these cases,
however, is not ordinarily whether a particular search was "reasonable," but
whether a search had occurred at all. The usual starting point is *Katz v. United
States*,[22] which established the principle that has consistently guided the Court's
analysis for many years: The focus is not so much the reasonableness of the
government's action as it is "whether the individual has an expectation of privacy that society is prepared to recognize as reasonable."[23]

Thus, similar to *Bartnicki*'s use of privacy to understand speech, *Kyllo* makes
clear that the concept of privacy affects the concept of "search." But the fundamental question of analytical orientation is the same: Which concept is the
cheese and which the hole? Are we most worried about personal protections
or law enforcement?

The sense of privacy relevant in this case is, as Justice Scalia's majority opinion notes,[24] a combination of these so-called subjective and objective elements.
Privacy will not be defined solely by the individual himself or herself, but by
society. The "expectation" involved here is not a psychological fact that a defendant could establish with his or her own testimony. It is instead a philosophical proposition—a normative, value-based concept that is determined
by courts rather than juries. Yet a judge's conclusion that a search has or has
not occurred will nevertheless be informed by an understanding of psychology
and modern circumstances. In other words, in trying to determine whether a
"search" has occurred, "is" and "ought" will both require attention.

For Justice Scalia, "ought" clearly dominates the analysis, making privacy the cheese, as it were. The details of the heat-sensing technology did not matter so much. He was not limiting his thinking to the "relatively crude"[25] technology in this case, but sought instead to accomplish something more visionary: "[T]he rule we adopt must take account of more sophisticated systems that are already in use or in development."[26] But to look forward in this way, his technique was to look backward—at the original basepoints for Fourth Amendment thinking. What mattered to him was the place at which the technology was aimed. *Kyllo* did not involve a phone booth or a wire running from a building or business and utility records. It involved a home, which Justice Scalia characterized as the central element of the Fourth Amendment: "At [its] very core ... stands the right of a man to retreat into his own home and there be free from unreasonable governmental intrusion."[27]

This is a somewhat unusual emphasis because, as Justice Scalia also acknowledged, the analysis of searches under the Fourth Amendment had long ago lost its anchor in common law understandings of property rights and trespass. From *Katz v. United States* on, the question was more personal than tangible: just as the Circuit Court had reasoned, whether the individual had formed a "subjective expectation of privacy," and, very important, whether that expectation was one "that society recognizes as reasonable."[28] But to give this vague test some particular meaning for this case, Justice Scalia returned to those common law roots:

> We think that obtaining by sense-enhancing technology any information regarding the interior of a home that could not otherwise have been obtained without physical "intrusion into a constitutionally protected area" ... constitutes a search—at least where (as here) the technology in question is not in general public use. This assures preservation of that degree of privacy against government that existed when the Fourth Amendment was adopted.[29]

The degree or "significance" of the intrusion did not therefore matter, as it did to the dissent. The key was drawing "a firm line at the entrance to the house."[30] This cheese was therefore going to have few holes.

Justice Stevens in dissent took a very different analytical approach: circumstantial rather than categorical. He was not at all impressed by the talisman of "the home." Instead, the details of the technology mattered critically. He distinguished between, on the one hand, "through-the-wall surveillance," like x-rays, that can effectively reach into the interior of a space, and, on the other, "'off-the-wall' surveillance," which is inferences drawn from information released into the public domain, like light rays or smells.[31] While Justice Scalia rejected this distinction as "mechanical,"[32] rather like the trespass requirement of older cases, Justice Stevens argued that it accurately characterized the state of current science, which should be the limiting focus of the decision:

> Just as "the police cannot reasonably be expected to avert their eyes from evidence of criminal activity that could have been observed by any member of the public," ... so too public officials should not have to avert their senses or their equipment from detecting emissions in the public domain such as excessive heat, traces of smoke, suspicious odors, odorless gases, airborne particulates, or radioactive emissions, any of which could identify hazards to the community.[33]

None of these potential "hazards" would require an intimate knowledge of activities in the house; they would just require some external manifestation that could then be interpreted by police officials to yield useful insights.

Justice Stevens was also therefore critical of the majority's effort to fashion an ambitious rule that would anticipate future technologies. He noted, for example, that Justice Scalia's reference to technologies not "in general use" meant that the actual application of the majority's rule would float with future "subjective expectations of privacy,"[34] to return to Justice Brandeis' phrase. The issue of appropriate police conduct would then seem to hinge on what the police and the technological community have managed to get us to accept over time as inevitable and appropriate. One example emphasized by Justice Stevens is a "dog sniff" for the purpose of disclosing narcotics, held by the Court long ago not to constitute a search.[35] The majority's overly ambitious rule was therefore in his opinion both too broad and too narrow: it called into question too many police surveillance techniques, many of which have already been held by the Court to be reasonable; and it was limited too strictly to the "home," when so many other contexts raise legitimate privacy concerns.[36]

Once again, then, what is the appropriate focus here? Is *Kyllo* a "search case" with a privacy twist or a "privacy case" with a search twist? And once again, the difference is critical: Is the heat-sensor technology to be assessed within the principle of the kind of privacy to which citizens are entitled, or within the principle of, as Justice Stevens puts it, "entirely reasonable public service"?[37] Does privacy define reasonable searching, or reasonable searching define privacy? At least at this level of abstraction, Justice Stevens is quite consistent between *Bartnicki* and *Kyllo*: In both cases his opinions have placed privacy in the secondary position. But if he is consistent, a significant number of his colleagues are not: Four members of the Court took one approach in one case and a different tack in the other.

These two cases are significant not only for the breadth of analytical disagreement they display about fundamental legal concepts, they also have interesting implications for future cases involving yet another modern issue: Rather than free speech and ordinary police surveillance, what importance will be attached to government claims to "national security"? What direction will analysis of the right to privacy take in a post-September 11 world of serious concern about the clandestine activities of terrorists? Will "security," like "search," be defined by privacy, as *Kyllo* suggests, which will limit government authority? Or, to the contrary, as *Bartnicki* implies, will security be treated as a dominant concern, like free speech, that defines and reduces our sphere of privacy?

No less dramatically, what implications should we attach to the *Kyllo* majority's emphasis on "the home"? Although that concept may have been stressed primarily because of Justice Scalia's consistent effort to root constitutional doctrine in historical "originalist"[38] terms (imagining, in effect, that the Founders were most directly and immediately worried about government intrusions into private domestic spaces), nevertheless one must bear in mind that the vast majority of instances of spousal and child abuse occur in "the home." Which, then, is the key idea: the place or the people within it?

B. The Canadian Case: Heat Detection, Again, but Methodical Reasoning

Precisely these sorts of lingering questions were on full display four years later in the decision by former Justice Ian Binnie of the Supreme Court of Canada in *R. v. Tessling*.[39] Its factual context was basically identical to *Kyllo*: A heat-sensing device was used by police (along with other evidence) to obtain a warrant to search the defendant's home, which proved to contain a marijuana farm. The legal context was also identical: The Canadian Charter of Rights and Freedoms establishes a right to be free from "unreasonable searches and seizures," and the right of privacy, recognized in Canadian law,[40] is critical to determining when that protection has been violated. But the Court, in a unanimous decision, expressly rejected the reasoning and result of the *Kyllo* majority, and agreed instead with the dissent, holding that the search was reasonable.[41]

Although there was no disagreement among the Canadian Justices, the opinion nevertheless reversed the holding of the Ontario Court of Appeal, and that Court was in turn reversing a trial court's ruling—thus giving us another example of contrasting judicial approaches. The trial court had found the heat-sensor technology "unobjectionable,"[42] but the Court of Appeal viewed the purpose of the technology, much as Justice Scalia did, as seeking to determine what was going on *inside* the house, and thus going beyond mere observation and ordinary police surveillance. Interestingly, this Court also thought the subject matter of the search was itself of no serious public importance, noting the "public, judicial, and political recognition that marijuana is at the low end of the hierarchy of harmful drugs."[43]

The Supreme Court reversed, based on a very thoughtful, meticulous analysis of the relationship between the concepts of privacy and reasonable searches. Most interestingly for our purposes, Justice Binnie began with an appreciation of both these concepts at the level of "text" much like the analysis presented in Chapter Five. He developed, in effect, a structured "set" of instances for both terms, anchored by central elements.

Privacy, for example, was understood as containing three basic dimensions:[44] "personal" interests, like bodily integrity, which is clearly the most central concern; "territorial" interests, particularly concerning places "where our most intimate and private activities are most likely to take place"; and "informational," involving facts or data "about ourselves and activities we are entitled to shield from the curious eyes of the State." This grouping is illustrated in Figure 9.1:

Figure 9.1

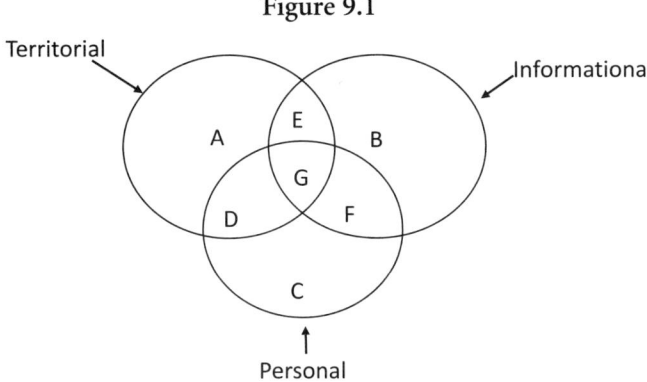

Both the arrangement of this diagram and its labeled segments are significant. The vertical order of the three circles corresponding to the elements identified by Justice Binnie is relevant because he makes clear that the most important of them is the "personal." Hence, it is the bedrock on which the other two aspects of privacy rest. Nevertheless, the depiction does not match the "central case" linguistic model employed in Chapter Five simply because that version is not somehow required as an analytic matter. In the present case we must acknowledge that while the circumstance of "bodily integrity" is indeed critical, privacy claims can arise without direct reference to that element. Thus, as the letters in the diagram identify the different kinds of privacy claims that could be made, areas A, B, and C would be demands for privacy related to only one of privacy's possible strands—in other words, being upset simply with, respectively, a bodily intrusion or a home invasion or a loss of information. Nevertheless, each of these areas would be entitled to "privacy protection." The other points present potentially stronger instances of legitimate claims: Segments D and F would be situations of bodily intrusion that occur either within your residence or involve the dissemination of your medical records. The most egregious circumstance would be segment G, where, for example, the police burst into your home to extract bodily fluids to determine and then make public whether you are taking illegal drugs.

The question here is where the *Tessling* case fits. It would seem to be within E—an invasion of one's personal space coupled with an intent to develop and use personal information (criminality). So in the first instance, the case would not involve the highest level of scrutiny that a court might give the government's actions (no bodily intrusion), but it would nevertheless be serious enough to merit attention. Yet perhaps that attention will not be all *that* serious, because this case could be viewed as a spot at the very edge of that area E: Although we might be within the overall area of possibly legitimate privacy claims, there is no actual entering of the house, and the information being gathered is not about innocent personal activities, but instead criminality. Hence, the claim to privacy by this defendant might be inherently weak—which is precisely the Court's approach.

Concerning the other major variable of the nature of a "reasonable search," the analysis would naturally turn to a focus on the actions of the police: What were they doing, and why should we care? But this inquiry inevitably overlaps with the concern about privacy. Here, however, the analysis moves from the "is" of various forms of invasion to the deeper "ought" of privacy. In Justice Binnie's similarly very detailed review of factors relevant to government searching, he noted initially (as an "is") that the search in this case was not particularly intrusive because the police were only measuring, quite generally, levels of heat emanating from the structure as a whole. Nevertheless, these government observations implicated "the underlying values of dignity, integrity, and autonomy"[45] of individual citizens embodied in the "biographical core of personal information"[46] that citizens were entitled to protect.

These overlapping foundational points were then the basis of the Court's assessment of whether the "search," if there was one, invaded the defendant's "reasonable expectation of privacy." Justice Binnie organized much of his analysis around the two ideas that had been relevant as well to the U.S. Supreme Court: Did the defendant have either a personal, subjective expectation, or a socially defendable objective expectation, to be free from police scrutiny of the exterior of his home? The former was of little consequence to the Canadian Court—the defendant had not testified at the hearing about the search, so any conclusion here would be guesswork. And Justice Binnie seemed to view the defendant's thinking, whatever it might have been, as more of a vague hope that he and his activities would not come to the attention of the police. Instead, the objective factor was the key to the decision and boiled down to the question "whether the police technique was intrusive in relation to the [defendant's now rather minimal] privacy interest."[47]

It was not, and Justice Binnie directly and explicitly rejected the reasoning and result of the majority in *Kyllo*. The key to the case was not the "place" involved, but the "person" making the privacy claim.[48] This required the focus of the analysis to be on the underlying theory of privacy, noted above, involving dignity, autonomy, and intimacy. These values were *why* the categories of personal, territorial, and informational were relevant.

From the perspective of this approach, the defendant had no legitimate claim to privacy that would invalidate the search. As a matter of "is," the "intrusion" into his life was itself minimal, as the only thing ever "seized" was general images of heat emanating from his home. So his "person" was certainly not violated, and his "territory" was never actually invaded. And the "information" obtained was not at all specific to his criminal activity—it required inferences by the police from other sources to make the heat sensing meaningful. As a matter of "ought," none of the basic values animating the right to privacy seemed to be meaningfully implicated as well.

Now let's go deeper. The question becomes whether the dimensions of legal reasoning that have been identified thus far in the discussion of these cases— implicitly most often in the U.S. Supreme Court cases while nicely explicitly in the Canadian opinion—can be organized further to show the *reasons* for the range of disagreement among the Justices. I think so, if we return to the previous discussions of context, hypertext, and subtext.

C. Using Legal Reasoning to Provide Additional Analytic Perspective

The aim here, of course, is not to develop comprehensive theories of privacy, search, free speech, and so on, but to accomplish a more limited, yet nevertheless ambitious, goal. Rather than argue what each of these complex legal concepts should "actually mean," we hope to make observations about how these concepts "take on meaning" through competing values. That effort can help explain why cases like *Kyllo* and *Bartnicki* will always generate a range of judicial conclusions.

The thesis of this book has been that, despite the vast variation in what judges might and can say in any opinion, the great bulk of those possibilities can be organized around a few key analytic elements that anchor, and then narrow, the range of possible directions their attitudes might take. The result of dropping back to this "meta" level of inquiry is the model that has appeared earlier in the book depicting this inevitable disagreement—even when the base concept, like privacy, is agreed to deserve respect.

In a modified version of the diagrams that have been developed earlier, the content of legal reasoning in these kinds of tough, controversial cases will be divided along two dimensions, one based on context—the "scale" at which the circumstances in a case are understood—and then a combination of hypertext and subtext—involving the basic philosophical and political orientation the court will take toward its decisional task. The first, as we noted earlier in Chapter Six, is based on the distinction between macro-level political philosophy and micro-level moral philosophy; the latter, as discussed in Chapters Seven and Eight, on the distinction between categorical and consequential perspectives.

1. The Context of Analytic Scale: Justice and Fairness

First, scale: In summary form, macro is the realm of the political—the values associated with large-scale governmental institutions: Who do we want making governmental decisions, and why? About what do we want government to be making these decisions? What propositions should guide this decision making? Micro is the realm of the moral—the values that animate interpersonal and small group relationships, values traditionally associated with "ethics": How should you and I treat each other? About what can we legitimately be concerned as we interact? Where does your "moral space" begin and mine end? Political philosophy is therefore ordinarily connected to our sense of justice and the institutions of government, and in turn most often associated with the activities of legislatures; while moral philosophy is ordinarily connected to fairness and individual dignity, and hence associated with the judiciary (recall Prof. Dworkin's distinction between "legal principles" and "policies" from Chapter Five).

The particular decisional angst in which we are interested here is determining the relative strength of claims to privacy in the face of competing claims to free speech and public safety. The background "meta" question, then, as a first step, is how interpersonal and institutional values interact in this legal situation. Individual people are being targeted for exposure or interference, or are being silenced or subjected to increased personal risk; but their circumstances involve social institutions such as courts, legislatures, the police, news organizations, and so on. Does the value of privacy, for example, exist to vindicate the moral dignity with which we are all endowed, or to limit potentially dangerous social institutions such as the police? Is a search unreasonable because it interferes with a particular person's life too much, or because those doing the searching are not subject to appropriate oversight? Although any decision will obviously force these perspectives to mix to some degree, reasonable people can disagree about which is key to defining the proper legal outcome.

2. The Values of Hypertext and Subtext: Categorical and Consequential

The second dimension we will add to the analysis is directly about the kinds of values themselves that could be applied at either of the levels of scale—what this book has labeled philosophical hypertext and political subtext. They will be combined here because the circumstances of judicial decision making necessarily involve simultaneously questions of both what values will be most relevant and which government institution should be applying them.

This element of reasoning also naturally divides itself into two camps (as we have seen earlier): (1) categorical theories (also labeled deontological or Kantian or sometimes rights-based or duty-based); and (2) consequential (also teleological or goal-based), grounded in social well-being. To summarize, but nevertheless repeat, aspects of this book's earlier discussions, one shorthand for this distinction is the separate focus one can have on the "means" by which something is done, and the "ends" this something produces. For example, lying could be morally criticized either because it is simply inherently bad in that it demonstrates a lack of respect for the innate dignity and worth of other people, or because it leads to a society filled with distrust and wasteful self-protective, rather than productive, activities. In the usual parlance of philosophy, categorical theories focus on the "right," or the intrinsic values of human existence, with all other guidance for behavior being derivative or secondary. Consequential theories, on the other hand, focus on the "good," in the sense of some goal or end that would define or enhance human society, with all other values being derivative or secondary. Hence, in general, for the former, "the right precedes the good," while for the latter, "the good precedes the right." (Illustrations you might recall from earlier Chapters are the family member with seemingly inconsistent attitudes about assisting the destitute and the analysis of a theory of freedom of speech.)

D. The Resulting Analytic Model

1. *Four Predictable Analytic Perspectives*

The contention here is that both elements of the dimension of scope—micro and macro—can be approached from either perspective of the dimension of orientation—values themselves or valued results. This then leads to a classic four-part box, shown in Figure 9.2, depicting the range of value-based "world views" from which any policy issue might be analyzed and assessed:

Before we analyze each of the boxes in detail, we must emphasize again that the boxes do not depict particular sets of values, either generally, like "political

Figure 9.2

CONTEXT: Scale		
Micro: • Individual focus: litigants as key	(1) Classical liberal: • Rights based Kantian • Emphasizing autonomy and individual rights (society as a salad?)	(2) Civic liberal: • Rights based contextualist • Acknowledging interpersonal connectedness, but tempered by respect for individual rights (society as a stew?)
Macro: • Social emphasis: litigants as representatives of sub-communities	(3) Liberal communitarian: • Goal-based Kantian • Acknowledging the legitimate demands of cohesive community, but tempered by respect for the importance of the individual (society as a layer cake?)	(4) Classical communitarian: • Goal-based contextualist • Emphasizing social goals and interpersonal connectedness, and the interactive values that allow one to flow into the other (society as a mousse?)
	Categorical: • deontological • "right" • "means" • individual autonomy and dignity • emphasis on courts	Consequentialist: • teleological • "good" • "ends" • responsibility to one's context • emphasis on legislatives

HYPERTEXT AND SUBTEXT:
Political Philosophy Generally

conservatism," or specifically, like "pro-gun control." They identify instead forms of value thinking. Thus, Box 1, for example, could contain both sides in a particular dispute where each determines its position based on values themselves (the "right") rather than on any measure of benefit to society (the "good") from the application of these values. Aspects of the debate over the right to an abortion have this character: Both supporters and opponents of the right can proceed from value-based, rather than end-based, conclusions about the nature of moral dignity, one group focusing on the woman, the other on the fetus.

But even if this four-part box has not separated these two combatants, it has nevertheless identified the nature of the dispute more accurately, and thus served at least three useful purposes. First, it shows that the two sides are talking about the same philosophical category at the meta level, and must therefore mount careful and comprehensive categorical arguments to wage this battle. Second, and perhaps more significantly, it will show when one side or the other goes "off story" to gain some additional edge in the debate—when, in other words, the two sides are not arguing from the same normative perspective. An example would be the argument made by proponents of the right to abortion that restrictions on the right will cause women to go "underground" for medical assistance, thus creating more health risks and fostering disrespect for the rule of law—both primarily consequential rather than categorical arguments.

Third, perhaps most significantly, the four-part model allows contenders for a particular public policy choice—say, the right to abortion—to anticipate the range of arguments they must make to satisfy all the normative analytical perspectives that will arise in the debate, and correspondingly to anticipate the range of arguments that will be made against them in the debate. Contenders for this right, for example, who base their argument solely on the woman's claim to a version of individual dignity will have done a poor rhetorical job, for the model predicts that attacks will be made against their conclusion from other directions not addressed, such as the claim that the right to an abortion will be exercised most often by the poor and minorities, thus having racial effects on society otherwise unanticipated; or, moving from hypertext to subtext, that the right as a constitutional right denies legislative supremacy and distorts our democratic ideals; and so on.

2. The Substance of the Four Perspectives

Now, on the details of the four analytic perspectives identified by the model:

Box (1) relies entirely upon the individual person for philosophical substance.[49] One's micro/moral responsibility is to respect the autonomy of others; political theory, quite consistently, demands that the state focus on protecting individual rights. Hence, individuals create their own community. Through their independent, unforced choices, they generate and maintain a collectivity that remains legitimate only as a defender and facilitator of the rights necessary for voluntary interpersonal interactions. This form of community is no larger or more important than its constituent members; the separate ingredients in this concoction matter more than the concoction as an entity. To use an analogy to food, from this normative perspective society looks like a salad rather than the familiar idea of a "melting pot"—while we may all share the same bowl, rather than blending within it, we maintain our rights to individual distinctiveness.

Box (4) is the mirror image of this approach.[50] Individuals are not ignored, of course, but they are understood quite differently as the product of community, rather than the other way around. One's micro/moral responsibility, then, is to treat others in ways that will maintain and enhance this community, which is in turn producing morally aware and responsible individuals. Individual values are therefore derivative of community values. Political theory follows suit: The state's principal purpose is to maintain and enhance at the macro level a sense of community that fosters and reinforces the sense of community established at the micro level.[51] Macro values are the community's micro values writ large, and vice versa. But the political community has a life and legitimacy of its own transcending that of its individual components. The focus from this perspective is on improving the larger end-product regardless of the impact on particular social elements. Those elements matter, of course, but only as contributors toward the larger enterprise rather than directly in and of themselves. The food analogy here is something like chocolate mousse—a smooth blending into a pleasing whole.

The possible alternatives to these approaches, in the upper right (2) and lower left (3) boxes, seem potentially attractive because they might be less strident in their perspectives and dogma, but, for precisely those reasons, they can then seem a bit mushy and confused in their inconsistent emphasis of values and consequences.

Box (2) is a kind of constrained individualism, but its nature depends in part on whether one describes it starting with the moral level or the political level. The moral theory of Box (2) again puts the individual in a context of micro-community: We cannot ignore the fact that our immediate community preceded us as individuals, and we must therefore acknowledge that our sense of ourselves—our sense of our "dignity"—is shaped and directed by that context.[52] Moral values are necessarily then rooted in this interconnectedness, and are for that reason consequentialist: We value those forms of individual interaction that will maintain an appropriate sense of interpersonal connection rather than dislocation. But this attention to functioning relationships is tempered by a political theory that requires the state to refrain from imposing values at the macro level. Rather than being directly in the business of value-definition, government's function is to foster small-scale community by focusing on the protection of individual rights—in other words, protecting the rights of individuals to participate or not participate in various communities as they choose. Thus, the focus of the state would be on preserving *systems* of interaction. By the same token, the constituent elements within this political community certainly matter in and of themselves, because each has individual rights, but these are not rights to fundamental disassociation from others, but instead *rights to choose appropriate forms of association.* To return to the food metaphor, the social result here is more of a stew—cooking blends but does not transform and merge the ingredients.[53]

Box (3) is a kind of constrained communitarianism. Moral theory here emphasizes autonomy rather than connection, but political theory introduces a sense of community at the macro level. This community has, as a whole, a sense of its long-term destiny or character, and therefore the political rights it extends to its citizens may vary from time to time as these social goals are sought and rethought. But this social effort is made in the context of a fundamental respect for individual autonomy. Although a recognizable end-product may animate this approach, its production depends to some significant degree upon the free choice of the ingredients. And, as with the development of Box (2), we can get different nuances of this version of metaethics by "starting" with, or emphasizing, either the moral or political dimension in the analysis. The food image that comes to mind here is a layer cake—more of a finished product than that of Box (2), but still not a homogenous blending like Box (4).

E. From Boxes to Variables

Because the model depicts the range of any normative debate—the categories of value thinking rather than values themselves—it follows that the four categories it isolates are not "absolutes" of any sort that demand or require that a person arguing for a particular policy stay within any one of them. Quite the contrary, these categories are more accurately understood as "beginning points" or opening "default positions" in a debate, even a debate going on inside the head of a single thinker. None of us is confined to or "locked into" any one or more of these categories; we wander among them as we attempt to decide what course of action to endorse. What Figure 9.2 shows, then, is the background difficulty in understanding any given policy debate, for the contentions will vary not only according to the values themselves argued by different positions, but also by the kind of values (metaethically) being argued. Given this background, normative disagreement, as this book has emphasized throughout, is inevitable.

But the circumstances are even worse. As a last step in appreciating what our model of normative disagreement is depicting, we note that we are not claiming that these four categories—even as mere "beginning points" in one's normative thinking—are themselves clean or neat. Picturing the normative categories in the form of boxes masks a further characteristic of the interaction of the basic perspectives (moral and political, categorical and consequentialist) that is important to note: Just as discussed in earlier Chapters, all these elements, rather than being specific categories of normative thinking, are more accurately perceived as variables that create a complex functional relationship. That is, one's attitude toward context can vary from extreme micro-focus to extreme macro-focus, and concomitantly, hypertext and subtext can range between extreme categorical to extreme consequential values. We are not, then, actually depicting "boxes" but areas in a graph where similar, but not identical, beginning or default positions would be grouped. So a graphic representation corresponding to the earlier boxes would appear as illustrated by Figure 9.3:

One important lesson emerges from this more complex picture. Now that the categories of normative reasoning have become areas on a graph, the lines that demarcate the boundaries of each are, of course, arbitrary rather than the result of scientific study. Placing the lines as depicted simply indicates that the

Figure 9.3

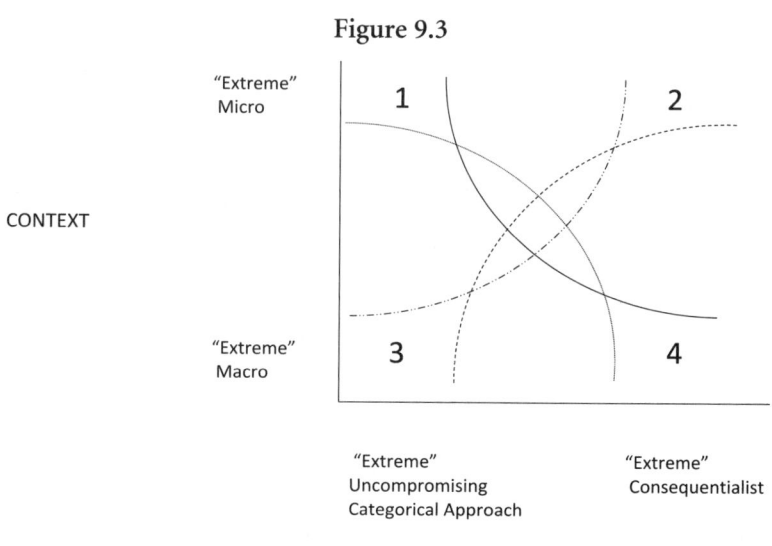

different perspectives exist, but the degree of "purity" of any point of view can vary—not just person to person, but issue to issue. The argument here is that in every public policy dispute the meta-perspectives of micro and macro, and means and ends, will come into play to some extent. It should come as no surprise, then, that the lines of these categories overlap, and may indeed have an area of complete overlap in the middle, suggesting that many policy discussions will find their way to that muddled centrality of grudging, unstable agreement.

F. Confirming the Analytic Model:
Back to the Privacy Cases

If the separation of normative disagreement into separate categories has merit, then we ought to be able to apply it to the three cases discussed above. The model predicts that a right as fundamental and abstract as privacy will generate a range of points of view even where everyone involved in the discussion accepts the existence of the right itself. The several opinions in the three cases confirm this proposition quite nicely.

A summary depiction of the meta-perspective from which those opinions spring is shown in Figure 9.4:

Figure 9.4

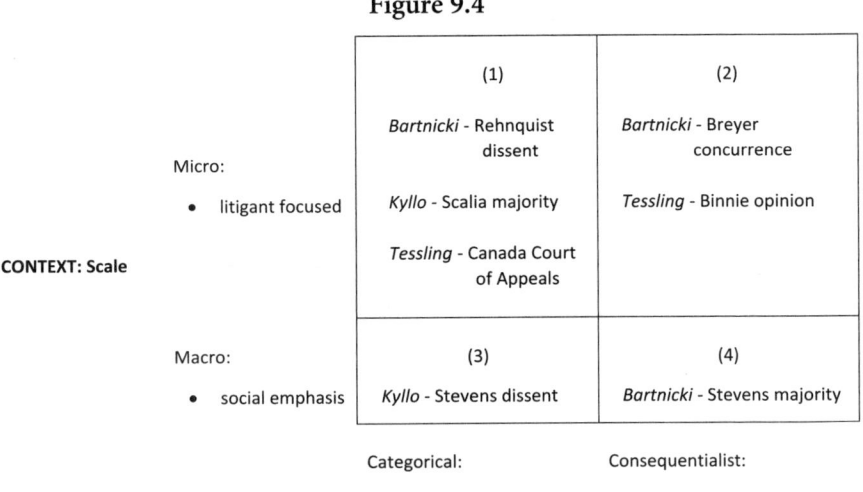

HYPERTEXT AND SUBTEXT:
Moral and Political Philosophy

To explain the placement of opinions in any of the boxes, some general observations about the nature of the dimensions in the model, mentioned earlier, need to be repeated here. The essential difference between the contextual factors—between fairness and justice—will be whether the author of an opinion emphasizes the circumstances of the litigants who prompted the case or the political institutions that must determine what to do about these kinds of situations. If a Justice does not pay much attention to this distinction, then the opinion will tend strongly to fall into either Box (1) or (4). Within the dimension of hypertext and subtext, the split between categorical and consequential will mean roughly the following: Regarding political subtext, the issue will be whether the institution primarily charged with a responsibility for individual rights—the courts—will have a strong role to play in determining the appropriate outcome in the case, or whether instead the courts should be more humble and acknowledge the superior normative role to be played by the institution primarily charged with the social good or ends—the legislature. Regarding philosophical hypertext, as the circumstances of the litigants are assessed, the division will be between values associated with the litigants themselves (or persons similarly situated in the future) or values associated with the larger social circumstances or sub-community of which these litigants (or similarly situated others in the future) are a part (or from which they spring).

The opinions in the three cases thus separate themselves as follows.

Box (1): The emphasis on rights

We can now see that the dissent in *Bartnicki*, the majority opinion in *Kyllo*, and the intermediate appellate court in *Tessling* share an important orientation: Each is classically "categorical" in its approach to the issue of privacy and its relationship to other claims, emphasizing the importance of key values in and of themselves—both morally and politically—rather than any social consequences that might flow from the result in the case. Interestingly, the two American opinions were both authored by Justices associated with the Court's "conservative" wing. Justice Rehnquist's *Bartnicki* dissent focused on the circumstances of the speaker whose cell phone conversation is intercepted, and stressed the appropriateness of the speaker's own, individual (moral) expectation of not being forced to share that private conversation as part of a public debate. The fact that the speaker might be a member of the larger group of "public figures" was not apparently significant. Justice Rehnquist did, however, add an important political subtextual twist: the appropriateness of Congress' endorsement of that expectation of privacy in the anti-wiretapping statute involved in the case. Yet the opinion contains no discussion of the utility—either at the micro level of individuals or the macro level of social welfare—of adopting his view of the importance of privacy in this context.

Justice Scalia's opinion in *Kyllo* similarly emphasizes the "right" rather than the "good": Even though society might be better off to some degree if the police could use their new technologies to gather more information about our activities, doing so by invading our homes in ways we cannot predict or detect simply goes too far. We have a right to privacy, based both on our status as citizens (moral) and on the dangerous nature of the police left unchecked (political), that causes the heat sensor to be an "unreasonable" search.

The *Tessling* Court of Appeals opinion similarly worried primarily about the legitimate expectations of privacy that citizens have concerning their domestic spaces, and the ability of the new heat-sensing technology to reach "inside" the home by demonstrating something unusual going on in there. These categorical matters easily overpowered the minor negative consequential result of letting a mere marijuana grower avoid detection.

Box (4): The ends justify the means

The clearest contrast to these normative perspectives is Justice Stevens' majority opinion in *Bartnicki*. Freedom of speech trumps privacy because the public "good" requires it. The person individually whose cell phone call was intercepted was not the key to the case; instead, it was this person as a public figure who must accept his or her circumstantial fate. Nor was the individual broadcaster's right to speak the key to the decision, for his role was less important in the Court's reasoning than the function of free speech within our political system. Similarly, the claim to cell phone privacy more generally was viewed by reference to the larger social interest in robust free speech. Hence, "good" dominated "right" quite thoroughly.

Box (2): Some ends, and narrower means, make a difference

Justice Breyer's concurrence in *Bartnicki* occupies this category of the civic liberal because of his insistence on limiting the scope of the result in the case. Rather than allowing the public character of a matter to swamp the claim to privacy so completely, Justice Breyer limited the impact by focusing on the more immediate potential impact of the speaker's statement on the lives of others within the speaker's sub-community.

This had two implications for his normative reasoning: First, at the moral level, he could agree with the majority's outcome because the context of the individual's claim to privacy mattered. Nevertheless, the consequences to his fellow citizens could not be ignored, thus reducing the viability of the speaker's claim to privacy. Second, however, Justice Breyer then differed from the majority hypertextually by emphasizing the "rights" at stake—the clearly established legal rights of all persons to be protected from assault and the speaker's clearly established legal (statutory) right to some degree of telephone privacy. He seemed to discount the macro contextual issue of the general social good that might follow from protecting the dissemination of information. While both the majority and Justice Breyer in *Bartnicki* allowed the "end" of speech to define privacy, Justice Breyer considered differently the "means" of a narrower legal holding as a key factor. For him, then, the courts, rather than legislatures, were the more serious institutional players in this kind of case.

Although Figure 9.4 suggests that the next topic now ought to be Justice Binnie's opinion in *Tessling*, we will postpone it for a moment.

Box (3): Legal flexibility matters more than categories.

Justice Stevens' dissent in *Kyllo* is a good example of why the initial diagram of rigid-looking boxes became a more flexible graph with general areas. It shares an important perspective with his majority opinion in *Bartnicki*: primarily that large-scale social circumstances (and hence social "ends") matter more than the specific situation of the litigants (and hence the legal "means" by which ends will be accomplished).

This was an important factor in his rejection of the majority's talisman of "the home"—he was much more consequentialist: Public safety will be unnecessarily compromised by ultra-respect for a particular physical location that already emits lots of data that law enforcement is entitled to capture and use (light, smells, and so on).

But his dissent ends up in Box 3 rather than Box 4 because of his hypertextual concern with individual rights: The right to privacy might actually be narrowed by this emphasis on the home, for technological invasions of our personal "space" are occurring in many more contexts than just the home. The Court's responsibility, then, was not to develop an ambitious, legislative-like approach to privacy-related cases, but let future circumstances—both future litigants and future legislation—be the venues for such decisions. The Court's role was therefore cast as a more limited and traditional one, based on a rights analysis that nevertheless had serious concern for the public interest.

So now we must fill in the previous gap in the analysis by confronting an interesting question: Where should we place Justice Binnie's *Tessling* opinion? It too, like the Stevens *Kyllo* dissent, is a good example of why the initial diagram using boxes became a more complicated graph, because his thinking exhibits all the analytical elements available in this legal area. This does not demonstrate a defect in the depictions, however, for the point of these exercises is not to place his work "precisely" within the matrix. Instead, it is to try to identify his default position—that is, the direction or background perspective from which his reasoning seems to emanate, and thus influence where he ends up. On that basis, even though he explicitly adopts aspects of Justice Stevens' *Kyllo* dissent, Binnie's opinion seems to fit better, surprisingly enough, in Box 2 along with Justice Breyer's style of reasoning.

Justice Binnie's result actually has the flavor, indeed, of Box 4, for it vindicates the public interest in drug enforcement. So it sounds like it might be based in a macro contextual orientation and a consequentialist philosophical and political perspective. But not really. Contextually, his analysis was consistently micro. He was much more carefully focused on the circumstances of the particular defendant, rather than homeowners in general or even marijuana-growing homeowners as a group. And he was also not concerned with search technology generally, but with this particular form of surveillance. But he ends up in Box 2 because his philosophical and institutional perspectives were primarily consequential. He rejected the *Kyllo* categorical notion of "the home" and, although he invoked other basic values like dignity and autonomy, these were not of consequence because the police activity never violated these precepts. Instead, he believed that the police certainly were entitled to develop *inferences* from all sorts of information they gather, basically non-intrusively, in the name of law enforcement. Whatever categorical values might have been relevant, they were secondary to larger social concerns.

What we glimpse in Justice Binnie's reasoning is, by reverse engineering, an insight into thorough advocacy: An effective argument to him would not be one that tried to tie him relentlessly to any of the extreme edges of the possible arguments suggested by the reasoning model. Instead, you would need to offer nuanced argument from each of the perspectives this book has developed: Words would have to be defined carefully; that would demand attention to both the facts and values inherent in that language; and the values would have to be both philosophical and political, micro and macro. When precedent is invoked, its authority will rest on its relationship to all these analytic points as well.

G. Legal Reasoning and Good Lawyering

Thus, applied rigorously and consistently, the analytic model should provide a rhetorical roadmap or checklist for an advocate. The questions become: What different kinds of normative perspective do I need to address in my arguments to best encourage a single judge or group of judges to agree with the result I seek in a particular case? If my goal is legislation, how do I best develop the consensus that will be necessary for success? How can I show that my result reflects both fairness and justice, and both appropriate means and ends? Although any successful advocate probably understands this range of necessary argument intuitively, unpacking some of the detail of these different contentions and the way they interact ought to be useful.

The lawyering point of this book's reasoning model is that *every* time clients seek legal advice about furthering their rights or interests in the face of significant opposition, a complete and thorough answer in a tough case will require their lawyer to note this full range of (at least) four possible perspectives. The disagreement at stake might involve micro, individual-level considerations of categorical values suggesting one kind of outcome, but that approach might be blocked or minimized by arguing for macro, social considerations that involve either different categorical values or a category jump into consequential values. And so on. The professional bottom line in challenging cases, as consistently observed in this text, is answering client questions with a *range* of structured answers, rather than just apologizing for the daunting complexity of the law.

The same considerations would apply on the other side of the policy question—the decision makers. The rhetorical issues are essentially the same: When is it "best" for a judge to understand, and apply, the law in a rigidly categorical form, or instead in a flexibly circumstantial, consequential form? When do the circumstances of the litigants themselves matter most, and when should social ramifications sway results? How can one judge best express his or her reasoning to develop a consensus among judicial colleagues for a particular result? What does it mean for a decision maker to be "ideological" or "pragmatic"?

And concerning the analysis of the work of any decision maker, the reasoning model provides avenues for assessment that perhaps have not been fully exploited: A decision maker's possible analytic inconsistencies can be exposed by focusing on the elements behind particular conclusions—inconsistencies that could be mistakes or at least require additional justification. For example, in *Kyllo*, Justice Scalia categorically emphasized the home as an essential nexus in our right to privacy, despite the impact that that approach might have on other interests like law enforcement. Yet a decade earlier in *Employment Division v. Smith*[54] he had no qualms in holding consequentially that the social interest in enforcing drug laws trumped an individual's right to free exercise of religion. In other words, in *Kyllo*, privacy dictated the limits of a legitimate *search*, while in *Smith* privacy did not impact the relationship between *religion* and *drug policy*. Why not? Do other values justify what seems to be a switch from the categorical to the consequential, or a switch from a micro to a macro orientation? Is the difference between *Kyllo* and *Smith* just the passage of time and thus differing social views associated with various activities? And while Justice Scalia may give categorical significance to the home for the right to privacy, he certainly does not show similar respect for the relationship between doctor and patient for purposes of the debate over the constitutional status of abortion rights.[55] Why is the home more central to privacy than personal medical procedures? And as noted earlier, would he be so sanguine about the importance of the home if the case involved child abuse?

All these questions may well have defensible answers. For example, *Kyllo* and *Smith* could be distinguished on the basis that searches for drugs are one thing while arrests for actual drug use are something else. But what makes this factual difference significant? Is it different contextual circumstances, like territory versus one's body? Or is it these contexts connecting with different hypertextual values, like dignity versus public safety? And quite distinct situations like home searches versus abortion regulation could be viewed as having little in common—one being essentially a demand to be left alone, while the other is a claim to be entitled to *do* something with one's body that could be seen as affecting someone else's bodily integrity. Which values, then, would be most relevant in each? Is a reference to autonomy the same idea in both?

The concern here is not that these myriad distinctions create disastrous conundra in the law, but instead simply that they are relevant issues that must be addressed systematically if we are to maintain our faith in precedent and the rule of law. One central element of both is simply consistency—treating like cases alike—but the challenging qualities of similarity and connection require complex, multifaceted thinking.

Notes

1. Bartnicki v. Vopper, 532 U.S. 514 (2001).

2. Kyllo v. United States, 533 U.S. 27 (2001).

3. 532 U.S. at 519-520.

4. U.S. Const. amend. I.

5. 532 U.S. at 526–528.

6. *Id.* at 534.

7. *Id.* at 532, 529.

8. *Id.* at 534.

9. *Id.* 536.

10. For example, speculation has always abounded about the degree to which health and medical information concerning major public figures (President, Vice-President, mem-

bers of the Cabinet, members of Congress, the members of the Joint Chiefs, and so on) should be more public than private.

11. 532 U.S. at 522–27.

12. *Id.* at 539.

13. *Id.* at 540.

14. *Id.* at 542.

15. *Id.* at 543.

16. *Id.* at 554–55.

17. *Id.* at 556.

18. 533 U.S. at 29–31.

19. *Id.* at 30.

20. *Id.* at 31.

21. *Id.*

22. Katz v. United States, 389 U.S. 347 (1967).

23. 533 U.S. at 34.

24. *Id.* at 36.

25. *Id.*

26. *Id.*

27. *Id.* at 31 (quoting Silverman v. United States, 365 U.S. 505, 511 (1964)).

28. *Id.* at 33.

29. *Id.* at 34.

30. *Id.* at 40 (quoting Payton v. United States, 445 U.S. 573, 590(1980)).

31. *Id.* at 41.

32. *Id.* at 36.

33. *Id.* at 47.

34. *Id.*

35. *Id.* at 48.

36. *Id.*

37. 533 U.S. at 47.

38. *See generally* ANTONIN SCALIA, A MATTER OF INTERPRETATION: FEDERAL COURTS AND THE LAW (1998); RANDY BARNETT, RESTORING THE LOST CONSTITUTION (2005); Antonin Scalia, *Originalism: The Lesser Evil*, 59 UNIV. OF CIN. L. REV. 849 (1989).

39. R. v. Tessling, [2004] 3 S.C.R. 432 (Can.).

40. *Id.* at 440.

41. *Id.* at 460.

42. *Id.* at 438.

43. *Id.* 439–440.

44. *Id.* 436.

45. *Id.* 445.

46. *Id.*

47. *Id.* at 448

48. *Id.* at 452.

49. You can think of this box as classical liberalism. *See* Richard E. Flathman, *Liberalism, in* 2 ENCYCLOPEDIA OF ETHICS 702 (Lawrence C. Becker ed., 1992). But it is also related, of course, to libertarianism. *See, e.g.,* ROBERT NOZICK, ANARCHY, STATE AND UTOPIA (1974).

50. Correspondingly, you can relate this box to modern communitarianism. *See, e.g.,* Maurizio Passerin d'Entreves, *Communitarianism, in* 2 ENCYCLOPEDIA OF ETHICS, *supra* note 49, at 181. One well-known background source on this topic is MICHAEL J. SANDEL, LIBERALISM AND THE LIMITS OF JUSTICE (2d ed. 1998).

51. One can find this approach in Immanuel Kant's approach to political, as opposed to his more famous moral, theory. *See* IMMANUEL KANT, TOWARD PERPETUAL PEACE: A PHILOSOPHICAL PROJECT (1795).

52. I would connect this version of Box (2) to the work of Prof. Ronald Dworkin, with his sense of pre-existing fundamental norms like "equal concern and respect," combined with his emphasis on individual rights. *See* the discussions of Prof. Dworkin's work at various places in this text. *See also* RONALD DWORKIN, A MATTER OF PRINCIPLE (1985).

53. Much the same result is reached, but with a different flavor, by starting the description of Box (2) with the political element. From this perspective, political theory is again oriented toward process rather than substance. Long-range social goals are viewed with suspicion, the emphasis instead being on the importance of interaction and interchange that can produce varying outcomes. Individual rights are therefore critical—the constituents within a community matter more than any particular social end-product. But the interplay of individuals is not as freewheeling as might be endorsed by Box (1). A certain responsibility attends the process that is based in a recognition of legitimate moral demands that we can make on one another to respect the interconnections from which we each spring. All values are therefore not up for grabs in the political realm—some at the moral level in effect preceded that game and are entitled to be maintained by it. Hence, while our system of justice may emphasize individual rights, it must do so within a context in which our individual dignity is defined by interdependence rather than separateness.

This version of Box (2) is, I think, close to the political theory of Prof. James Fishkin, with his emphasis on the "good" being produced, by definition, from time to time by appropriate interchanges among very well-informed citizens. JAMES S. FISHKIN, THE DIALOGUE OF JUSTICE (1992).

54. Employment Division v. Smith, 494 U.S. 872 (1990).

55. Justice Scalia's attitude is well-documented in a range of opinions. *See, e.g.,* Planned Parenthood v. Casey, 505 U.S. 833 (1992); Webster v. Reproductive Health Services, 492 U.S. 490 (1989); Stenberg v. Carhart, 530 U.S. 914 (2000); Gonzales v. Carhart, 550 U.S. 124 (2007).

Chapter Ten

The Never-Ending Disagreements over Statutory Interpretation: The Primacy of Subtext

A. Textual Ambiguity and Legal Reasoning

The concern I expressed in the brief preface to this last portion of this book could, of course, simply be unique to me. Perhaps everyone else finds it unremarkable that a fundamental aspect of our legal system—the interpretation of statutes by courts—remains so deeply controversial. The situation seems deceptively simple, because nothing directly associated with this activity seems debatable:

- "Statutes" themselves are clearly a legitimate element of our law.
- "Interpretation" is always required, as we noted earlier in this book, due to our imprecise and general language attaching itself to unpredictable specific future events.
- "Courts" are the primary place where this interpreting will occur because there will always be a dispute that has caused this legislation to be examined, and in our legal system the judiciary is where we typically resolve such disagreements.
- At the personal level, no one seriously doubts that the people doing both of these primary tasks—the drafting and the interpreting—are intelligent, well-educated, dedicated, and conscientious (and if you do doubt this, then this Chapter is a waste of your time).
- And also at the personal level, but now crassly political, even if we assume that statutory interpretation is simply a function of partisanship—say, conservatives battling liberals, or business battling labor—no particular interpretation *technique* can be attributed to any particular point of view

or agenda, simply because a method that yields the "correct" result in one case will not necessarily and consistently do so in the next.

So you might think, as a reasonable person, that a statute's words would, by and large, direct all readers consistently to a determinate, clear outcome— something akin to Justice Roberts' comforting reference to "calling the balls and strikes." If a statute's language was nevertheless occasionally challenging to understand precisely, you might again reasonably think that at least the *method* employed by judges to develop determinate meaning would be largely agreed upon and established over time—again something like "if you are unsure about the import of the statute's words, then resolve the issue by defining the words by doing X." After all, we all speak English in this situation.

But, of course, both assumptions would be quite wrong.

Although the *activity* of statutory interpretation, unlike trying to understand and apply the substantive legal doctrines that a statute embodies (like, for example, criminal penalties or standards of tort liability), would seem to be basically apolitical, it isn't, of course. The disagreements that fuel the debate over interpretation are simply a good example of a shift from a fight over legal substance to a fight over legal process: The issue is not what rights people may have, but how those rights are to be identified and who gets to do the identifying. Not surprisingly, the "what" is often intimately interconnected with the "how" and the "who," but they are sufficiently separate squabbles to deserve separate attention.

Nevertheless—which now brings us to the actual point of this Chapter—debates about both substance and process have a similar basic structure regularly recognized and employed in legal commentary: As we have seen, surface disagreements about particular legal outcomes are said to be fueled by a deeper disagreement about more fundamental "policies" or "theories" or "principles" or "values" that create the normative context within which the issues must be appreciated. Statutory interpretation, for example, is claimed to implicate political values involving nothing less than the "rule of law" itself, and therefore different perspectives on and approaches toward it should not be a surprise. What interests us here, however, is what may lie beneath that normative debate—how we might explain the seemingly endless struggles to determine the appropriate judicial approach toward legislative language. Do we actually disagree that much about the relationship of courts and legislatures in our political and legal systems, or is that debate actually fueled by disagreements over what we should even be *thinking* about as we attempt to define our political and legal values *themselves?*

This question becomes, then, in the context of this book: Can the debate about statutory interpretation be better understood as a debate about *legal rea-*

soning, which is the phenomenon underlying the entire controversy? This Chapter seeks to demonstrate precisely that.

To the cynic, of course, all this discussion of deeper analytical effort is a waste of time, for the simple conclusion should be that judges read statutes to achieve the results they want, period.[1] The problem with this view, however, is that it does not match the data well, unless judges as a group are remarkably adept liars and actors. Their expressed efforts to understand and apply legislative material seem, to the contrary, to demonstrate real struggles with the appropriate relationship between courts and the governmental branches that generate particular statutory language. Nevertheless, it is also quite clear that the method (or methods) of interpretation employed by any judge will be influenced to some degree by considerations larger, more fundamental, and more personal than just the words on a page. Judges are human, after all, and cannot completely escape their own pre-existing values and perspectives. But the relationship between interpretation and outcome determination seems much more complicated than crass.

It is that relationship and its complexity that are the subjects of this Chapter, but approached from a different analytical perspective. The range of possible methods of interpretation have been examined countless times by very capable scholars and judges, and I do not have a new technique to suggest, or some other unique synthesis to offer, that will resolve the debate. In fact, I will also not offer a new "theory" or approach to statutory interpretation that will help us choose among the various interpretative techniques. Instead, my argument will be that we *cannot* resolve the debate—that another difficulty lies "underneath" the struggle with statutory interpretation, if you will. This problem then guarantees continuing disagreement about all aspects of the topic—not just how judges should interpret statutes, but also which theory of judicial interpretation best explains or justifies the use of any particular interpretative technique.

It is this inevitability of controversy that I find more interesting and illuminating than the arguments for and against any particular interpretative method. The underlying struggle, not surprisingly, is about important values—but not the values reflected in the statutes themselves that are to be interpreted, nor the political values inherent in the relationship between courts and legislatures. Rather, it is about how we *think* about all those values, how we put any value into a larger analytical framework whenever we bring it to life. The approach to statutory interpretation in this book, then, while about values, is not actually normative, but epistemological—with normative implications.

As in previous Chapters, what we are concerned with is how we frame legal and policy questions, rather than the substance of the occasional, often short-lived, answers we might, or "should," reach on a given issue. Indeed, my contention has been that if we could better understand the disagreements, we might better be able to create and maintain the instances of agreement.

The question here is whether we can identify different ways in which various judges and scholars in fact *approach* the task of statutory interpretation itself even *before* the substance of the statute is addressed and even *before* they worry about the political values or policies that are at stake. If we can, then these epistemological differences may orient the disagreements about the meaning of the statute, and do so in a manner that is predictable. And then if so, in turn, the analytical approach suggested in this book becomes practical as well as theoretical: You should be able to use this approach to anticipate the arguments that will be made against any value or policy you espouse to others, allowing you more effectively to develop your defenses.

This Chapter proceeds in four steps, the first two being background. Part B identifies, in very summary form, the now-familiar approaches to statutory interpretation generally recognized and applied by courts. Part C then reviews some of the academic literature on these approaches to discuss the general political and legal theories on which this range of approaches is said by courts and commentators to be based.

Part D then applies the epistemological analytical approach developed in earlier Chapters to organize this range of techniques and normative theories systematically, using the now-familiar elements of text, context, hypertext and subtext. The result, just as we have seen earlier, is that the tensions within each of these elements then generate yet another four-part range of possible categories into which we would predict that interpretive techniques would divide themselves. These methods will be a surprise to no one, for they are the familiar gaggle of plain text, legislative purpose, legislative intent, and so-called dynamic interpretative approaches.

The point of rehashing these traditional categories will *not* be (as you would expect at this point) that any one of them is "correct" or "most appropriate" in some deeper sense. It will be instead that *none* of these approaches is necessarily to be privileged—that the full range is, and will continue to be, inevitable. This conclusion will in fact be developed more fully in Part E, where the inevitability of controversy will be linked to a review of the much-maligned decision by the Supreme Court in *Holy Trinity Church v. United States*,[2] which can be criticized not only for some of its unfortunate attitudes toward immigrants to this country, but also more important for our purposes, for trying to be too analytically ambitious.

B. Open Texture and the Traditional Responses

In the first place, and most obviously, statutes are notorious breeding grounds for dispute, no matter how smart or capable a drafter or reader might be, because legislation has several well-known background characteristics that produce, in H.L.A. Hart's famous phrase, linguistic "open texture," or inevitable degrees of ambiguity:[3]

- political circumstance: Statutory language is frequently (if not always) the result of difficult political compromises, only some of which may have ever been expressed openly in the legislative process, and those compromises may push the statute's language into ever-higher levels of generality or abstraction to achieve the agreement necessary for passage;

- epistemic and predictive imperfection: All statutes have been enacted by people who, by definition, have an incomplete and imperfect understanding of the context to which the statute will be applied, and who will be unable to predict all future contexts in which the statute might prove relevant;

- subject and behavioral generality: The people to whom the statute will be addressed and on whom it will be imposed will necessarily be large, diverse groups within the population, rather than a few specific individuals, and the behaviors to which the statute will be relevant will likewise usually be somewhat broader than just requiring a single, specific action; hence, the ability to imagine all the circumstances to which the statute will be applied is even more attenuated.

Yet these are only the most obvious problems inherent in interpreting statutes. Much subtler, and more relevant to the inquiry here, is the underlying issue of the *reasoning* to be applied to each of these challenging statutory circumstances. As it turns out, lawyers and judges cannot even agree on *that* point—on the "when in linguistic doubt, consider X" in the summary above—thus guaranteeing considerable disagreement about the statute's appropriate meaning.

Nevertheless, the debate about how to respond to linguistic messiness has developed, over time, some traditional grounding-points, or perhaps more accurately, some "schools of thought" concerning appropriate judicial analysis of legislative work—that is, what the X is that should be considered to resolve the interpretive problem. The most commonly recognized are these four:[4]

- identifying the "purpose" the legislature was trying to achieve;
- understanding the "intent" of the legislature in enacting the measure (if that is different from purpose);

- exploring more widely the moral and political values that the statute may have been attempting to further or vindicate—what has come to be called a "dynamic" approach to interpretation; or
- much more narrowly, relying solely (or as nearly as one can) on the "plain text" itself that the legislature actually enacted, without resort to other psychological or normative "fillers" of any kind to supplement the actual words of the statute.

The approach to these traditional perspectives in this book should not be viewed in isolation from the prior literature on this topic, however, for much of that work is exploited here—just arranged rather differently for important reasons. The section below explores a small portion of this immense body of work that seems particularly appropriate for exploring the relevance of legal reasoning to interpretive efforts. The point for our purposes will be to note that their approaches all involve, and can be better appreciated by reference to, the analytic categories we have developed: linguistic text, contextual scale, hypertextual values, and particularly political subtext.

C. Examples of Scholarly Efforts to Organize the Interpretation Debate

Only three examples from the literature on statutory interpretation will be developed here, each of which represents a particular type of scholarly endeavor, and each of which provides an extensive review and assessment of the range of interpretative techniques. The first is a casebook—ELEMENTS OF LAW,[5] by Professors Hanks, Herz, and Nemerson (which I will refer to by using the title). It is intended for law school courses usually labeled "Legal Methods," with one of those methods obviously being the drafting and implementing of statutes. The second is a respected treatise on statutory interpretation—LEGISLATION AND STATUTORY INTERPRETATION,[6] by Professors Eskridge, Frickey, and Garrett (which I will reference as INTERPRETATION)—which presents a more ambitious effort to reorganize the debate conceptually. The third is an article by Judge John Walker[7] of the U.S. Court of Appeals for the Second Circuit (which I will reference using his name), who, from his perspective on the front lines of the battle over interpretation, seeks to explain and justify a practical understanding of the effort.

In the most general sense, and consistent with the traditional approaches in this area, each of these sources dissects the interpretation debate quite similarly: Rather than just present a laundry list of available interpretative techniques that have been suggested or employed from time to time, the authors first identify an underlying theoretical debate about the proper role of courts in confronting the work of another branch of government. These deeper perspectives (which will obviously be combinations of hypertext and subtext) then help explain the categories into which interpretative techniques are regularly grouped. While the three sources vary in their description of the deeper theoretical issues, they all ultimately divide the various techniques themselves into three basic categories: "plain text" or "textual" approaches; approaches attempting to identify legislative "intent" or "purpose"; and more creative "dynamic" approaches that search more widely for normative or pragmatic justifications for statutory meaning. Of primary interest here are the theoretical backgrounds the sources identify, the relation between these theories, and the way the three categories are then described.

Both ELEMENTS OF LAW and Judge Walker orient their discussions initially around two fundamental political (subtextual) perspectives on the appropriate relationship of courts to legislatures. In the terms employed by ELEMENTS, judges can think of themselves as mere "agents" of the legislature, simply applying statutory directives as written, with no expectation that they have any role in refining the legal rules presented to them. Or judges can understand themselves to be "partners" with the legislature in the joint enterprise of supplying and applying legal guidance to the populace.[8] Judge Walker describes the dichotomy as one between a judge being "faithful" to the statutory text or being interested instead in "improving" it.[9]

These perspectives then produce a continuum, rather than neat categories, so that different interpretative techniques are specific manifestations of different amounts or degrees or mixes of a judge's belief about his or her role as faithful agent or improving partner: Judges adhering to a more constrained understanding of their legal role will favor the constraints offered by the statutory text, and those with a more expansive view will favor the much wider range of dynamic interpretative methods. Hence, a simple continuum is evident, as shown by Figure 10.1:

Figure 10.1

Interpretative Technique:	textualism	intent or purpose	dynamic
Background Theory:	court as agent		court as partner

Of course, both ELEMENTS OF LAW and Judge Walker develop the three basic interpretative categories in much more detail than presented here, with Judge Walker being particularly interested in the historical sequence that has led to the current range.[10] But only one facet of that development is relevant to the present analysis: the troubling middle category of "intent" and "purpose."

Here, the sources diverge and struggle, as everyone seems to do. Judge Walker does not discuss or develop any meaningful distinction between these two terms, in part, one can surmise, because judges and commentators have for so long used them seemingly interchangeably. ELEMENTS OF LAW, on the other hand, does make an effort to do so, relating "intent" to a narrower, possibly more objective, psychological concept (a narrower context), and "purpose" to a broader sense of social goal (a broader context).[11] This psychological version of intent is perhaps most clearly manifested in Judge Richard Posner's concept of "imaginative reconstruction"[12] of a statute by a judge, in which the judge imagines how the legislature would have responded to the precise circumstances faced by the judge—that is, rather like a hypothetical situation presented to the legislators prior to their vote. Correspondingly, inquiry into a legislature's general purpose or social goal in enacting a statute (often argued to be reflected in a statute's legislative history) seems more naturally to be a wider opportunity for a judge to apply his or her own policies to a particular situation.[13] But the blend of "agent" and "partner" in this middle area remains murky.

The analysis in the INTERPRETATION text is richer in detail and ambition concerning both the theoretical background of interpretation and the number of possible categories that this background spawns. The authors identify three underlying theories concerning judicial efforts to understand legislative pronouncements—each more theoretically substantive than the "agent/partner" dichotomy—and then the range of interpretative methods increases to six. The problem that develops in the INTERPRETATION text, however, is a disconnection between the theories and the methods.

The various theories or "norms," as the authors put it, at work behind the interpretative techniques are three "ideas":[14] "rule of law," "democratic legitimacy," and "pragmatism." The first is characterized by a court's concern with the predictability and political neutrality of its decisions, the second by an emphasis on judicial deference to the legislature's dominant law-creating role in our legal system; and the last by the judiciary's general interest—shared by all good citizens—in contributing productively to the common good. The authors then suggest that these (as I would label them) subtextual/hypertextual perspectives can be related to the three basic categories of interpretative devices—which they label as "textual," "intentionalist," and "dynamic"—by asking how the different devices "contribute" to any of the norms. The connection between theories and methods is therefore quite straightforward:[15]

rule of law	→	textualism
democratic legitimacy	→	intentionalist
pragmatism	→	dynamic

But the analysis of interpretation in the text becomes more complex and nuanced than this simple set of relationships suggests. Although the theories remain the same, each of the methods expands to add variations as the authors consider other factors at work in the interpretative exercise.

For example, in the examination of "textualism," a key element becomes the distinction between the goals of (or, as this book would express it, the hypertextual theory underlying) the interpretation of the statute, and the source of information about what the proper interpretation should be.[16] Thus, references to a statute's text might simply be the strongest source for achieving the goal of implementing the legislature's intent. As a consequence, the method of interpretation labeled "textualist" has, according to the authors, two subcategories: "soft plain meaning,"[17] which is actually more related to intentionalism, and the harsher, more dogmatic "new textualism,"[18] which seeks to limit interpretation more rigorously to the words on the page.

In a closer look at "intentionalism," the question becomes how rigorously psychological the analysis of "intent" will be. The authors see three possibilities:[19] A judge could attempt to identify the actual, real, "specific" intent of legislators; or, as noted earlier, the effort could be to approximate the intent of this group by "imaginatively reconstructing" what they *would have done* with the particular issue now faced by the court; or, the judge could generalize the idea of psychological intent into an inquiry into the legislature's "purpose" in enacting the statute. The difference among these approaches, the authors note, is basically the degree of abstraction used within them, but the book also acknowledges that these differing degrees implicate the interpretative theories lying in the background: "As the inquiry becomes steadily more abstracted from specific intent [which is the most legitimate basis for an "intentionalist" theory], not only does its democratic legitimacy fade, but the inquiry becomes less determinate and perhaps more driven by nonlegislator value choices, hence in tension with the rule of law."[20]

This suggests that there is some continuum involved here—a sliding scale of some kind that relates the theories and the interpretative methods.

One possible version of that spectrum is then revealed when the authors examine what they label as "dynamic" theories of interpretation.[21] Approaches in this category quite simply abandon "sources" in favor of "goals": Interpretation is understood as an exercise in making (hypertexual) value choices, and those values ought therefore to be the honest focus of the discussion.

The question then becomes how well any judge understands the values that are at stake in a given case. INTERPRETATION's authors acknowledge that here too we have a range of possibilities. At the extremes would be somewhat simplistic efforts to provide a "best answer" to the interpretative issue. These answers would themselves be of several possible kinds, ranging from "morally" best in some deontological sense, to more "pragmatically" best in the sense of emphasizing coherence within the law, to more extreme "critical" efforts at deconstructing statutory language to discard or eliminate the hegemonic forces that may have spawned them. Somewhere in the middle of this muddle, however, lies the methodology the authors clearly favor (as does Judge Walker ultimately): a "pragmatic"[22] approach that acknowledges that "the goals of statutory interpretation may be multiple and the sources may be various."[23] Turning from prescription to description, the authors argue that what really goes on out there in the judicial mind (and again Judge Walker largely agrees) is a consideration of all the possible interpretative methods at various points for various pragmatic reasons.[24] The only actual difference between the methods, then, is the degree of conceptual abstraction that the court is willing to employ in a particular case.

This is getting to be a very complicated picture indeed, with several different strands of interpretative nuance. In an effort to get some perspective on and control over the range of possible interpretative results, the authors suggest a form of continuum along which the interpretive methods and sources fall, which the authors call the "funnel of abstraction," shown in Figure 10.2:[25]

Figure 10.2

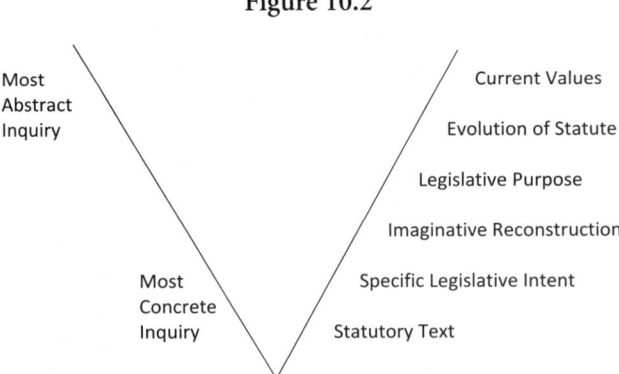

By implication, then, the levels of abstraction on the left of this diagram could be replaced, perhaps, with the three basic underlying theories the authors earlier identified, starting with "dynamic/pragmatism" at the top, "democratic legitimacy/intentionalism" in the middle, and "rule of law/textualism" at the bottom. If so, the methods of interpretation, in normative if not descriptive terms, relate to, and overlap with, each other along a spectrum much like that suggested by the ELEMENTS casebook and Judge Walker.

The point of this review, as stated earlier, is not to show inconsistencies among these sources or to argue that any of them got the analysis wrong. Quite the contrary, it is their consistency and thoroughness that is important. If we accept the accuracy of the analysis in these sources, the question is whether a further structure might lie underneath them that would have predicted the common features we find. In turn, that structure might predict and endorse the idea that interpretative methods employed by courts do not fall into neat, separate categories or typologies, but instead array themselves in some interconnected way along an even more complex continuum of some kind. Finally, that underlying structure might also give us some additional insight into the troublingly vague middle category of "intentionalism" in particular.

It is that next step into deeper structure and interconnections that Part D explores.

D. Explaining, and then Structuring, Continuous Disagreement

1. Explaining

The explanation for the continuous disagreement that swirls around these traditional interpretative methods, and the efforts to identify some interconnective continuum among them, lies within the nature of legal reasoning this book has developed: The four perspectives of text, context, hypertext, and subtext immediately suggest significant complexity, but they also simultaneously suggest a method to organize aspects of that complexity. To make matters a bit simpler, we will assume that we have a "text" with the usual problem of words that demand attention to the distinction between the "is" and "ought" of their use. The question then becomes how to approach that analysis—how to determine the meaning of the statute's words. *Legal tradition* would send us into an examination of legislative purpose, intent, and so on. But which should we choose, and why?

To resolve these questions, we will first examine each of this book's analytic elements in turn, and then integrate them all into a single comprehensive picture of the debate plaguing interpretation.

First, *context*: Chapter Six established that a court's perspective on a statute will certainly require (simply because this is a *court* at work here, and not a legislature) that the judge determine the "scale" that will be most critical to its understanding of the legislation: Will the key to its application be the micro level of the persons who have brought this issue to the court's attention ("fairness" from their perspective), or the macro concerns of the legal system, or society more generally, associated with the statute's topic ("justice")? To what extent, in other words, should it be relevant to the court that this *specific* case involves these *specific* litigants? Never? For example, should the judge focus on only the words of the statute alone, regardless of the impact on these people? Or should instead the litigants always matter? For example, should the judge bend the statutory language as necessary to achieve what he or she believes is an "appropriate" result for the people in this case? Although any judicial decision will quite obviously to some degree involve a mix of these two considerations— of moral philosophy and political philosophy—the point is that there will indeed, and inevitably, be a mix, and that mix will be one concerning which reasonable judges could disagree as they try to determine a proper outcome to the case. Thus arises an immediate analytic tension.

But why is this a tension at all? Why does the distinction of scale matter? The problem is that the difference between macro and micro becomes both quite evident and quite difficult when one realizes that both of these aspects of scale— of "is"—can in turn create different perspectives on the "ought" of the case— the substantive normative values that will be applied to determine a winner and loser. The statute's text, then, implicates not just context, but hypertext.[26]

Thus, *hypertext*: Chapter Seven argued that all values relevant to any judicial decision maker could be divided between two very large categories: categorical and consequential (corresponding generally to the philosophical distinction between deontology and teleology). One example used there to illustrate the difference was the right of free speech: Was the foundation of this right to be found in the values of human dignity that it protected and vindicated, or in the beneficial results enjoyed by society if many ideas get discussed rather than just a few?

To this illustration we could add another that is well-known in the philosophical literature: Immanuel Kant's argument[27] for an absolute duty to tell the truth, regardless of the consequences of doing so. Let us take the harmless situation of your host at a dinner party asking if you enjoyed the meal that was served. In fact, you hated it. But what do you say in response to a direct question where you cannot easily evade the point (i.e., "the meal was interesting")? A categorical approach to telling a lie ("the meal was superb") would attempt to determine the rightness or wrongness of the falsehood by identifying the values implicated by the statement. That is, lying could be understood as inconsistent both with the speaker's (your) own sense of personal integrity and with the responsibility to respect the dignity of others, even though the lie would allow you to avoid hurting your hosts' feelings. The categorical values would thus trump psychological impact.

A consequentialist approach, on the other hand, would assess the goodness or badness of lying by its actual impact on the personal and social relationships and circumstances at stake. If, for example, the result that is deemed best is a social setting with less tension, embarrassment, and animosity, then telling a lie to avoid hurt feelings would be entirely appropriate, despite the negative impact on other normative values like "dignity" and "integrity." Or quite the contrary, the outcome that you believe most appropriate could be retaliation for a prior hurt inflicted on you by this host, in which case an equality of injury guides the analysis (getting even). In fact, you could use either hypertextual perspective to dominate the other: You could use categorical values (like dignity) to tell you which consequences will have any relevance, just as you could use consequential values (like domestic tranquility) to define the nature of your categorical values (what dignity actually means in this setting).

The relevance of hypertext to statutory construction then becomes, in turn, determining whether the text of the legislation, and its context, should be approached categorically or consequentially. The former would identify the values most relevant to the interpretative *process*—values such as consistency and predictability in the law, or enforcing the will of the legitimately established political majority, or vindicating and honoring certain key human, political, or legal rights. The latter would be most concerned with the *substance* of the statute involved—the social results that the statute was apparently meant to produce, such as benefiting a particular racial group or protecting certain kinds of workers or whatever. These perspectives need not necessarily clash with each other, of course, for in the easiest cases they will point the judge toward the same result, and will suggest a straightforward interpretive strategy for getting there. But they also do not necessarily coincide. Interpreting words one way might yield consistency, but at the cost of an absurd or counterproductive result in a particular setting. Read another way, the words might produce a happy result at the cost of stretching or manipulating the meaning of various terms beyond established, accepted, or familiar understandings.

But as complex as these analytic steps have become, we are still not done. Finally, we must also address *subtext*. In the background of the discussion of both context and hypertext has been the fact that we are dealing here with a *court's* interpretation of the output of another branch of government—either the legislature or an administrative agency. Thus, we must also recognize the impact on the entire analysis thus far—on both the circumstances involved in a case and the values implicated by that case—of the court's political situation. The judiciary knows quite well that it does not operate in a vacuum. One key to its ability to perform its function, then, is its relationships with the other branches of government: A court's attitude toward its proper place in the political landscape will certainly have an influence on its determination of which circumstances are appropriate for it to consider, and which values should guide the normative assessment of those circumstances. Indeed, this analytical concern will in many ways be the dominant consideration, for it influences particularly heavily all other aspects of the court's reasoning.

2. *Structuring*

The result of all these perspectives can be summarized and depicted, at least initially, in what has become by now a familiar format: a four-part box. What is immediately intriguing, however, is that while this method has consistently yielded this number of perspectives on any issue, the topic of statutory interpretation is already grounded in four approaches. The task now is to demonstrate that no one should be surprised by this correspondence.

a. Factors Create Categories

From previous discussions, the dimensions that will create the multiple methods of interpretation are equally predictable. We already have our challenging "text"—the statute the court must apply—and now we need to determine how the factors of context, hypertext, and subtext interact to produce a structure—but not a resolution—to the debate. We can start by accepting the traditional four methods—plain text, legislative purpose, legislative intent, and dynamic judicial creativity—as our anchoring points, and then watch as they predictably emerge in relation to (and in competition with) each other.

To turn our three remaining dimensions into two so that we can match earlier analytic pictures, we must acknowledge that both context (scale) and subtext (political institutional considerations) are suffused with hypertextual values that give them content. Hence, the two sides of the box will be combinations of subtext *and* hypertext, and context *and* hypertext. The structure thus becomes that shown in Figure 10.3:

Figure 10.3

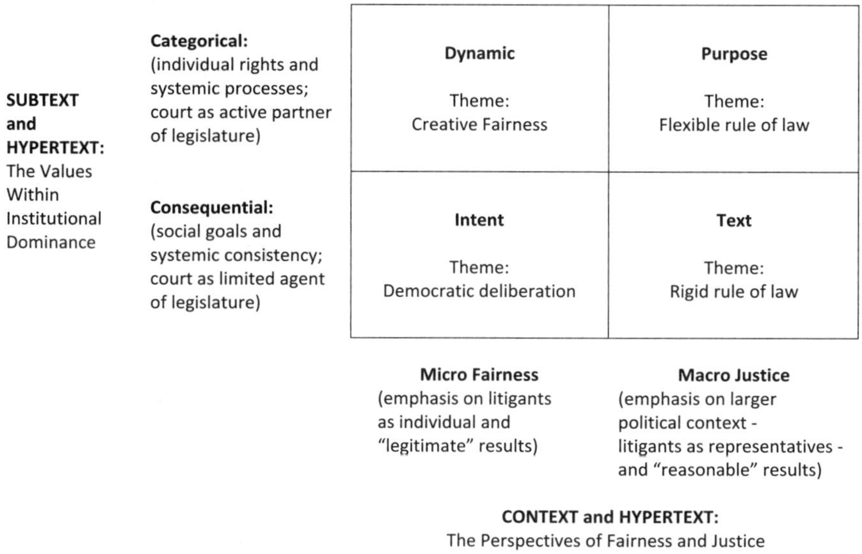

		Dynamic Theme: Creative Fairness	Purpose Theme: Flexible rule of law
SUBTEXT and HYPERTEXT: The Values Within Institutional Dominance	**Categorical:** (individual rights and systemic processes; court as active partner of legislature)	Dynamic Theme: Creative Fairness	Purpose Theme: Flexible rule of law
	Consequential: (social goals and systemic consistency; court as limited agent of legislature)	Intent Theme: Democratic deliberation	Text Theme: Rigid rule of law

Micro Fairness
(emphasis on litigants as individual and "legitimate" results)

Macro Justice
(emphasis on larger political context - litigants as representatives - and "reasonable" results)

CONTEXT and HYPERTEXT:
The Perspectives of Fairness and Justice

The two polar opposites of dynamic interpretation and strict textualism are now easier to explain. The former permits courts, which are uniquely positioned to consider the circumstances of individual litigants, to manipulate the legislation in question as necessary to achieve appropriate rights-based outcomes. The latter, in contrast, limits the court's role severely, focusing on the fact that the court is reviewing not its own prior work (precedent), but the work of a separate political branch of government, which is by definition thinking macro rather than micro. Hence, the job of the court should be to do likewise by limiting itself to the words themselves that the legislature employed, not imagining supposed normative considerations that might have lurked within their complex groupthink process. The court's task in interpretation, then, is not to "improve" the legislative product, but simply apply it. If that yields uncomfortable results, let the legislature deal with the fallout.

For our purposes, then, the clash is this: The dynamic approach to interpretation may permit normatively praiseworthy creative outcomes that achieve individual fairness, but it does so at the cost of denigrating equally normatively praiseworthy legal elements like consistency, predictability, and political accountability. And concomitantly, the textual approach creates systemic consistency that perhaps everyone, including even the legislature occasionally, now regrets. The four-part box does not, by itself, tell you which method you should find compelling.

The other two boxes are more interesting because they are not as obviously at war with each other—but they are quite distinct nevertheless. They demonstrate the important tension that lurks beneath references to "intentionalism," which conflates legislative intent and purpose.

A court's exploration of a legislature's supposed purpose in enacting a statute is the proactive effort of a political equal—the court may be stuck with the legislature's words, but it can look beneath them to discern the social goals sought to be pursued. The court, despite having individual litigants before it, can nevertheless think macro by viewing these people or entities not particularly but generally—as illustrators of the legislation's social impact. But distinct from simple textualism, one relevant element in that impact is the court's independent institutional responsibility to ensure that social goals do not leave our political, systemic concern with individual rights in the dust.

In contrast, but not sharply so, a court concerned with legislative intent is (at least facially) engaged in a psychological inquiry—not trying to discern social goals but identifying more specific thought processes. The effort can be understood quite nicely by reference to Judge Posner's idea, noted earlier, that a judge, in interpreting a statute, should try to imagine how the legislature would have responded to the judge's specific case if its circumstances had been presented to the legislature as a hypothetical. This analysis turns the court back to its more traditional micro role, but, unlike the dynamic approach, does not turn the judge loose to consider various hypertextual values rooted in individual rights. And, although the court views its political role as deferential to, rather than equal with, the legislature, an inquiry into intent is unlike the textual approach because the court does not view itself as so dramatically saddled by the words alone with which they are confronted.

Hence, the distinction between purpose and intent reduces to something like this: An effort to implement legislative purpose may further the legislative agenda, but do so through encouraging a court to act (inappropriately) like a legislature. Or a reference to purpose may quite appropriately save a great deal of political time and trouble by avoiding more legislative work, but do so at the cost of insufficient attention to the litigants themselves who are caught up in this effort to achieve a social goal. By the same token, discerning the intent of the legislature could be a way to show respect for individuals without turning courts loose to think macro themselves. Or looking for intent could be an empty, impossible psychological exercise that is actually meant to disguise judicial creativity. You choose.

b. Further Implications: Structure Based on Variables

There are, consequently, two points to this extended analysis of the various methods of statutory interpretation. The first is that this exercise, like earlier ones, demonstrates that the neat categories of the four-part box are misleading. The two basic dimensions of subtext/hypertext and context/hypertext are, as we have seen, not easily divided between two simple approaches, but are more akin to variables ranging between two extreme positions: concerning the former, between a sort of "total" categorical or total consequential thinking, and concerning context, relentless micro or relentless macro. Hence, the more accurate depiction of the relationships returns us to the graph version, with "areas" of interpretative methodology, rather than sealed boxes, as shown in Figure 10.4:

Figure 10.4

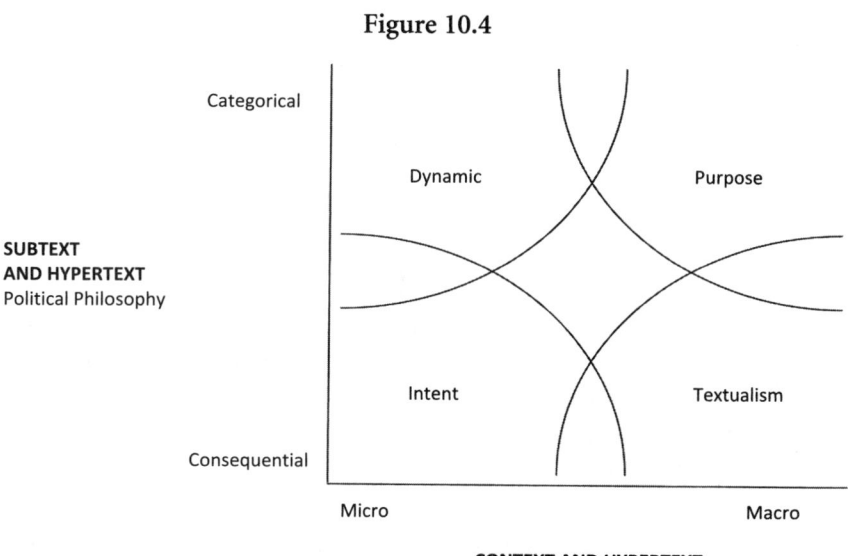

From this perspective, each method blends into the others, with only the most strident ideologues holding down the extreme corners. The rest of us struggle within the muddled middle areas.

The second implication is that various interpretative methods that have been identified in the literature from time to time[28] can now be seen as slight variations within the range of possibilities already traditionally established. Because we can now think in terms of areas rather than boxes, we can easily imagine numerous overlapping segments that might get their own particular label, each still being nevertheless a function of the same fundamental analytic dimensions provided by our understanding of legal reasoning. The depiction could then become that shown in Figure 10.5:

Figure 10.5

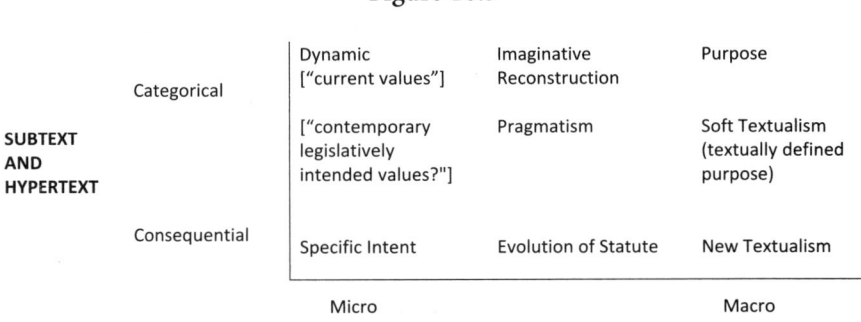

		Dynamic ["current values"]	Imaginative Reconstruction	Purpose
	Categorical			
SUBTEXT AND HYPERTEXT		["contemporary legislatively intended values?"]	Pragmatism	Soft Textualism (textually defined purpose)
	Consequential			
		Specific Intent	Evolution of Statute	New Textualism
		Micro		Macro

CONTEXT AND HYPERTEXT

Some interesting implications emerge from this array, I believe. Note that pragmatism is here (more accurately) understood as a rejection of every dogmatic approach. It is not, as INTERPRETATION suggested, associated with freewheeling judicial dynamism, but instead with an effort to accomplish practical ends that may demand that normativity be avoided, not embraced. But their idea of a "soft textualism" does seem to be an element in the debate, as a blend of text and judicially understood purpose. And the concept of making sense of a particular statute by linking it to prior legislative work—"evolution"—gives textualism a different twist by connecting it to a form of legislative psychology.

The array of choice in this interpretation circumstance is certainly now very daunting, but that should come as no surprise. Instead, the point here, as it has been from the beginning, is this: Going deep into legal reasoning reveals that any judicial effort to determine the "correct" method of statutory interpretation will be plagued by inevitable, and continuous, disagreement.[29]

E. Rethinking *Holy Trinity Church*

At the very foundation of all discussions of statutory interpretation is a judicial decision that illustrates precisely this proposition. The usual beginning point for law school teaching on this topic is the Supreme Court's struggle to understand and apply a particularly messy immigration statute in *Holy Trinity Church v. United States*.[30] It is famous in part because it seems to be just as much an analytic jumble as the legislation. It is usually therefore criticized for its failure to identify and then stick to *any* particular interpretative method, instead pushing and pulling in various directions.

But rather than being condemned, it should be praised (in a way) for trying to support its interpretative result in every possible way. Whether this judicial approach is one to which courts should aspire I leave to others to decide.

The case involved a restrictive immigration law aimed (apparently) at reducing the flood of unskilled, and hence, cheap, workers coming into the country in the late 1800s (the image here being Chinese immigrants helping to build the American railroads) by prohibiting employers from paying the travel expenses of those they hoped to employ. If an employer did so, a fine would be imposed. The problem that arose for the Court was, as is always the situation, a circumstance that no one had apparently considered: a major New York church seeking to import, so to speak, from England a famous preacher. The question became whether this fellow and his occupation fit within the broad categories of workers targeted for the no-travel-expenses requirement within the statute, or whether he was some sort of exception. The lower courts had viewed the situation as straightforward, and imposed the statute's fine on the church.[31] The Supreme Court, however, gives every impression in its opinion that it knew quite well where it would end up—which was to allow the church to avoid the fine—but it had to figure out how to get there.

The text of the statute was, of course, the problem. It could hardly be more thorough, making it unlawful:

> ... for any person, company, partnership, or corporation, in any manner whatsoever, to prepay the transportation, or in any way assist or encourage the importation or migration, of any alien or aliens, any foreigner or foreigners, into the United States, its territories, or the District of Columbia, under contract or agreement, parol or special, express or implied, made previous to the importation or migration of such alien or aliens, foreigner or foreigners, to perform labor or

service of any kind in the United States, its territories, or the District of Columbia.[32]

But, as the Court noted, the statute did contain some exceptions—although all things considered, they seem today almost comical as an acknowledgement that Congress did not want the legislation to affect the lives of its members too directly: "professional actors, artists, lecturers, singers, and domestic servants."[33] These exceptions, however, actually added to the statute's clarity because it meant that the reference to "labor or service of any kind" was otherwise apparently all-encompassing.

The Court therefore had to acknowledge that the case before it was "within the letter" of this statute[34]—its language was so broad and inclusive that it would seem hard to imagine how to dodge the result the Court did not want. But dodge it would, using every angle it could think to include.

Although the Court certainly conceded that legislative text ought ordinarily to control any judicial analysis, the Court quickly noted that texts can sometimes not be sufficiently clear:

> It is a familiar rule that a thing may be within the letter of the statute and yet not within the statute, because not within its spirit nor within the intention of the makers ... This is not the substitution of the will of the judge for that of the legislator, for frequently words of general meaning are used in a statute, words broad enough to include an act in question, and yet a consideration of the whole legislation, or of the circumstances surrounding its enactment, or of the absurd results which follow from giving such broad meaning to the words, makes it unreasonable to believe that the legislator intended to include this particular act.[35]

So we seem to be well within Judge Posner's intent approach that attempts to imagine how these legislators would have handled this church and preacher if asked at the time. But how will we do this imagining? Although the statute's text seems to have been declared clear, the Court focuses on a different piece of the legislation to find wiggle-room: the statute's title. And although "the title of an act can [not] control plain words in the body of the statute,"[36] nevertheless "[w]here the mind labors to discover the design of the legislature,"[37] everything—even headings—become fair game.

The title in turn allowed the Court to move from legislative psychology to legislative purpose. The title made clear that

> the thought expressed ... reaches only to the work of the manual laborer, as distinguished from that of the professional man. No one

reading such a title would suppose that congress had in mind any purpose of staying the coming into this country of ministers of the gospel, or, indeed, of any class whose toil is that of the brain.[38]

And this loops the Court back to text:

The common understandings of "labor" and "laborers" does not include preaching and preachers, and it is to be assumed that words and phrases are used in their ordinary meaning. So whatever of light is thrown upon the statute by the language of the title indicates that an exclusion from its penal provisions of all contracts for the employment of ministers, rectors, and pastors.[39]

An inquiry into legislative purpose, however, can be a powerful weapon, because it is so closely allied with dynamic judicial creativity, and the Court employed these concepts to an extent embarrassing to modern readers. As the Court put it, "[a]nother guide to the meaning of a statute is found in the evil which it is designed to remedy."[40] That social nastiness the Court found in other judicial precedent and the hearings before congressional committees. These sources made clear that the legislation's target was "great numbers of an ignorant and servile class of foreign laborers"[41] whose low wages were undercutting those of workers already here. "[C]heap, unskilled labor ... was making the trouble, ... the influx of which Congress sought to prevent."[42] As if this wasn't enough to make the English preacher an exception, the Court's use of the Congressional Record wasn't finished. These people, according to this legislative history,

are ignorant of our social condition, and, that they remain so, they are isolated and prevented from coming into contact with Americans. They are generally of the lowest social stratum, and live upon the coarsest food, and in hovels of a character before unknown to American workmen. They, as a rule, do not become citizens, and are certainly not a desirable acquisition to the body politic.[43]

As a consequence, the "title," "evil," and "circumstances" combined to create the textual doubt the Court needed to reach the nice result it wanted. The irony, of course, which seems lost on this Court, is that in order to do so, the Court had to attribute remarkable classism and racism to Congress to assure us that at least we took religion seriously. You could say that this is an example of "pragmatic" judicial interpretation with a vengeance, but the effort of this Court is not at all simply motivated by practicality. It is instead suffused with values, at which today we cringe.

This is not, however, a fault of legal reasoning itself, I hasten to add, but of the substance of the elements themselves that comprise it. Thinking isn't bad, although thoughts can be.

Notes

1. This would be a crass form of "legal realism." *See, e.g.,* Yosal Rogat, *Legal Realism, in* 4 ENCYCLOPEDIA OF PHILOSOPHY 420 (Paul E. Edwards ed., 1967) ("Judges ... must acknowledge their [personal] responsibility instead of attributing their choices, through tortured technicalities, to compulsions of legal doctrine.").

2. Church of the Holy Trinity v. United States, 143 U.S. 457 (1892).

3. COL, *supra* ch. 1 note 12, at 124–136.

4. *See, e.g.,* Timothy P. Terrell, *Statutory Epistemology: Mapping the Interpretation Debate,* 53 EMORY L.J. 524, 544 (2004).

5. ELEMENTS OF LAW, *supra* ch. 2 note 9.

6. WILLIAM ESKRIDGE, JR., PHILIP FRICKEY & ELIZABETH GARRETT, LEGISLATION AND STATUTORY INTERPRETATION (2d ed. 2009) (hereinafter referenced as "INTERPRETATION").

7. John M. Walker, Jr., *Judicial Tendencies in Statutory Construction: Differing Views on the Role of the Judge,* 58 N.Y.U. ANN. SURV. AM. L. 203 (2001) (hereinafter referenced as "Walker").

8. ELEMENTS OF LAW, *supra* ch. 2 note 9, at 253.

9. Walker, *supra* note 7, at 205–206.

10. *Id.* at 210.

11. ELEMENTS OF LAW, *supra* ch. 2 note 9, at 261–63.

12. RICHARD A POSNER, THE FEDERAL COURTS: CRISIS AND REFORM 286–87 (1985). Judge Posner applied this approach in *Friedrich v. City of Chicago*:

> When a court can figure out what Congress probably was driving at and how its goal can be achieved, it is not usurpation — it is interpretation in a sense that has been orthodox since Aristotle — for the court to complete (not enlarge) the statute by reading it to bring about the end that the legislature would have specified had they thought about it more clearly or used a more perspicuous form of words.

Friedrich v. City of Chicago, 888 F.2d 511, 514 (7th Cir. 1989).

13. This is why, of course, this approach is controversial. *See, e.g.,* Pub. Citizen v. United States Dep't of Justice, 491 U.S. 440, 473 (1989) (Kennedy, J., concurring) ("Where it is clear that the unambiguous language of a statute embraces certain conduct, and it would not be patently absurd to apply the statute to such conduct, it does not foster a democratic exegesis for this Court to rummage through unauthoritative materials to consult the spirit of the legislation in order to discover an alternative interpretation of the statute with which the Court is more comfortable."). A particularly entertaining example of the Court's negative reaction to a sifting of legislative history to determine statutory meaning is *Exxon Mobile Corp. v. Allapattah Services, Inc.,* 545 U.S. 546 (2005), in which the Court rejected the effort of a couple of law professors to educate the courts on what they meant when they helped Congress draft portions of the Federal Rules of Civil Procedure.

14. *See* INTERPRETATION, *supra* note 6, at 220.

15. *Id.*

16. *Id.* at 231.

17. *Id.*

18. *Id.* at 235.

19. *Id.* at 222.

20. *Id.*

21. *Id.* at 245.

22. *Id.* at 249.

23. *Id.*

24. Walker, *supra* note 7, at 233.

25. INTERPRETATION, *supra* note 6, at 250.

26. A good example of an analysis that turns on the micro-macro distinction in the legal situation of interpreting environmental legislation is William W. Buzbee, *Standing and the Statutory Universe*, 11 DUKE ENVT'L L. & POL. F. 247 (2001). Standing based on an "injury in fact" would vary potentially based on whose perspective—the individual plaintiff or the society more generally—was the focus. *See also* Friends of the Earth, Inc. v. Laidlaw Environmental Services, Inc., 528 U.S. 167, 181 (2000).

27. The morality of lying is one of the famous examples examined by Immanuel Kant. *See* Immanuel Kant, *On a Supposed Right to Lie from Philanthropy*, *in* PRACTICAL PHILOSOPHY 611, 611 15 (Mary J. Grego ed. & trans., Cambridge Univ. Press 1996) (1797). His conclusion, true to the rigorous logic upon which philosophy must be based, is that one cannot lie even to save a friend from a murderer. *Id.* One is thus led to wonder how many friends he had.

28. Although the INTERPRETATION book discusses sources for the range of interpretative methods that it lists on the right side of its V-shaped diagram (noted earlier in the text), other examples include the following. INTERPRETATION, *supra* note 6, at 250. On the idea of "legislatively intended values," see William W. Buzbee, *The One-Congress Fiction in Statutory Interpretation*, 149 U. PA. L. REV. 171 (2000), which argues against the assumption that all statutes in a given context (like environmental regulation) come from a single "Congress," rather than a group reacting to different circumstances at different points in time. *Id.* On the idea of "textually defined purpose," *see* Robert A. Shapiro & William W. Buzbee, *Unidimensional Federalism: Power and Perspective in Commerce Clause Adjudication*, 88 CORNELL L. REV. 1199, 1269–70 (2003), which argues that the purpose provisions at the beginning of a statute be given special emphasis. *Id.*

29. As another bit of detail in this area, I would note that Prof. Dworkin, in his development of the idea of "integrity" in judging, which was discussed in Chapter Six, also has a legislative element—integrity in legislation—which Professors Eskridge and Frickey note and summarize as follows:

> Ronald Dworkin ... argues that judges can advance progressive social policy without imposing their own values onto statutes ... [Dworkin's] "integrity in legislation" requires lawmakers to try to make the total set of laws morally coherent ... The courts' role is to interpret authoritative statements of law (the Constitution, statutes, common law precedents) in light of the underlying principles of the community. Thus, in the "hard cases" of statutory interpretation, the best interpretation is one that is most consonant with the underlying values of society and

> makes the statute the best statute it can be (within the limitations imposed by the language).

William N. Eskridge, Jr. & Philip P. Frickey, *Legislation Scholarship and Pedagogy in the Post-Legal Process Era*, 48 PITT. L. REV. 691, 721–22 (1987). Thus, Prof. Dworkin's approach would seem to be reflected in several areas of the graph in the text.

30. Church of the Holy Trinity v. United States, 143 U.S. 457 (1892).

31. *Id.* at 458.

32. *Id.*

33. *Id.* at 458–59.

34. *Id.* at 458.

35. *Id.* at 459.

36. *Id.* at 462.

37. *Id.* (quoting United States. v. Fisher, 6 U.S. 386 (1805)).

38. *Id.* at 463.

39. *Id.*

40. *Id.*

41. *Id.*

42. *Id.* at 464.

43. *Id.* at 465.

Conclusion

Babe Pinelli's Moment of Truth: Suspending Cynicism

A strike in baseball isn't simply a physical space, even if that variable tangibility usually dominates the analysis of it. A lease isn't simply the document that seeks to memorialize an agreement between a landlord and tenant, even if the words on that paper usually dominate the understanding of the relationship. A statute isn't only the words that comprise it, even if the initial inquiry into its meaning inevitably begins there. The art of legal reasoning is the ability to understand any of these legal concepts thoroughly, which requires more analytic sophistication than commonly believed.

But that skill will inevitably involve anxiety occasionally as well. Thanks to Stephen Jay Gould's remarkable essay, Umpire Pinelli's dilemma illustrates particularly well the struggle of the conscientious decision maker to do "the right thing." In facing any issue of "line-calling," where something must be declared to be inside or outside the boundary of some concept, like a strike, the judgment we hope will be applied will always involve attention to the texts that attempt to communicate and define the matter, the circumstantial contexts within which the matter is to be approached and appreciated, the normative hypertexts that make the matter significant to us, and the political subtexts relevant to the institutions assigned to decide the matter. To respond to Justice John Roberts' offhand comment, there simply is no "simply" in "simply calling the balls and strikes."

On the other hand, making these calls is not impossibly difficult either. The argument here has been consistent with the classic texts on legal reasoning in that the emphasis has been on reasoning rather than particular results: An analytic process exists for assessing claims to, in the case of a strike zone, in-ness or out-ness, and it is that method we demand of judges of all types. And their efforts should be watched carefully. Reasonable people can always disagree about outcomes—they cannot, however, deny that a complicated, challenging, but accepted and respected, process lies underneath all those conclusions.

Kierkegaard's comment, then, noted in Chapter Eight, was clearly an exaggeration: Decisions are not "moments of madness." Judges do not leap into some ontological abyss, nor do lawyers argue that they should do so. Instead, decisions are, like the reasoning and arguments that lead to them, instances of suspended cynicism. Lawyers and judges alike accept, I have argued here, that their goal is not perfection, but *legitimate imperfection*. Just as Prof. Gould suggested, decision making in complex human circumstances like "the law" is not about "inviolable truth" but rather "truthful *moments*," when one acknowledges that the job is not to impose agreement on contending parties, but to manage their disagreement appropriately. The classic texts in legal reasoning thus enjoy their status because they are correct: Legal circumstances are murky, but they can be analyzed logically and rigorously, even though the thinking will be suffused with values and points of view over which we clash.

This is inevitable; it is difficult; and it breeds controversy. Welcome to the law—the challenge of legal reasoning and the angst of judging.

Index